Health Economics

An International Perspective

Barbara McPake, Lilani Kumaranayake
and Charles Normand

London and New York

First published 2002
by Routledge
11 New Fetter Lane, London EC4P 4EE

Simultaneously published in the USA and Canada
by Routledge
29 West 35th Street, New York, NY 10001

Reprinted 2003

Routledge is an imprint of the Taylor & Francis Group

© 2002 Barbara McPake, Lilani Kumaranayake and Charles Normand

Typeset in Times by Graphicraft Limited, Hong Kong
Printed and bound in Great Britain by TJ International Ltd, Padstow, Cornwall

British Library Cataloguing in Publication Data

A catalogue record for this book is available from the British Library

Library of Congress Cataloging in Publication Data

McPake, Barbara.
   Health economics : an international perspective / Barbara McPake, Lilani
Kumaranayake, Charles Normand.
        p. cm.
   Includes bibliographical references (p.) and index.
   ISBN 0-415-27735-3 — ISBN 0-415-27736-1 (pbk.)
     1. Medical economics. 2. Medical economics—Case studies. I. Kumaranayake,
Lilani, 1966– II. Normand, Charles, 1952– III. Title.
RA410 .M398 2002
338.4′33621—dc21   2002021332

ISBN 0-415-27735-3 (hbk)
ISBN 0-415-27736-1 (pbk)

To the memory of
Alan Murray McPake, 1920–2001
and John Murray Normand, 1918–2002

Contents in Brief

Contents in Full

....

Figures

Tables

Boxes

Preface

The authors have been teaching health economics at the London School of Hygiene and Tropical Medicine and the London School of Economics for the past ten years. Our students come from a wide range of backgrounds and disciplines, from over one hundred countries, and have varied experience of planning and managing health systems. We have attempted to provide courses that meet the needs of people training for jobs in public health services in the United Kingdom and Europe, for students who are planners and managers in low- and middle-income countries, for health-promotion specialists and for those working on infectious disease control. Some students want only a basic introduction, and others aim to work as health economists. Some are mainly interested in applied work, and others focus on research.

Despite this extraordinary diversity, we hold the firm view that economics principles remain constant, and there is a great deal of overlap between the needs of the different groups. Students often ask for examples related to a setting in which they have experience and where they are likely to work. We try to accommodate this, but we also believe that people can gain additional understanding and insight from seeing economic principles applied in other settings. Understanding how services are provided in other settings can also help people to reconsider their expectations and prejudices about how things should be organised.

This book aims to provide an international perspective – that is the issues and principles are explored in diverse settings, and reflect where we have worked and our experience in different parts of the world. Examples are chosen because they illuminate the ideas, whatever the setting. It also aims to cover material at different levels and with different degrees of technical complexity. Readers have some choice about how to read the book, with some more formal presentation put in boxes. For some access to the ideas in the later chapters will require careful study of the introductory chapters, and those coming with a grounding in economic principles can move straight on to the higher-level material.

There is inevitable controversy about what should be the content of a book on health economics. In the US the focus of much of the material is on insurance, financing and issues related to paying providers of care. In Western Europe the early developments were mainly in economic evaluation, although recently the scope of work has widened considerably. There is increasing interest in looking at whole health systems, and how our ability to manage them can be improved with better use of economic analysis. Our aim has been to reflect the different traditions and needs, but also to provide a coverage of the approaches and issues we expect to be of interest in the future. As teachers and researchers in a public health school our aim is to improve health through excellence in teaching, research and policy development. We hope that the material in this book can help to achieve this goal.

B.M.

L.K.

C.N.

Acknowledgements

....

The authors are all members of Knowledge Programmes supported by the UK Department for International Development, the Health Economics and Financing and Health Systems Development Programmes. We consider this text a joint output of the two programmes. We would like to thank Nicola Lord, Melissa Texeira, Isabel Sinha, Francis Peel and Sandra Russell for their tireless assistance with the production of this manuscript. This administrative team supports the two Knowledge Programmes and, without it, the book and much of the work that underpins it might never have seen the light of day. Finally, we are grateful to the generations of students who have helped us to hone our approach to the teaching of this subject through their questions, evaluative feedback and mistakes! We hope the future generations who make use of this text appreciate their inputs.

Part I

Introductory Health Economics

Chapter 1

Introduction

Health Economics in International Perspective

1.1 The Role of Economists in the Health Sector

Why do economists work in health? The health sector is not usually the first place people associate with economists. It is not supposed to be about money, profit, production and markets. Should it not be about medicine, nursing, caring and the difference between life and death? Surely, an economist has no wisdom to bring to bear here? Such views were virtually universal until quite recently but they demonstrate a limited understanding of the role and content of economics. In principle economists are concerned with better choices and in particular making the best use of existing resources and growth in the availability of resources. As economists started to work on problems in the health sector, the new discipline of health economics emerged. Many of the concerns in health economics are also those of other health scientists – how can we improve survival, quality of life and fairness in access to services? What economics brings is a different framework for analysing such questions. We think this framework offers important and useful insights.

Economists in all sectors are concerned with the allocation of resources between competing demands (Samuelson and Nordhaus 2000). Demands are assumed to be *infinite* – there is no end to consumption aspirations. Resources (like labour, raw materials, production equipment and land), in contrast, are always *finite*. Thus *scarcity* of resources (not in the sense of 'rarity' but in the sense of resource availability *relative* to demand) becomes the fundamental problem to which economists address themselves. Some readers will have difficulty with this description of the world. It is not necessarily 'true' but is, in a broad sense, a model on which economics is based. See Box 1.1 for further discussion of the nature and purpose of models, and of this one in particular.

In the health sector, such scarcity can be recognised in a host of questions that concern all who work there or use its services. Why has the volume of resources absorbed by the sector increased so fast over the last four decades worldwide? Why does it seem that no matter how many nurses and doctors are employed, new technologies adopted, new drug therapies introduced, that even the rich countries of the world do not seem to be able to provide the highest quality of care for all citizens? Are we investing in the wrong kinds of health services? (Are we organising

Box 1.1 *Realism and the Need for Simplification: the Use of Models in Economics*

In the teaching of health economics, we have found that students often raise objections to the assumptions of economic models and the characterisation of all-pervasive scarcity on which economics is based. Others object to the concept of the 'rational economic man' that underlies demand theory (see Chapter 2), and the assumptions of the theory of perfect competition (see Chapter 6).

At least part of the concern comes from a misunderstanding of the role and usefulness of theories and models. Models are not intended to describe reality. They deliberately abstract from it, in order to simplify the relationships between key variables so that we can see them clearly and analyse them. Models should never be 'realistic', they should always be simplifications. Models deliberately ignore variables we are less interested in, or consider to play only a small role, either by holding them constant or setting them to zero. Economists use the expression *ceteris paribus* (all the rest the same) to indicate that all variables which haven't been included in the model should be assumed to be constant. By simplifying, we aim to focus on the relationships we are interested in, examine the interactions between these variables, and avoid the 'noise' of the hundreds of other variables which will otherwise confuse those key relationships. An extreme position is that of Milton Friedman (1953) who has argued that a model is good if it predicts accurately. Its assumptions may bear no relationship to reality. Friedman uses the example of leaves deliberately seeking to arrange themselves so as to maximise the sunlight each receives. The assumption of 'deliberating' leaves may be unrealistic, but a model based on that assumption predicts accurately the pattern of leaf growth and development on a tree. Others (for example Hodgson 1988) consider that a model which predicts on the basis of very unrealistic assumptions fails to explain the relationships in question. We do not understand much about the process of leaf growth and distribution starting from this assumption. Explanation is often as useful a function of models as prediction.

Take the particular assumption that demands are 'infinite'. Are they really? Levels of consumption enjoyed in the rich economies of the world have grown beyond the imaginations of previous generations – and of the 50 per cent of the world's population who live on less than $2 per day today (*Human Development Report*, UNDP 1999). The consumption levels of the richest in the world demonstrate that when resource constraints are low, people consume goods that would in other circumstances be considered of very low priority. If demand exists for psychiatric services for pet dogs, cars capable of speeds exceeding the maximum permitted on public roads, and dancing snowmen singing 'Jingle bells', where can limits be found? Observing some spectacles of consumption, one might conclude that increased wealth and command of resources increases greed and aspiration to consume even more.

In the health sector, one might reach similar conclusions based on the rapid development of technology, which makes available almost unlimited opportunities to extend and improve the quality of life. There seems no limit to the resources that might be consumed with the objective of improving the health of a population.

However, it is also clear that not all members of the world's population aspire to such levels of consumption. Many widely held systems of philosophic and religious belief from Calvinism to Islam eschew consumerism. And even if the levels of demand which might potentially be

Continued

expressed are very large indeed, could they really be infinite? Is there not a maximum rate at which any individual could possibly consume resources?

The discipline of economics needs an assumption which is realistic enough to generate useful analysis and conclusions. What is unarguable, is that the extent of demands on resources far outstrips the capacity of available resources to deliver, and does so to such a great extent that there is no prospect of ever meeting all demands with available resources. This is sufficient to make the economist's characterisation of all pervasive 'scarcity' a reasonable basis on which to proceed.

Of course, current distribution of resources leaves some high-priority demands unmet at the expense of some of the low-priority demands listed above. For the cost of the dancing snowman, several people might have their sight restored through cataract surgery. In this insight lie the concerns of economists. Why do the current resource-allocation mechanisms choose snowmen over cataract surgery? If we take the normative perspective that surgery is 'better' than snowmen as a starting point, what kinds of intervention might help us move towards a situation in which more demands for surgery and less demands for snowmen are met? These questions are the business of economics.

services so as to best improve the health of the population? Are we investing in technologies that have a low health output compared to alternative investments?) In poor countries, questions of resource scarcity are starker still. Can we afford, at all, universal access to high-cost services such as cancer care?

All societies must make choices as to how to allocate whatever resources are available to the production of health services, and how to distribute those health services produced between those who want them. These choices are the subject of the discipline of health economics. Health economics (and economics in general) is often seen as having two branches: the *positive* branch which is concerned with describing and explaining how such choices are actually made, and the *normative* branch which is concerned with judging which choices should be made. For example, a health economist might be concerned with health insurance coverage of a population. She might take a positive perspective. Why are there so many uninsured? What are the characteristics of those that are uninsured (are they unable to

afford the cost of insurance premiums, or do they judge themselves unlikely to need health services?)? From a normative perspective it is necessary to establish criteria according to which the situation can be judged. If equity of access to health services is one criterion, and ability to pay is a dominant explanation of non-coverage, the situation might be judged 'bad', and alternative interventions to reduce the problem evaluated.

There are two ways in which society can make choices about the allocation of resources to production in the health sector, and the distribution of the services that are produced among those that want them. A society can leave these decisions to the *market* – letting demand, supply and prices determine resource allocation – or it can *plan*, usually by giving its government the task of collecting resources from the population, allocating those to defined production activities and distributing the produced services among the population. The debate as to which approach is best has divided the world's population through the whole of the twentieth century, underlying the formation of political parties, coups d'états, and hot and cold war, and will not be settled in this volume! Societies worldwide have taken different stances on this question, and have evolved a wide array of mixes of plan and market in the attempt to reach a satisfactory choice as to how to produce and distribute health services.

Health economists have evolved different approaches to analysing and evaluating resource allocation in the health sector which reflect the plan–market dichotomy. In societies in which health services have been largely planned, the main activity of health economists has been the development and application of a set of tools which collectively make up the field of *economic evaluation*. Economic evaluation aims to consider whether appropriate services have been adopted in the health sector, or whether there is a mix of technologies and interventions which would better meet health sector objectives, such as the improvement of the population's health, or the equity of access to care. You might notice that in terms of the positive–normative dimension, this is an essentially normative activity. It requires the definition of objectives and asks, 'What should we do?'

Where there has been a greater role for the market in health sector resource allocation, more effort has been made by economists to understand that market to predict its pattern of development, and to analyse the implications of interventions such as regulation, subsidy of insurance coverage or the introduction of planned activities. Even in the most market-reliant health sectors, such interventions are always present. Understanding markets involves the understanding of demand (how consumers of health services express their preferences through their ability and willingness to pay), supply (conditions in input markets, cost, and how provision is organised, for example by one big firm or by many) and their interactions. This is essentially a positive activity – explaining what is happening and predicting the effects of introducing a change – but it can be normative. If it is decided that a particular effect is desirable, such analysis can be used to evaluate whether a change should be introduced.

As health sectors have evolved, especially over the last two decades, richer mixes of planning and markets have been developed in a large number of countries. In health sectors which have traditionally been planned, elements of market mechanisms have been introduced, for example through 'internal markets'. In health sectors which have traditionally relied to a greater extent on market mechanisms, more planning has been introduced – for example through more intrusive public regulation, or through the use of capitation payment mechanisms (consumers pay the provider a fee per year rather than per service) which shift risk on to providers and thereby pass on the planning role usually carried out by a public sector body. This has led to a certain cross-over of interests in the health economics fields. US health economists are now much more interested in the techniques of economic evaluation which can assist Health Maintenance Organisations (providers paid by capitation) in developing their strategies, and economists interested in the welfare state health provision of northern European countries are increasingly interested in the operation of markets and the implications of different kinds of regulation and other public intervention for market behaviour. On both sides of the Atlantic, there is now interest in capturing the insights of economic evaluation to enable better planning by actors in the market place, and to better understanding how public intervention can improve outcomes associated with health markets.

These two traditions of health economics can be detected by comparing the outputs of health economists in northern Europe, Australia and New Zealand (largely planned health sectors), and the US (where market forces have been allowed greater rein). Canadian health economics has perhaps been least categorisable, located in a health sector which is characterised by planned approaches to resource allocation, but strongly influenced by the academic environment of the US. Some prominent contributions to health economics from Canada have provided a critique of US analysis. There has been a perceived need in Canada to provide a rigorous defence against the spread of American ideas and approaches to health care – what Marmor (1999) describes as intellectual acid rain.

Although most work in health economics has been produced in these regions, trends in health sector development affect those conducting economic analysis in the health sectors of almost all countries. It is no longer safe to assume that one is working in a planned environment, that an understanding of market forces is unnecessary, and that topics in economic evaluation provide the only useful tools required. Similarly, it is unlikely that the US will ever return to the market conditions of the 1970s. Technology assessment, facility planning and the mandate of insurance packages are likely to feature for the foreseeable future, and economic evaluation will continue to play a major role in the operation of these.

It is therefore increasingly the case that, wherever their work takes them in the world, a health economist needs grounding in both branches of the discipline. This book is founded on that belief. It aims to explain basic health economics across the spectrum of the discipline and to demonstrate applications on a worldwide basis. The work of the three authors of this book covers a wide geographic span, taking in the UK, the US, Canada and Australia, many of the countries of the former Soviet Union and Eastern Europe, Uganda, Zambia and Zimbabwe, Bangladesh, Laos, Cambodia, Chile, Colombia and Peru – in fact countries from all continents except Antarctica. Obviously, the problems faced by these different countries in trying to ensure that public health problems are thoroughly addressed and that all citizens receive high-quality health services are quite different – in type and degree. Nevertheless, the tools of economic analysis presented in this book have provided us with a good basis for seeking to understand and evaluate the problems encountered and the measures taken to respond to them irrespective of the context. We believe that contrasting experience of applying these tools in different countries is helpful in understanding issues and undertaking analysis in any particular country. The aim of this book is to provide an introduction to these tools and to show ways that the same approach can inform health policy in widely differing contexts.

1.2 Economists, Health Policy and Equity

Economic analysis in health and health care is often undertaken with a view to helping governments and other agencies better achieve the goals of their health policies. An obvious requirement is to know what these goals are. Where explicit goals are specified it is common for two to dominate – improving the health status of the population and fairness or equity. Health economists have therefore focused on assessing how to maximise the impact on health and equity. In economics it is recognised that choices must be made – it is not possible to get everything you want. While some policies may offer the opportunity to increase both equity and health improvement, others require a choice between equity and health improvement – in other words we must sometimes choose to trade-off efficiency (the achievement of better health) and equity (the fairer distribution of health).

Fairness and equity are difficult concepts, and a whole literature exists just on how they should be defined. As ideas they inevitably carry strong moral overtones. To be against fairness seems impossible almost by definition. To be openly in favour of widening gaps in health between the rich and poor is understandably uncommon. Being clear what is meant by equity or fairness is also uncommon, and it is important to define the concepts and desired outcomes more precisely. There can be many reasons why health and access to health care are unequal. Some people happen to be born with diseases or disabilities, or the predisposition to become ill. Some people are just unlucky, and become ill. Those without jobs or housing may live in risky or unhealthy conditions. Others take risks, such as rock climbing or smoking, and the outcomes may be bad. And some people would benefit from treatment or care, but cannot find the resources to pay for it.

A significant part of this book is devoted to analysis of markets in health and health care, how they work, how they fail and what can be done to make them work better. Even if they work well, poor people are poor, and without help can afford only limited access to care. They are also more likely than richer people to have illness and disability. In most countries in the world, and in all developed countries, there are government measures to reduce the disparity in access to care between richer and poorer people. Despite this the

gaps remain between the health experiences of different groups – better health is enjoyed by richer people, by professionals and by women. Access to care does not reflect fully these differences.

In countries with government funding of health care, or some system of funding that is heavily regulated by government, it is common for there to be a system of allocating resources to take account of differences in needs in different parts of the population. The most common approach is for allocation to be based on population, weighted for needs factors such as age, gender and morbidity. The allocations are then proportionate to the measures of need. This approach has done much to weight funding towards those with worse health. However, there are obvious problems, since it is not clear that the appropriate level of funding should be proportionate to a particular measure of need. This illustrates a difficulty in making operational a desire to create vertical equity (that is the unequal support for unequals). The other common notion of equity is horizontal equity, the equal treatment of equals. In principle this is easier, since all that is needed is the same access to health or health care opportunities for people in the same situation. Putting this into practice is not so easy.

Economists often focus on the trade-off between efficiency and equity. Take the example of urban and rural populations, and the different perinatal mortality rates. It is common for rural areas to have worse rates of such deaths, so it may be expected that the efforts of public health and health services would focus on reducing this difference. However, it is also likely that the cost of lowering the rate of perinatal deaths in rural areas will be higher (for example because service users are more costly to reach), so that a given expenditure might do more to lower the *number* of deaths if applied in the urban area. A real choice might be to lower the number of deaths by 100 if the focus is on urban areas but only by 80 if the same funds were spent on the rural programme. A difficult choice faces policy makers – spend the money on the urban areas and more deaths are prevented, but at the same time the disparity between urban and rural areas would become wider. Of course we would all like to see both fewer deaths and less inequality, but for any given spending we cannot avoid making this difficult choice between a more efficient intervention (i.e. fewer deaths) and a more equitable one. Is the additional fairness worth twenty deaths?

The example of perinatal deaths is based on a real choice that was faced by a health agency. It represents one of the most difficult dilemmas. There are also many occasions when there is no trade-off between efficiency and fairness, since people with worse health have more scope to recover with treatment. Take another example, based on experience in an urban area in England. Due to differences in referral rates, people in the poorest part of the district had the highest rates of treatable coronary heart disease, but were getting less treatment than those from more prosperous parts. In effect those with the least capacity to benefit were getting more, and those likely to benefit more got less. In this case the allocation of resources is inefficient (since more improvement in health could be achieved with the existing budget), and greater efficiency would also lead to greater equity. Being ill or at risk is a necessary condition for being able to benefit from treatment, so that it is often the case that those who can benefit most are those with low incomes and above-average morbidity. In some cases it is more expensive to treat poorer people, since they may need longer in hospital. There are

also cases where there are higher costs of running a prevention programme for poorer people. For example, those choosing to attend for screening programmes tend to be those who are richer and have less disease. Recruiting those from poorer families may be important, since there is likely to be more diseases detected, but it may cost more to organise such a programme.

These examples aim to shed light on several aspects of equity. There is no simple definition of equity. It is also important to consider equity in the health sector in the context of overall equity. Poverty leads to ill health, and constrains access to health care. Action to improve equity in access to health services can help, but tackles symptoms more than causes. To a large extent the problem of health inequalities is a problem of more general economic and social inequalities, and the solutions lie outside the health sector. There is some evidence that it is relative (rather than absolute) poverty that is associated with poor health, although recent studies cast some doubt on this. It is certainly the case that countries with great social inequalities have worse health on average than those that are more equal. The rapid changes in Central and Eastern Europe were associated with rapid increase in income inequality, and worsening of health.

It can be useful to distinguish within the health sector between structures that lead to unequal access to services and the failure of health systems to work as they are planned to. Countries with state funding or social insurance funding for health care normally aim to provide nearly equal access to important services. The rules normally state that care should be offered on the basis of need and not income or ability to pay. The reality is often different, since there may be user charges (whether official or unofficial), medicines may not be available at the hospitals, staff may be rude and careless with poorer patients, and buildings in a poor state of repair. The design may be for a system of equal access, but the reality is that those with more money get better access. This may be contrasted to systems that do not aim to provide equal access. In the US access depends on income, employment, age and disease. Those who are employed and insured get excellent services. Those who are very poor or old get free or subsidised services. Those with renal failure may get free dialysis, but those with low-paid jobs, and no insurance, may be excluded from many parts of the system. Even if each part of the system were to work as planned, the system does not aim to provide the same health care opportunities to all users. This is not to argue the superiority of systems that aim to be equitable but which fail, but in such cases the solution may be to make the system work as planned. In a fragmented system such as in the US any moves to greater equity are likely to require some changes in structures.

This book does not have a separate chapter on health equity or equity in access to care. However, many sections touch on these issues. The analysis of markets considers the consequences for who gets what access to what health opportunities. Economic evaluation may affect priorities and therefore access. In some cases better management and implementation of existing policy more fully will also reduce inequalities. The final part of the book on health systems addresses the implications of different health system structures for rationing principles. Where there is a trade-off between more health gain and more equality in health, those making policies must be clear – greater equity will be achieved only at the expense of worsening the overall levels of health. This may be

deemed to be desirable, but equity, like most desirable ends, has a cost.

1.3 The Structure of the Book

Part I introduces basic micro-economics and its applications in the health sector. These topics – demand and elasticity, production and cost, perfect markets and market failure – provide the basic building blocks for any more sophisticated micro-economic analysis whether of the operations of markets, or the economic theory underlying topics in economic evaluation such as shadow pricing, and willingness to pay as a means of valuing benefits.

Part II introduces economic evaluation. We have noted above that any normative economic analysis must start out with clear criteria by which to evaluate the goodness or badness of any proposed policy, or change to current practice. This part starts with an introduction to welfare economics which is the branch of economics which has developed the system of criteria on which economic evaluation is based. The rest of the part focuses on the philosophical and practical difficulties encountered in trying to evaluate policy and practice in the light of these criteria, and provides a running case study through which these difficulties are exemplified and explored.

Part III covers topics which enable a more sophisticated analysis of market behaviour and applications to the evaluation of market intervention such as regulation and contracting. On the basis of this part, the reader will start to understand the insights that can be gained from the application of market theory and analysis to health sector scenarios – whether in more or less planned health sectors.

Part IV provides an overview of the insights that economic analysis can provide to the understanding of health systems at a macro level. It starts with a review of the shape of health systems around the world and an overview of the performance characteristics associated with different systems. It proceeds to provide a framework for explaining the patterns of performance through an understanding of the resource allocation mechanisms associated with different health systems, and the nature of the institutions which finance and provide health services. It concludes with an introduction to health sector reform debates in which reforms are viewed as interventions aiming to reshape health systems, informed by an economic analysis of the strengths and weaknesses of alternative configurations.

The book is designed to be read in different ways. The aim has been to keep the text as readable as possible, and to use technical terminology only where necessary. Where possible the ideas are illustrated with examples taken from the authors' experiences of applying economics to health and health care issues. A more technical approach is provided in parallel. Text boxes offer fuller explanation of some points, mathematical presentation of some of the theory and background to some ideas and individuals. The presentation in Part I assumes no previous knowledge of economics. The later parts build on this foundation. Readers with previous training in economics should find these quite accessible, but those new to economics should not attempt to read them without a reasonable grasp of the material in the first part.

Chapter 2

The Demand for Health and Health Services

....

2.1 *Demand and Demand for Health Care*

Medicine and health care have a long history of being treated as special. There are some obvious ways in which the way we interact with the health sector is different from our dealings with other providers of goods and services. Doctors advise us on what services we need and often also provide them. Some health services are used when we are very ill and may not be able to make sensible decisions. Some health care decisions are literally about life and death. In many cases interventions have very uncertain effects for any individual. Another problem is timing. In general we are healthier when relatively young and relatively rich. These are times when we are least likely to need health care, but most likely to be able to afford it. Perhaps the most important feature of our need for health care is that we seldom know in advance what we will need, when we will need it and how much we will need. Another interesting feature is that few of us actually want to use health services – we do so because we hope they will improve our health. Indeed, use of health services is often unpleasant. Most things we buy are more enjoyable to consume.

On the other hand not all health interventions are uncertain, few are really about life and death, and in many cases the intervention is well understood by the patient. For example, you have myopia, and need optometry services. You can calculate with almost perfect accuracy how often you need eye tests, and, unless you sit on them, how many pairs of spectacles you will need for the rest of your life. For many people dental care is almost as predictable. There is no significant uncertainty in the need for many childhood vaccinations – unless the child dies the content and timing of immunisation is predictable.

Many health services are about comfort, mobility, feeling healthy and having good quality of life. Relatively little of what is done extends life to a significant degree. In an absolute sense health care is less necessary than many other necessities, such as food and clothing. This chapter introduces the economic theory of demand, and applies it to health and health care. The features of health that are special are explored.

There are several reasons why we should be interested in demand for health and health care. The first is to help us to predict likely reactions and behaviour. For example, if we charge people a fee for eyesight tests what will be the effect on the number of people using the service? How will such a charge affect the frequency of use of optometry services? Second, knowing something about people's demand for health care may tell us something about how much they value services. This point will be explored in greater depth below.

2.2 *Preference and Indifference*

The theory of demand is normally built up in two stages. First, we look at the patterns of preference or indifference between different goods or services. For example, do I prefer a twenty-minute phone call to my mother or twenty minutes of free Internet access? Do I prefer one television set to one bicycle? Do I prefer a 20 per cent reduction in the size of classes at school or twenty sets of textbooks? Of course our preferences are complicated, and normally we want both the products or services offered. The best way to think about preference is 'Which would I choose?' The most reliable information comes from actual choices people have made, but at times we have to rely on what they say they would choose. It is obvious that what people say may be affected my other factors, such as a concern about what others will think.

Normally we like more rather than less. But normally the more we have of a service the less we value extra amounts. Take the phone call to your mother. After twenty minutes all the important news has been given. If offered another ten minutes this would allow more detail. It is not clear how much value would be put on an extra two hours. Similarly, when offered twenty minutes on the Internet, this allows important information to be found. With subsequent minutes there may be enjoyable surfing, but most people

Table 2.1 Preferences for combinations of Internet time and telephone time

Minutes on the Internet	Minutes on the phone to mother	Order of preference
20	0	5
15	5	3
10	10	2
5	15	1
0	20	4

would place a lower value on this. The normal response to the choice of the phone call and the Internet access would be to say 'can I have some of each?'

We can imagine an experiment in which we are given different combinations of Internet time and telephone time, and are asked to state our preferences. Table 2.1 shows combinations and the preference order given by a senior health economist who loves his mother. All combinations of time on each are preferred to time only on the Internet or only on the phone. When the time is split, the senior health economist prefers more to be available for the phone call and less for the Internet. In a similar way we can devise combinations of minutes on the phone and on the Internet between which the economist would have no clear preference. The fourth option had previously been the preferred one. Now the others have been improved so that they are considered to be just as good. This is illustrated in Table 2.2.

Since he cannot choose between the different combinations he is said to be *indifferent* between the different combinations. We can illustrate the data in Table 2.2 in a diagram, showing the combinations of minutes on the phone and minutes on the Internet between which he is indifferent. The points in Figure 2.1 are those between which he is indifferent. If we identify all the other combinations of

Table 2.2

Minutes on the Internet	Minutes on the phone to mother	Order of preference
35	0	?
22	5	?
13	10	?
5	15	?
3	20	?

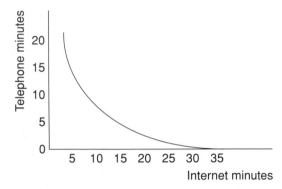

Figure 2.1   Indifference curve

phone and Internet minutes to which the person is indifferent we can plot his *indifference curve*. There are reasons to expect that for most individuals, for most pairs of goods, the indifference curve will have the shape outlined above in Figure 2.1, that is be convex to the origin. As we see in this example, the more he has of either service, the less he values additional minutes. This is not surprising.

If two goods are perfect substitutes for each other the indifference curve will be a straight line. If they are perfect complements, that is to say they can only be used in fixed combinations, then the indifference curves are L-shaped, as illustrated in Figure 2.2. For example, syringes and needles are needed in fixed combinations, and neither is useful without the other so they are complements. For most people an effective treatment for a headache can be either aspirin or paracetamol, so they are near substitutes.

For most goods and services we prefer more to less. Figure 2.1 showed combinations of phone and Internet minutes between which the person was indifferent, but he would prefer more of both. We can draw a series of indifference curve sets of combinations between which a person is indifferent, as in Figure 2.3. The person prefers all points on I3 to all on I2, and all on I2 are preferred to all on I1. This means that he judges that his welfare is higher if he can achieve I3 than it would be on the lower indifference curves.

Figure 2.2   Indifference curves for near-perfect (a) substitutes and (b) complements

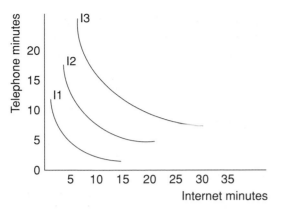

Figure 2.3 Indifference curve map

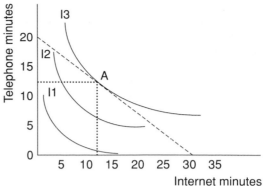

Figure 2.5 Optimum combination of Internet time and telephone time, given the budget line

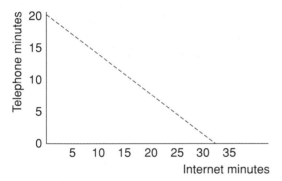

Figure 2.4 The budget line

Each of the indifference curves represents different levels of welfare – since the person prefers more to less. Economists sometimes use the term 'utility' to describe the person's level of welfare, so in this case his utility is higher on I3 than I2 or I1. The idea of utility is key to some theories of welfare.

Within his limited resources, the health economist in this example wants to maximise his utility. In other words, he wants to be on the highest achievable indifference curve. What limits him is his income. In this example, assume that he buys only these two goods. He will use all his income on phone calls and Internet access. We can calculate how much of each he can afford if we know his income and the price of each service. Figure 2.4

illustrates his budget constraint. If he were to buy only phone calls the total number he could buy can be represented by his income divided by the price of phone minutes. Similarly, the maximum number of Internet minutes is his income divided by the price of Internet minutes. In this case his income in euros (€) is €100, the price of telephone minutes is €5, and the price of Internet minutes is €3. This line representing the choices available to a person is normally described as a *budget constraint* or *budget line.* Since the ends of the budget line cut the axes where the income is divided by the prices, it follows logically that the *slope* of the line is the ratio of the two prices.

We can put the information in Figures 2.3 and 2.4 together to work out his best combination. Put another way, his best strategy is to choose the combination that allows him to be on the highest indifference curve. This is shown in Figure 2.5. His best combination is at point A, where his current income gets him his most preferred combination of thirteen phone minutes and thirteen Internet minutes. Despite the fact that he prefers phone minutes to Internet minutes in general, the lower price of the Internet minutes persuades him to consume more of them.

It is clear from the example that this model makes some important assumptions about how people make decisions. (Recall Box 1.1 on the use of models in economics.) By choosing the combination at point A he is maximising his utility (subject to the constraints imposed by his limited income). He looks at the different available combinations, and chooses the one that provides the highest utility. This may not fully reflect the complexity of how people take decisions, but may be a reasonable simplification. A further simplification is that we are looking at a choice involving only two services. We can of course think of the same process with three (where indifference curves become indifference surfaces, and budget lines budget planes). However, to retain the convenience of two-dimensional diagrams we can simplify things by comparing a particular good or service to a composite good ('all other goods').

The slope of the person's budget line is the ratio of the two prices. The slope of indifference curves also has a meaning. What it represents is the rate at which the person is willing to exchange one service for the other. This is called the *marginal rate of substitution.*

2.3 From Preference to Demand

In section 2.2 a two-stage decision process was described in which the consumer identifies his preferences between two services, and then chooses using this information and information on his income and the relative price of each service. This analysis allows us to develop the theory of demand. Keeping all other factors constant we can show that the effects on the choices made change as we vary the price of one good, or vary income. Figures 2.6 and 2.8 illustrate the effects of a change in price or a change in income

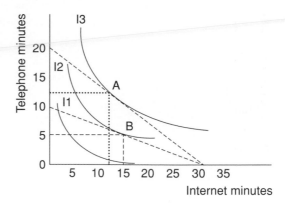

Figure 2.6 Demand for telephone time, given change in price

respectively on the demand for phone call minutes.

Consider Figure 2.6, in this case the price of phone calls has risen to €10, with the effect that the person buys fewer phone minutes (five instead of twelve) and more Internet minutes (seventeen instead of fourteen). This is what you would expect. But note also that in effect the person is also now poorer, in the sense that his money buys him less. We can analyse the effect of the price rise as having a *substitution effect*, which is the pure effect of the change in relative prices (i.e. a shift along I3 to the point where its slope matches that of the new budget constraint) and an *income effect*, which is the effect on demand of the person being poorer. Substitution effects are negative – the higher price leads to less consumption. Income effects are also normally negative, but may be positive in the case of certain goods.

From Figure 2.6 we can calculate the effects on the amount of each service that will be bought at each price (keeping income and the price of the other service constant). We could draw a series of budget constraints, each representing a value of the price of phone minutes. From the information in Figure 2.6 we can identify two combinations of price

Figure 2.7   Demand curve

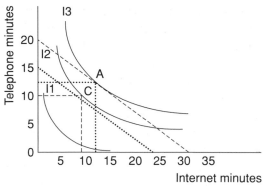

Figure 2.8   Demand for telephone and Internet time, given change in income

and quantity chosen. (At price €5 he bought twelve minutes, and at price €10 he bought five minutes.)

These two points are shown in Figure 2.7. If we did this exercise a large number of times we would produce a *demand curve*, as illustrated. In this model of demand, the quantity chosen is a function of the price

Q = f(P)

Mathematical purists will notice that this diagram has been drawn with price on the vertical axis and quantity on the horizontal axis. This is the opposite of the normal convention in mathematics for the dependent and independent variable. Alfred Marshall, who first suggested this analysis in the nineteenth century, used the axes in this way, and the habit has stuck.

Figure 2.8 illustrates the effects of a fall in income on demand for each service. In this case the person chooses less of both, but there are times when a fall in income will lead to one good facing increased demand. This most often happens if income falls, and people choose to decrease consumption of luxury goods and consume more of basic ones. A fall in income can be represented by a paral-

lel shift of the budget constraint to the left. In this case the effect is to shift choices to point C, where the person consumes ten minutes of each of the two services.

2.4 *Determinants of Demand*

The analysis above suggests a number of determinants of demand for a service. First, individual tastes and preferences are important in determining the shape of individual indifference curves.

A preference function contains a set of arguments or components, for example:

U = f(X, Y, L, H)

where U is utility, X and Y are goods, L is leisure and H is health, meaning that the individual's utility is dependent on the consumption of a set of goods, leisure time and health status. Each individual's preference function is considered unique. Preference functions may be more or less stable – some things change with fashion, and others are more predictable.

Second, the price of the goods will influence the amount chosen. Third, demand will be affected by the price of other goods, both substitutes and complements. In general a fall in the price of substitutes leads demand for the service to fall, and a fall in the price of complements for it to rise. Fourth, the income of individuals is a determinant of demand. More formally we can express this as

$$D = f(P, P_s, P_c, Y, T)$$

where P is price, P_s is the price of substitute goods, P_c is the price of complement goods, Y is income and T is tastes.

We know that, in general, demand falls with price, increases with the price of substitutes, decreases with the price of complements, increases with income and increases as tastes and preferences increase.

In developing this simple theory of demand two features were highlighted – the person's tastes and the person's income. The decision to spend money shows a *willingness to pay* and an *ability to pay*. We can therefore interpret the demand curve as representing the person's willingness to pay given that person's income. This idea of demand as willingness to pay is useful, and underlies some of the ways in which we can assess benefits (see Chapter 11).

What is illustrated in Figure 2.7 is the demand curve for one person. Clearly the overall demand for the good depends on the demand of all people who potentially are in the market. To get the community's demand curve we just add together the demand curves for all individuals, horizontally (at each price, the total demand is that of all the individuals in the market added together).

2.5 From Demand to Demand for Health and Health Care

The example chosen to illustrate the basic theory of demand was not taken from a health setting. The question is to what extent the principles can usefully be applied to understanding demand for health and demand for health care.

The first obvious point is that health is complicated. It has many dimensions. We enjoy it for itself, and use it to help us earn a living and to enjoy other goods and services. In order to produce health we can do a number of things – live healthier life-styles, eat healthier food, live in better housing, avoid contaminated water, stop smoking, take more exercise, have vaccinations, take part in screening for risk factors or early symptoms of disease, or have medical or surgical treatment.

Demand for health care depends in part on how much we value health – it is sometimes therefore described as a derived demand, since the real demand is for health, and the demand for health care is to help achieve the desired health. Indeed it is often actually unpleasant to have treatment or care. Of course many goods and services have this feature. The demand for cars might be described as the demand for hours of happy family motoring, or demand for bicycles as the demand for access to different places.

In our behaviour we can observe trade-offs between health and other goods and services. When someone smokes they (presumably) enjoy the taste and the ending of the craving for an addictive substance. The decision to drive to nearby shops is a decision not to get the health benefits of some exercise. Crossing roads at pedestrian crossings reduces the chance of death or injury, but many people save themselves a few minutes and cross heavy traffic. Driving fast is exciting, saves time and increases chances of death or injury. In these senses people constantly make a trade-off between consuming more health and consuming other goods which give utility. We may claim that our health is of paramount importance, but our behaviour does not always support this claim. By observing our choices of health-enhancing or health-damaging goods and services we can in principle impute the demand for health.

Perhaps a more important consideration is that health is not something that is very directly traded. We cannot easily buy it and sell it, and it is closely attached to us. In that sense it is a characteristic rather than a product. Since it is difficult to trade, and is in some senses part of us, it is different from phone calls or bananas.

Another important feature of health is that it is surrounded by uncertainty. Only some illness is predictable, and there is huge variation. We all know of lifelong smokers who live healthily into their nineties, and sensible people who follow the health promotion messages and get sick. Of course we can change the risks, but cannot simply choose a good outcome. This further complicates matters.

Demand for health care is also affected by this uncertainty. In essence what we want to buy is access to care should we need it. This means that for some people the demand for health care is a demand for insurance offering guaranteed access to care should the need arise. Of course many other goods have this characteristic. A house being damaged by an earthquake or a freak hailstorm cannot be predicted, but we can insure against such eventualities. It is often claimed that health care is different from other goods because it is a necessity. To an extent this is true (although the proportion of health care that is devoted to reducing premature death is relatively small in most countries). Many goods are necessities for life, and many are more important for life than health care.

A feature of health is that in some senses it is like a capital good. If you invest in better health it remains with you, and health-damaging behaviour can leave it permanently lower. In this sense we may want to draw on the insights of demand theory applied to capital goods industries, and look at decisions to invest in durable products. Perhaps comparison should be with houses rather than telephone calls.

Another test of whether health care can be considered to be the same as other services is how demand responds to changes in income or price. What is found in all studies is that, all other things being equal, a rise in the price of health care reduces the amount consumed, and a fall in price increases use. Increased income is associated with higher demand for health services, and lower income with lower demand. Thus, in many important ways demand for health and demand for health care are like the demand for other goods and other services. However, the great uncertainty, limited information and the contexts in which health and health care are produced all make it somewhat special, and the analysis later in this book explores many of the ways in which applying economics to health and health care can be challenging.

Study of demand for health care has a long history. An important starting point for much of the subsequent work was the framework suggested by Grossman (1972). His model takes into account some of the special features of health – that it is both a consumption good and a capital good, and that it is in part a derived demand.

Chapter 3

Demand, Elasticity and Health

....

3.1 Elasticity of Demand

In Chapter 2 the ideas of preference, indifference and demand were explored. It was argued that demand is influenced by a range of factors, including income, tastes and preferences, prices of the good and prices of substitutes and complements. The demand curve was drawn showing how demand for the good or service may be related to price.

It is often useful to know more about how demand varies with price. Some services or goods are so necessary to life that we are likely to use them whatever the price. Others may bring benefits, but are less necessary or have more substitutes. The measure of how responsive demand is to price is known as the *price elasticity of demand*. In a similar way we can calculate the responsiveness of demand to income changes, and this is the *income elasticity of demand*.

3.2 Measuring Elasticity

Many studies have estimated demand elasticities. It is often useful to know what will happen if prices rise or fall. Take the example of legalising the use of heroin. The current price of heroin is high, largely as a result of the prohibition of production, importation and distribution of the drug. If the drug were legalised it is likely that the price would fall, since it is very cheap to produce. It is very likely that consumption would rise in this case, since demand normally increases as price falls. The question of interest is 'how much is demand likely to rise in response to a fall in price?' Policy makers would be keen to know the answer to this before embarking on legalisation. It might be argued that, since heroin is addictive, then users are not very sensitive to price. In other words demand is *inelastic*. But it would be useful to have estimates of elasticity before making the policy change.

Figure 3.1 illustrates the relationship between price and quantity of heroin demanded, per week in one market. From the information in Figure 3.1 we can draw up a table showing the relationship between quantity consumed and price. For example, at price €80, the demand would be 59 g. Table 3.1 shows all the combinations.

From the table what can be said about how responsive is demand to price? The fall in quantity seems quite large – the price rise from €20 to €80 reduces demand by 31 g.

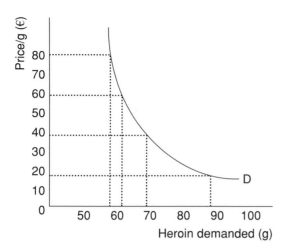

Figure 3.1 Demand for heroin

Table 3.1 Relation between quantity consumed and price, from Figure 3.1

Price (€)	Quantity of heroin sold (g)
20	90
40	70
60	63
80	59

But really to answer the question we need to compare the *proportionate changes* If price falls from €80 to €60, this 25 per cent fall leads to a rise in consumption of less than 7 per cent. This suggests that demand is not very responsive to price – what might be expected from the addictive nature of the drug. If we consider a fall in price from €40 to €20, this 50 per cent fall in price leads to a 29 per cent increase in demand. In this case we can see that demand is more sensitive to price changes at low levels of price, but is very insensitive at higher prices. This is important – we often find that the responsiveness changes at different levels of price.

Clearly this comparison of percentage increases in demand and decreases in price provides a measure of how much demand responds *proportionately* to price changes. This is the basis of the calculation of the price elasticity of demand. The normal way to calculate this is to divide the *proportionate change in the quantity* by the *proportionate change in price*. More formally

Price elasticity of demand =
$$\frac{\text{Proportionate change in quantity}}{\text{Proportionate change in price}}$$

$$\varepsilon = \frac{\%\Delta Q}{\%\Delta P}$$

where ΔQ is the change in quantity and ΔP the change in price.

In the above example, when price changes from €80 to €60

$$\varepsilon = \frac{\%\Delta Q}{\%\Delta P} = \frac{-7\%}{25\%} = -0.28$$

By the same calculation, when price falls from €40 to €20, the elasticity of demand is calculated at −0.58. It is clear from the calculation that elasticity is just a number – it has no units. Note also that in these cases the price elasticity of demand is a negative number. In the above example percentages were used, but of course exactly the same answer comes if proportions are used instead.

The price changes in the above example are large (we are calculating elasticity over an *arc* in the demand curve). The calculations have been carried out on the basis of lowering the price. If instead the price were raised from €20 to €40, then the percentage rise is 100 per cent. In this case it therefore matters if we are calculating the elasticity on the basis of a rise or a fall in the price. There are two ways in which we can get around this. First, the percentage rise or fall can be calculated on the basis of the mid point of the change. If we did this we would get a slightly different estimate for elasticity:

$$\varepsilon = \frac{\%\Delta Q}{\%\Delta P} = \frac{-4}{61} \bigg/ \frac{20}{70} = -0.23$$

If we are dealing with large changes in price or quantity it is preferable to calculate elasticity in this way. However, the better solution is to consider smaller changes. We could consider changes in price of €1, and there would be much less difference between the calculation using the mid point and the calculation using the starting price to calculate the percentage.

We can easily rewrite the expression for elasticity in two parts – the ratio of the changes, and the ratio of the price and quantity

$$\varepsilon = \frac{\%\Delta Q}{\%\Delta P} = \frac{\Delta Q}{\Delta P} \times \frac{(P2 + P1)/2}{(Q2 + Q1)/2}$$
$$= \frac{\%\Delta Q}{\%\Delta P} = \frac{\Delta Q}{\Delta P} \times \frac{(P2 + P1)}{(Q2 + Q1)}$$

where P1 and P2 are the initial and final prices, and Q1 and Q2 the initial and final quantities

The first expression approximates the slope of the demand curve. As we make the change in price smaller and smaller we can rewrite the expression for elasticity in terms of the slope of the demand curve and the ratio of price and quantity. Using normal calculus notation:

$$\varepsilon = \frac{\delta Q}{\delta P} \times \frac{P1}{Q1}$$

This expression is for the elasticity of demand for the good or service at the point P1, Q1 (and this is known as *point elasticity*). It is now clear that elasticity can vary along the demand curve, either because of changes in slope, or as a result of the changing ratio of price and quantity. Even if the demand curve is a straight line, elasticity varies along the curve. This is important to note – a flatter demand curve is on average more elastic, and a steeper one less elastic, but elasticity is not the same as slope.

In the example above the elasticity of demand was calculated to be in the range from −0.28 to −0.58. In describing price elasticity of demand we normally describe the range 0 to −1.0 as inelastic – that is to say demand responds to changing price by a smaller proportion than the change in price. When elasticity is −1 the proportionate changes in price and quantity are the same, a situation of 'unitary elasticity'. The range from −1 to −∞ is normally described as elastic. In this range the quantity demanded is highly responsive to changes in price.

3.3 Elasticity of Demand and Health Promotion

Knowledge of price elasticity of demand can be useful for a range of policy decisions in health care and health promotion. An obvious example is the use of taxes to raise the price of cigarettes and discourage smoking. In this case several questions are relevant. First, if prices rise, to what extent will this achieve a reduction in smoking? Second, who will be dissuaded – will it be the young or the old, heavy smokers or occasional ones? What will happen to government revenues? Will the tax fall disproportionately on the poor?

Many studies have been carried out on the demand for cigarettes (Townsend 1987; Stebbins 1991; Trigg and Bosanquet 1992). Estimates vary, but the consensus is that price elasticity of demand is around −0.5. Using this information we can make a number of judgements about the likely effects of a change in price on smoking and tax revenue, and examine how the burden will fall on different population groups.

Table 3.2 The effect of raising the tax on cigarettes

Variable	Before	After
Pre-tax Price (€)	10	10
Tax (€)	2	3
Consumption (g)	100,000	96,080
Total spending (€)	1,200,000	1,249,040
Tax revenue (€)	200,000	288,240

Let us assume that the current tax on cigarettes is an *ad valorem* tax (i.e. a percentage added to the selling price), and is set at 20 per cent of the selling price. What will be the effects of increasing this to 30 per cent of the selling price? Not all of this will be passed on to the consumer – the relative burden on consumer and seller depends on a range of factors. However, for simplicity let us assume that this tax is all passed on to the consumer. Since demand is inelastic, in order to produce any given percentage fall in consumption there must be a more than proportionate increase in price. Put another way, in order to produce a large reduction in smoking it is necessary to increase tax (and therefore price) substantially.

What happens to the tax revenue for the government? A simple example is set out in Table 3.2. The price increase is 8 per cent, and the fall in consumption 4 per cent. It can be seen from the table that spending has gone up despite the fall in consumption, and that tax revenue takes a larger share of the larger total spending. A simple rule of thumb is that, if demand is inelastic, a price increase caused solely by a higher tax *will always increase tax revenue*. It is sometimes suggested that governments are afraid to increase tax on tobacco for fear of losing revenue. This is almost certainly wrong. The example may understate the scope for government to

increase revenue by increasing tobacco tax. In this example we have ignored the fact that normally some part of the tax is paid by the seller, so that government can increase its tax revenue from both buyers and sellers.

Studies of elasticity of demand for tobacco have normally shown that demand is more elastic among young smokers, many of whom are recent starters. This means that the overall elasticity estimates are likely to imply that demand elasticity is even lower for older, more addicted, smokers. This would suggest that tax increases may be a good strategy for reducing smoking in younger people. However, although richer people may display lower price elasticity of demand than poorer ones, the effect of the tax is likely to fall more heavily on poorer people. Poorer people spend a higher proportion of their income on tobacco, so the tax is *regressive*, that is, it takes a higher proportion of income from those who are poorer. Taxes are described as *progressive* if richer people pay a higher proportion of their income on the tax than do poorer people.

Another point to keep in mind is that price elasticity of demand normally varies at different prices. If we know that elasticity is −0.5 at the current price we can safely predict the effects of a relatively small tax increase. What is not so sensible is to make predictions of effects of, say, a tax rise from 20 per cent to 80 per cent, which involves a move along the demand curve, possibly to a point where elasticity is much higher.

What can be said from this simple, although realistic, example? First, increasing tax on tobacco is likely to be an effective way of reducing smoking, but large tax increases will be needed to effect a moderate reduction. Second, the government is likely to enjoy an increase in tax revenue as a result of the increase. Third, it is likely that this policy will be particularly effective in reducing smoking in new, relatively young smokers. Fourth, such a policy may have undesirable effects on the tax burden, since it falls disproportionately on poorer people. In some countries this is an even greater issue since smoking rates are often higher in lower-income groups.

Low price elasticity of demand tends to indicate that the good is considered to be essential, and that there are few if any substitutes. Goods may be considered essential either because they are necessary to sustain life, or as a result of addiction. One indicator that a good is addictive is that it is not normally considered necessary to sustain life, but nevertheless has a low price elasticity of demand.

High taxes on health-damaging goods may be effective in reducing consumption. We can do similar calculations to investigate the effectiveness of subsidies to encourage healthy behaviours. For example, it would be possible to exempt all fresh fruit and vegetables from tax to encourage more consumption. Sports facilities can be subsidised in order to encourage use. We cannot say if these kinds of policy will be effective ways of encouraging healthier lifestyles without doing calculations of demand elasticity.

3.4 Cross-elasticity of Demand

Price-elasticity of demand is the more widely used measure. We can also measure other elasticities. For example, we can assess the *cross-elasticity of demand* between two goods – for example, how sensitive is the demand for needles to the price of syringes? Since they are complements, we would expect demand for needles to fall if the price of syringes rises. If Pn_1 is the original price of needles, and Qs_1 is the original quantity of syringes, the cross-elasticity of demand can be expressed as

$$\varepsilon = \frac{\delta Qn}{\delta Ps} \times \frac{Ps_1}{Qn_1}$$

If goods are complements, as in this example, the value of cross-elasticity of demand is negative. In the case of substitutes, then, the cross-elasticity of demand is positive. For example, if the price of aspirin increases, then we would expect a rise in demand for ibuprofen, since they are substitutes.

3.5 Income Elasticity of Demand

People on higher incomes can buy more of everything. Of course they do not do so – as income rises a person buys more of some goods, and less of some others. She may buy fewer bus rides and more taxi journeys, more housing and more expensive holidays. A good is said to be income elastic if the *proportion* of income spent on the good rises with income. Income elasticity of demand can be positive (i.e. with rising income more is bought) or negative. Goods with positive income elasticity are described as *normal goods* and those with negative income elasticity as *inferior goods*.

Income elasticity is calculated from the relative change in demand for a good and the relative change in income. Formally, the formula for income elasticity of demand is

$$\varepsilon = \frac{*Q}{*Y} \times \frac{Y1}{Q1}$$

where Y is income, and Q1 the original income.

3.6 Elasticity and Prices of Health Care

In the same way that we can use information on elasticity to inform policy on tax or subsidy to encourage healthier lifestyles, it can also be useful in developing policy on charging for health services. In most countries there are at least some charges for medical services, hospital care or drugs. If demand is inelastic, then the effect of such charges will be to raise revenue with little effect on use. If more elastic, then charges may deter people from using effective and useful care.

The evidence suggests that in general demand for health care is price inelastic, so that there is only a small effect on demand from raising charges (Gertler *et al.* 1987; Creese 1991; McPake 1993). However, the evidence also shows that the picture is more complicated. Poorer people display more elastic demand than do richer ones, so a simple policy of charges will deter them more. This may justify exemption from fees for people on lower incomes.

A potential role for user fees is to deter people from making unnecessary use of services. If people face a charge for access they will think carefully about their need for care. However, again the evidence suggests that such a policy cannot be applied simply. The depressing fact is that the deterrent effect of charges seems to be the same for clearly useful and probably pointless interventions (Newhouse 1993).

Studies on the income elasticity of demand for health services suggest that the values are positive and greater than one. In other words demand for health care is income elastic. As incomes rise the quantity of health care consumed rises *more than proportionately.* Goods with this characteristic are often described as luxuries, since richer people buy more. This does not imply that they are unnecessary, but only that they are chosen in much larger amounts as income rises. This phenomenon may also explain the finding that countries that are richer not only spend more in total on health care, but also spend a *higher proportion* of GNP on health services.

Overall the evidence from empirical studies of the impact of user fees suggests that they can be used to raise revenue without major deterrent effects on use of services. However, it also shows that care has to be taken since those on low incomes are most likely to be deterred, and are often those with the greatest needs. Understanding the patterns of elasticity of demand at different price levels and for different groups in the population allows policy to be developed to avoid some undesired effects.

Chapter 4

Production, Health and Health Care
Efficient Use of Inputs

....

4.1 Introduction

Health services are very diverse. Some parts use technically skilled staff, sophisticated equipment and expensive consumables, while others require caring and human skills. Some are highly automated, and others are more like craft industries. Some require teamwork, while in others professionals work alone. Health services are provided in many different settings. This chapter considers the general approach of economics to production, and explores how this can help in understanding production of health and health care.

4.2 Efficiency in Production

It is widely agreed that, given the scarcity of health care resources, it is important that services be produced efficiently. It is not always clear what we mean by efficient. Economists use a number of concepts of efficiency. At the most basic level we wish to ensure that the existing inputs are not capable of producing more services. For example, if ten staff are needed to produce a service and twelve are employed that is inefficient. But even if

production is efficient in this narrow technical sense, it may still be possible to lower cost by changing to a different technology, or by paying less for the inputs. When economists think about production they focus on the fact that we almost always have choices of the technology used and the mix of inputs. The third sense of efficiency is getting the best value from the resources. In this chapter the first two meanings are relevant.

4.3 Factors of Production and Efficient Use of Resources

Production is the process of 'changing the form or arrangement of matter to adapt it better for the satisfaction of wants' (Marshall 1920). Marshall goes on to suggest that it is when we 'adjust matter to make it more useful'. By putting together materials, equipment and skills we provide a service or produce a useful product. Many different combinations are usually possible, and the choice of how to produce services should depend on many factors. The explosive growth of the Internet has led to many changes in the ways services are delivered – music no longer needs to be put on discs, and insurance can be bought electronically. News can be delivered on air, on paper or online. Two important points emerge – first it is almost always possible to provide services in different ways, and the options open to us are constantly changing.

Production normally requires a range of inputs. (Various terms are used in economics to describe inputs – including factors of production and inputs. In this chapter the terms are used interchangeably.) There is a need for some or all of the following: buildings, equipment, vehicles, skilled staff, semi-skilled staff, energy and consumables. Once again, since paper is two dimensional, we will simplify the analysis to take account of only two inputs – equipment and staff. Although this may seem to be too much of a simplification, it allows the principles to be applied. The analysis has some similarities to the analysis of indifference curves in Chapter 2.

Economists always think in terms of inputs to production being, to a greater or lesser extent, substitutes. We can choose to use more equipment (and relatively *capital-intensive* production) or more staff and choose a more *labour-intensive* process. We can choose to use more experienced staff, or use staff with less training, but who are given more supervision or provide services following strict protocols. Tradition often dictates that certain professions do certain jobs, but if we go back to first principles it is not always obvious why this is the case.

The example below considers the options for providing immunisation services to a dispersed rural community. There are two options for transport – walking or cycling. In this example we define one unit of capital as one bicycle that is in working order for one week. Staff is measured as one person working for one week. In Figure 4.1 combinations

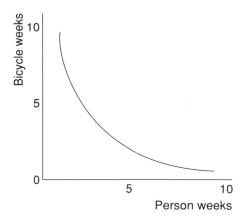

Figure 4.1 Combinations of units of labour and capital for the immunisation of 1,000 children

of units of labour and units of capital are shown that can be used to immunise 1,000 children.

The example suggests that there is a trade-off between bicycles and staff, but that they are not perfect substitutes. (Research suggests that bicycles seldom give injections to patients!) In this example, when there are eight bicycles available, there is no further advantage in having more. Intuitively this feels right. There comes a point when there is all the necessary transport, and what is needed is people to do the work. Equally, although we could provide the service with no bicycles, in order to reach the more remote areas we would need to send people on very long walks. Under these circumstances even one bicycle would make a great difference. Indeed, adding a second bicycle reduces the need for staff from ten to six.

This phenomenon is well known in economics. If we add more combinations of bicycles and staff we can show all the possible ways of providing the service as a curve, known as an *isoquant*, as shown in Figure 4.2. The curve shows all the combinations of staff

Figure 4.2   Isoquant

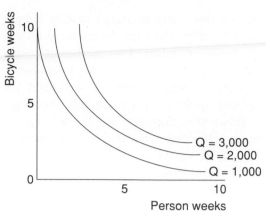

Figure 4.4   Isoquant map with increasing re-turns to scale

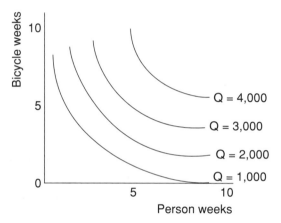

Figure 4.3   Isoquant map

and bicycles that allow the service to produce 1,000 immunised children. It is important to be clear what the isoquant means. It is possible anywhere above (i.e. north-east of) the curve is feasible. Nowhere below the curve is feasible. In essence the curve represents the boundary of the feasible set of combinations of inputs that can produce an output of 1,000. Put another way, the curve represents the *technically efficient* combinations of staff time and bicycles that can produce 1,000 immunised children.

The slope of isoquants is determined by the extent to which the inputs are substitutes for each other. As suggested above, this is likely to vary. The slope of the isoquant is a measure of the *marginal rate of technical substitution* between inputs.

We could draw similar curves for 2,000, 3,000 and 4,000 children immunised. This is done in Figure 4.3. These isoquants have all been drawn convex to the origin, suggesting that at all levels of output, the two inputs become less substitutable as we move to higher proportions of one input. Knowledge of the shapes and positions of isoquants (the isoquant map) allows us to describe certain features of the service. For example, in some cases production uses less inputs relative to outputs at higher levels of output. This is known as *increasing returns to scale*. When there are increasing returns to scale the isoquants become closer together as output increases, as shown in Figure 4.4. If there are decreasing returns to scale, then the isoquants are more widely spaced as output increases.

We can show different production methods, or uses of different technologies, as different rays from the origin. Figure 4.5 shows relatively capital-intensive and relatively labour-intensive production.

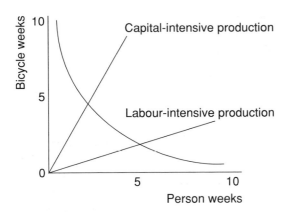

Figure 4.5 Rays of capital- and labour-intensive production

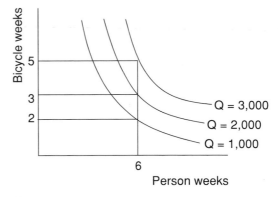

Figure 4.6a Decreasing returns to the labour factor

4.4 Mix of Inputs and Diminishing Marginal Returns

In Figure 4.1 it was shown that there was no further advantage in more bicycles once 8 were available. The argument was simply that without people to ride them, no additional benefits come from more machines. In general we find that if we hold one factor of production constant, then increasing the other will increase output, *but at a decreasing rate*. One factor of production is considered to be 'fixed' in the 'short run' – see Chapter 5. This is illustrated in Figure 4.6. In this example we hold the number of bicycles constant and observe the effects on output of increasing the number of staff. Similarly we explore the effects on output of changing the number of bicycles with the number of staff held constant.

Holding the number of bicycles constant at three, four staff produce 1,000, six staff produce 2,000, but to produce 3,000 requires an additional four staff. For this given number of bicycles, the extra output (the *marginal product*) of each member of staff falls as

Figure 4.6b Decreasing returns to the capital factor

the number of staff increases. This is not surprising since there are fewer bicycles to go round, and more staff spend more time walking.

In the second case we hold staff constant at six. Using two bicycles it is possible to provide 1,000, and a further one bicycle allows this to increase to 2,000. A further two bicycles are needed to achieve 3,000. In this case we can calculate the marginal product of bicycles as we increase their number while holding person weeks constant.

This pattern is well known in economics, and is known as the principle (or law) of eventually *diminishing marginal returns*. Holding one factor of production constant, additional units of the other increase output, but at an eventually diminishing rate.

4.5 Production, Efficiency and Health Care

The basic economic theory of production can be useful in giving a focus to some issues in delivery of health care. First, it emphasises that there are many ways to combine inputs to produce outputs. There is a tendency in health services for a belief to grow up that there is a 'best' or 'proper' way to do things. This can lead to inefficient choices about technology.

Second, isoquants define the (efficient) boundary of the set of feasible ways in which health services can be produced. Clearly most services, most of the time, are not completely efficient. The example chosen to illustrate production is very simple in comparison with most services. The service can be quite easily defined, and its production can be carefully planned and managed. In reality it is often not so simple. If we are running an emergency service, the product is not only treatment for those who have needs, but is also the readiness to provide care. This means that often the staff and facilities are ready for action, but are not actually busy. This can be efficient, but defining efficiency in this type of circumstance is not easy.

It can also be difficult to be sure that apparently greater efficiency is not just lower quality of care. Once again, the problem is often of definition of what is the output. In the case of vaccination, the service can be defined, and quality may not be a great issue.

However, in long-term hospital or nursing care, differences in inputs may reflect (hidden) differences in output. There is no easy way to know if this is the case. Part of the problem is the tendency in health care for the output to be described in terms of processes or intermediate outputs. Where possible this should be avoided. Taking the immunisation example, output can be described anywhere on the spectrum from children immunised, cases of disease prevented, death or disability prevented, life years gained or welfare. If we define it in terms of achievement (for example, as life years gained) then poor quality of service will reduce this. However, if the output is described in terms of number of children injected with the vaccine, then there is more risk that what is in reality poor quality will appear to be efficient production.

Production theory raises a number of important issues in health care. For example, are there increasing returns to scale? When we think about health care production it is likely that there are few. Large hospitals are not really large, at least in the sense that they are composed of many (largely separate) departments. West (1997) suggests that hospitals are really sheds with workshops inside. Baumol (1995) supports this view in his analysis of health care as a handicraft industry. What is clear is that only some parts of health care exhibit increasing returns to scale, and where these exist they tend to be in the automated, high-technology areas. Large hospitals may be large because of the *scope* of their services. Economies of scope depend on there being important links between the different activities (such as shared computer support, more efficient administration or shared use of diagnostic services). Evidence suggests that there are only limited economies of scope in health care. Indeed, since health care organisations are often highly complex, and present real challenges for management, it may be that there are decreasing returns to scale. The wider scope of activities of a general hospital may make all the activities more difficult to organise, and more expensive.

4.6 Health Care Providers as Multi-product Firms

It has been suggested that hospitals and other health care providers produce a wide range of services. The analysis above shows how there is a degree of flexibility in the use of inputs, with different combinations of staff and equipment being feasible. Similarly, there is a degree of flexibility in what the hospital can produce. Some hospital inputs are very specific to particular services, but to a large extent the skills of health care professionals are generic.

If we imagine a hospital that produces two kinds of service (say stroke rehabilitation and geriatric assessment), there is scope within any given staff, buildings and equipment mix to switch between the two. However, since there are some specific skills and items of equipment, it is unlikely to be possible simply to substitute one stroke case for one assessment case. Figure 4.7 illustrates the likely pattern of output.

The slope of the curve in Figure 4.7 is the *marginal rate of transformation* between the two services – that is, the rate at which it is possible to switch from producing one to producing the other within any given resources. This has been drawn in the diagram as being concave to the origin. The reason for this is that there is a mixture between generic and more specialised skills needed. If we move to one end of the curve, that is to a heavy concentration on one or other service, then it becomes increasingly

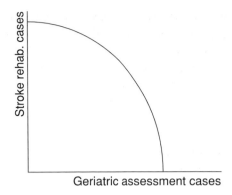

Figure 4.7 Transformation of production between two services

difficult to switch production to even more of that service.

4.7 Professions, Skills and Efficiency of Production of Health Services

The emphasis of this chapter has been very much that there is scope for variation in the mix of factors of production, and that there is scope for switching between outputs. However, constraints to doing this often come from the very specific bundles of skills held by health care professionals. It is interesting to consider the extent to which this is a logical system, or simply the accident of history. Changes in the technology of health care, and in the ways in which existing technologies are applied, tend to lead to a need to reconsider the packages of skills held by each profession or sub-profession. For example, as mental health services shift from institutions to the community, there is a need for the professionals to combine assessment, treatment and practical skills if they are to provide the required support. Nurses have to deal with their patients' housing, financial and social

31

problems as well as supporting the provision of medication. Similarly, it can often be efficient for nurses to be able to take simple x-rays, or for occupational therapists to carry out some (traditionally) nursing tasks. In many countries the roles of nurses are being widened, with some traditionally medical tasks being added. Some changes are driven by the desire of professions to enhance their position and status, but to some extent there is recognition that this offers more flexibility in the use of resources.

Chapter 5

Cost of Delivering Health Services

5.1 Production and Cost

The theory of production in Chapter 4 suggests that inputs can be used in various proportions to produce health care services. Isoquants define the technically efficient combinations and form the boundary of feasible production possibilities. However, it is not enough to know that production is technically efficient – we want to minimise the cost of production of services. What is required is a way to identify the technically efficient combination of factors of production that minimises cost. We do this by adding a set of *isocost lines* to the analysis. (Points on the isocost line are points of equal cost.)

When we refer to minimising cost, this is defined as minimising the cost of any given quality and volume of services. It is always possible to cut costs by doing less or doing it worse. This may or may not be a good thing. However, reducing the cost of any given quality and quantity of services always allows more to be achieved with the given resources.

If we know the wage rate for staff and the cost per week to rent a bicycle, we can work out how much of each, or combinations of

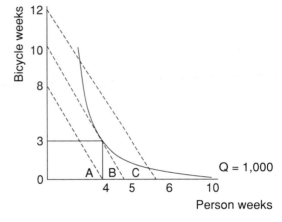

Figure 5.1 Production at minimum cost, based on the analysis of isoquants in Chapter 4

each, can be bought for any given budget. On each axis, the isocost line marks the maximum number of inputs that can be purchased from the budget if none of the other inputs is purchased. The slope of a budget line is the ratio of the factor prices (in this case the ratio of the prices of person weeks and bicycle weeks). If the wage is £500 per week and bicycle rental price £250 per week, we can draw isocost lines (A, B, C in Figure 5.1, where A = £2,000, B = £2,500 and C = £3,000). If we wish to produce 1,000 vaccinations, it is not feasible on line A – that is to say, a budget of

£2,000 is inadequate to produce 1,000 vaccinations even if it is used efficiently. Isocost line B is just feasible, and line C unnecessarily generous. In line B the budget is £2,500. The intersections with the axes are easy to calculate. If the entire budget were used on wages it would buy five weeks. If all were used on bicycle rental it would buy ten weeks.

In this example the lowest cost way of producing 1,000 vaccinations is to use three bicycles and four staff. At this point, the 'economically efficient' combination is determined (recall that all points on the isoquants are technically efficient – see section 4.3). Presumably some people live within easy walking distance, so there is no great advantage in providing a bicycle for each member of staff. This is an important point – depending on the prices of bicycle rentals and staff, we can determine the lowest cost way of providing the service. If the price of bicycles were to fall, then we would be likely to choose to provide each member of staff with transport. Equally, if wages fell substantially it might be cheaper to employ more people, and for them to walk to the nearer towns.

In the same way as the consumer chooses her consumption on the basis of preferences and relative prices, the lowest cost way of providing services can be determined from the map of isoquants (representing different outputs) and relative prices of inputs.

We do not observe isoquants in everyday life, but a version of this approach is used in the statistical analysis of production in health care. In estimating production and cost functions we are effectively going through this process. The important points are that there are almost always choices in how we produce health care, and the lowest cost method depends on selecting the cheapest of the efficient options.

5.2 Changes in Technology

Isoquants represent efficient combinations of inputs to produce a given level of output. Underlying the isoquant is a given technology. It may be that as we increase output different technologies become available, so that the efficient combinations can change with volume of service. In the health sector this is particularly apparent in pathology, where automated systems may only be efficient if large volumes of samples are tested. Many technologies are 'lumpy', that is to say, machines only come in certain sizes, so that they may only be efficient in use if at least a minimum volume of service is provided. The isoquant map tells us about the behaviour of the technology in any particular case. Changing slopes mean that the relative productivity of different factors changes, and increasing or decreasing returns to scale are reflected in changes in the gaps between isoquants. However, in choosing the lowest cost combination of inputs to use in production we need to remain aware also of any changes in the relative price of inputs.

There is constant evolution and development of health care technologies. This means that the efficient use of resources and the minimum costs of services are also likely to be changing constantly. Understanding the theory of production and costs can help remind us that budgets for particular services should not normally be left unchanged. It also helps focus on the fact that the potential for costs to fall with technical change varies between services, and across the board budget cuts fail to take this into account.

5.3 Changes in Relative Factor Prices

To some extent the prices of inputs depend on workings of the market. The prices of equipment, drugs, buildings and consumables are determined largely by market forces. Demand for and supply of staff with particular skills may also play a major role in determining wages. However, there are often other factors that have important influences on the determination of prices of inputs. The operation of trade unions (including 'professional' associations) may raise wages. Professional organisations can be effective in restricting supply of skilled staff, and thus can raise wages. Many countries have minimum wage laws that will affect the price of unskilled staff. However, in the long run supply and demand conditions are likely to be important determinants of these prices. For more detail of markets and how they can fail see Chapters 6–8.

In a growing economy there tends to be a rise in the wages of all workers. Cost of equipment normally falls over time (although this can be masked by increased sophistication and higher specification). Indeed technical change is an important source of lower costs, and it should be remembered that in itself technical change *cannot increase the cost of producing a given output*. There is widespread confusion because new technology can be associated with higher health care expenditure through improving quality and by making available new opportunities to treat disease, but cannot increase the cost of a given service.

The result of technical change is lower costs of equipment for any given unit of output. This process occurs throughout the economy, leading to gradual increases in wages for all workers. This means that the relative prices of labour and other inputs change, with labour becoming relatively more expensive than other inputs. For this reason it is important to remember that the lowest cost way of providing services is likely to change, even when there is no change in the underlying technology.

Once again understanding that it is normally possible to make some substitution between equipment and labour means that what is efficient production is likely to change over time.

As technology has developed, some goods and services have become much easier and cheaper to make. In agriculture the development of systems to allow oxen to be used greatly increased the productivity of farm workers, and the development of horse-drawn and mechanical technologies further increased it. In industry mechanisation, division of labour and new materials have allowed goods to be produced at much lower cost. However, some services are produced by 'handicraft' (Baumol 1995) industries, and these have more limited scope for technological progress and falling costs.

To some extent health care can be seen as such an industry. Although many elements of services have been automated, and new drugs and appliances can lower costs, a large part of most health service cost comes from staff who look after patients, and it is more difficult to get technical progress in this kind of work. The prices of handicraft goods generally rise over time relative to other goods. Whereas the workers in industries with rapid technical change may obtain higher wages from sharing in the gains from higher productivity, in health care higher wages are likely to lead to higher costs of care. The increase in the relative cost of health care may therefore be seen as an inevitable feature of an industry that is more handicraft than mass-production in its technology.

5.4 What do We Mean by Cost?

It is never easy to answer this question. The classic answer is that economists use 'cost' to mean opportunity cost – that is, the value of the output of the resources in their best alternative use. That much is simple. But what determines the price we have to pay for inputs, and what is the value of the best alternative use of the resources? Indeed, what is the best alternative use of the resources? Health care systems are normally subject to many rules and regulations – often these are important sources of safety and protection to the users. But restrictions can also distort prices. In many cases the prices of inputs (wages and prices capital and consumable inputs) include an element of *economic rent* – that is, they are paid more than is necessary to make them available. For example, I may be willing to work for €70 per day, but will happily accept €120 if it is offered. In this case the cost is €70, but in addition I accept an economic rent of €50 per day. In principle such rent payments are not part of cost, but it is very difficult to separate the two.

More complicated issues arise with patented devices and drugs. Development costs are recovered through charging prices that are above the direct costs of producing the goods and maintaining the equipment. Without compensation for the investment in research and development in new products it is unlikely that many new drugs would be developed and in many ways patent protection is an efficient way of providing incentives for innovation. But this does mean that the price charged is above cost.

The practical question of how we assess what is the opportunity cost is explored further when we discuss economic evaluation in Chapters 11 and 13. In this chapter the emphasis is on the normal determinants and patterns of financial cost.

5.5 *Estimating Cost Functions in Health Care*

The analysis of isoquants and isocost lines provides a framework for analysing the likely relationships between inputs to health care and the costs. Empirical investigation of the patterns of costs can be useful in understanding what is the lowest cost way of providing services in different circumstances. An obvious question is whether there are *economies of scale* (i.e. does the unit cost of production of services fall with scale of production?). If there are significant economies of scale in hospitals, then there are advantages in having fewer, larger hospitals. However, it is important to be clear why this might be the case. It is important to distinguish between the effects on unit costs of doing more of a given service (e.g. caesarean sections or cataract operations) and the effects on costs of being a larger hospital overall.

There is some evidence that costs of relatively high technology procedures fall with volume (e.g. Cronin *et al.* 1998), but much less that large-scale economies exist at the whole hospital level. In some cases it has been found that there are *economies of scope* – that is by combining certain different services in the same organisation there will be savings. These are likely to exist if some equipment or staff can usefully be shared between the different services. The history of the development of health care infrastructure over the last fifty years shows that there has been a widespread belief in economies of scale, with a common pattern being the closure of small hospitals and redevelopment of services in fewer larger settings. Although this trend may be now reversing, it is still common to hear planners and clinicians referring to such changes as *rationalisation*. In the past most

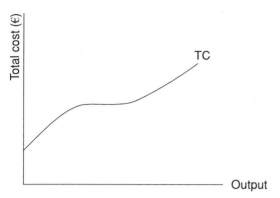

Figure 5.2 Total cost curve

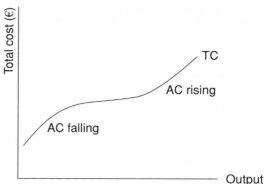

Figure 5.3 Average cost trends in different areas of the total cost curve

developments of health care infrastructure have been carried out without good evidence about the relationships between what is produced, how it is produced and at what cost it can be produced. Estimating cost functions for health care provision can allow better understanding.

Cost functions can be estimated by comparing data from different providers of care to explore the main determinants of cost. It is important in such studies to take account of case mix, and this can be very difficult. It is a constant problem that apparently similar cases in health care can have very different costs (Gray *et al.* 1997). There is a growing literature on cost functions in health care provision, and it is becoming clear that economies of scale are quite limited, but can be important in certain types of service. Case mix is normally very important. The evidence supports Baumol's assertion that health care has many of the characteristics of a handicraft industry.

The purpose of estimating cost functions is to discover more about the relationship between cost and the different ways in which services can be delivered. It is worth noting that since there are some fixed costs, at zero output there is a positive cost. This applies in

the 'short run' only since the 'long run' is defined as the period in which all factors of production can be varied – in other words there are no fixed costs. The cost relationships discussed below are those expected to apply in the 'short run'.

In this case total cost rises at a decreasing rate at lower output, and at an increasing rate at higher output. This suggests that at lower levels of output there are economies of scale, but these disappear and are reversed at higher output. For some purposes we are interested in the total cost of provision – for instance if we are setting a budget for the service. However, for most purposes we are interested in two other measures – the cost of each unit of service (the *average cost*) and the cost of one more or less (the *marginal cost*). From the total cost curve here we can calculate the average cost. We can see that at lower output the average cost is falling, since with each extra unit of service, all units become cheaper. However, as output rises this is reversed. This is shown on Figure 5.3.

From this pattern we can derive the average cost – it will be U-shaped in this case. We can also calculate the marginal cost. The marginal cost is the *additional cost of one more*

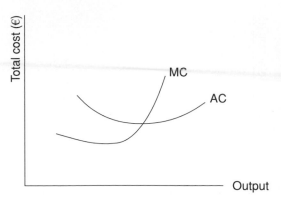

Figure 5.4 Average cost and marginal cost

unit of service. This can be described as the change in total cost divided by the change in output – and of course this just describes the *slope* of the total cost curve. This slope is positive all the way along the total cost curve, but the slope is initially decreasing, and later increasing. Similarly the marginal cost curve therefore starts by falling, and then increases. The average and marginal cost curves are shown in Figure 5.4.

The observant reader will notice that the MC curve crosses the AC curve at its lowest point. This is not an accident. If the average cost is falling, then it follows that the cost of one more unit of service (the MC) must be less than the average. If the average is rising, then the cost of one more must be above the average. Thus the MC curve always intersects the AC curve at its lowest point. In this short-run analysis, the shapes of the cost curves reflect the 'returns to a factor' rather than the 'returns to scale' since, as discussed above, they reflect how costs change when one factor of production (or input) is varied, while the other is considered fixed.

The normal interpretation of the cost of a treatment or operation is the average cost. For example, we might say that it costs €20 to immunise a child against the major infectious diseases, or say that percutaneous transluminal coronary angioplasty costs €2,000. As will be shown in Chapter 11, we need to be careful. Sometimes the relevant measure of cost is the marginal cost, since the policy question may be 'should we do more?' Many serious planning errors have followed from confusing average and marginal cost.

Chapter 6

Basic Market Models

6.1 Demand, Supply and Equilibrium

Previous chapters have explained the logic behind the demand curve and have argued that, while health is often 'different' from bananas or telephone calls, most of the differences are not unique to health. We argued that there were good reasons, both theoretical and from the observation of behaviour, to expect downward-sloping demand curves in health markets. For example, where prices for health services are charged or are implicit (for example in distance and waiting times), we expect less health services to be demanded the higher they are. We also normally expect suppliers of health services – such as suppliers of pharmaceuticals or of skills and labour – to supply more as the price increases *ceteris paribus* (although we will note important exceptions to that in the next three chapters).

Where we have downward-sloping demand curves and upward-sloping supply curves, the determination of price, output, and the allocation of production and consumption should, in principle, be straightforward. Figure 6.1 illustrates the expected process. Demand and supply curves intersect at the 'equilibrium' price (P*) and output (Q*) levels. The pressures exerted by demand and supply curves are

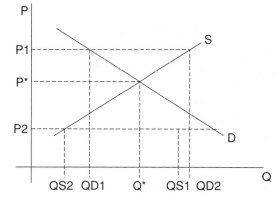

Figure 6.1 Interaction of demand and supply

expected to lead price to move towards P*Q*. Consider what would happen at any price away from this point. At P1, above P*, demand is QD1, less than supply QS1, suppliers are left with surplus goods to get rid of, and will have to lower the price to do so. At P2, below P*, demand is QD2 higher than supply at QS2. The result is a shortage of goods, and suppliers can increase prices and still sell what they want. Price can only be stable at the equilibrium point. At equilibrium, consumption is allocated to those willing to pay this price or more (those whose demands are illustrated to the left of the demand curve) and production to those willing to supply at this price or less (whose willingness is illustrated to the left of the supply curve).

This is a very simple model and, as much of the rest of the book will explore, does not capture the complexities of many real markets including health. However, it is an idea with enormous power to generate initial expectations about behaviour in markets which often turn out to be realised, even in health markets. For example, it suggests that if demands for dental services are increasing, *ceteris paribus*, prices of dental services are likely to increase, or that if numbers of medical graduates rise faster than demands for medical services, new graduates are likely to find themselves accepting jobs with a lower remuneration package than before. These types of predictions often hold.

6.2 The Perfect Market Model

An extreme set of simplifying assumptions lies behind the concept of the 'perfect' market. It is best to think of a 'perfect' market as you would think of a perfect square when studying geometry. It is not found in nature but it is an enormously useful tool to use to understand shapes which are. If you want to calculate the area of a complex shape it is useful to understand the principles behind calculating the area of a square. Similarly, if you wish to understand the operation of complex health markets, it is best to understand the operation of a perfect market which besides being 'perfect' in its efficiency implications (as we shall see) is also 'perfect' in its simplicity, like a square. It is safe to say that no perfect market exists, although we may be able to point to some markets which come quite close.

First, we need to step back and reflect further on what is happening 'behind' the demand and supply curves. The indifference curve analysis of Chapter 2 emphasised that price determines the rate at which an individual can trade off the good in question with other goods he also values. At the point at which the budget constraint is tangential to the indifference curve, the individual's marginal rate of substitution of one good for another (the slope of the indifference curve) is equal to the price ratio (the slope of the budget constraint). Price then captures the value of the last unit of the good purchased (the 'marginal value') to the individual, in terms of whatever alternative good is considered. (When all choices have been made, the value of the last cent spent must be equal for each good purchased – assuming that an independent decision can be made over each cent.) Money therefore represents all other goods the individual values and knowledge of how demand changes as price changes tells us about how much individuals making up a market value each individual good at the margin.

If this seems too involved, a simpler way of arriving at the same conclusion uses the individual's demand curve. Whatever the price is, the utility-maximising individual will purchase those units of the good for which his utility values are higher than the price and will stop purchasing at the point that his values fall below the price. *At the margin*, he equates his value to the price. The individual's demand curve therefore measures his value of each additional unit of the good – or his marginal value. At the market level, all individuals are making the same assessment. It follows that demand curves are powerful tools for telling us about how individuals value the goods they purchase, and indicate the aggregate marginal value or marginal utility of goods in that market (see Box 6.1).

On the supply side, we have seen that typical short-run cost functions are expected to take 'U-shaped' forms, reflecting 'diminishing

Box 6.1 Consumer Surplus

The idea that demand curves 'reveal preferences' and are indicators of marginal values to consumers can be extended to produce the concept of 'consumer surplus'. Consumer surplus is defined as the value to a consumer of trading in the market at the given price. It is measured by the area under the demand curve, since this sums the additional value to the consumer of each unit purchased (above the price, or marginal cost to the consumer of purchasing it).

Consider the diagram, which represents Mrs Brown's purchasing decision and value for aspirin. The demand curve then reveals her marginal value of each additional packet of aspirin consumed per year.

Figure B1   Mrs Brown's demand for aspirin

Suppose the price is 500 francs. Mrs Brown will purchase the first packet of aspirin (for which she would have paid up to 1,000 francs; the second packet of aspirin (for which she would have paid up to 750 francs) and the third packet (for which the 500 francs represents the most she would pay). However, she pays the going price – 500 francs – for all three packets. By interpreting the maximum she would have paid as her marginal valuation, we can identify a surplus value in the first packet of 1,000 – 500 = 500 francs; and in the second packet of 750 – 500 = 250 francs; and of zero for the third packet which cost exactly the most she was willing to pay. The total consumer surplus is equal to 500 + 250 + 0 = 750 francs.

The example uses large units in relation to the total amount bought, and the area of consumer surplus is 'stepped' rather than smooth, and does not equal the area under the demand curve. Under these circumstances, the demand curve is really stepped too – if the price fell to 375 francs, Mrs Brown could not purchase a further half-packet of aspirin. Unless items can be bought in infinitesimally small quantities (e.g. dry goods by weight, liquids by volume), a smoothly drawn demand curve is really a stepped one. As the quantities considered get larger (either because we consider smaller units like individual aspirin for Mrs Brown, or because we consider markets involving large numbers of people), it becomes more accurate to draw a smooth demand curve, and more accurate to consider the area of consumer surplus as a triangle, underneath the demand curve and above the price line.

Consumer surplus has been used in cost–benefit analysis as a measure of the value of an intervention, and also underlies the use of 'willingness to pay' as a source of consumers' values.

marginal returns' (see sections 4.4 and 5.5). Where the firm is a 'price taker' (is not powerful enough to control the price but must accept the price given by the market), the firm's supply curve can be derived from the marginal cost curve. Total revenue is equal to the price multiplied by the quantity sold. In other words, it is the firm's income before its costs have been taken into account. Under price-taking circumstances, the given price indicates both the average revenue, and the marginal revenue which is generated by selling one more unit of output. While the revenue to be gained from producing and selling one more unit of output is greater than the cost of producing that unit, a profit-maximising firm will produce it. If the marginal revenue is less than the marginal cost, a profit-maximising firm will not produce another unit. Such firms will choose to set production levels at the point at which marginal revenue equals marginal cost. In other words, the supply curve can be traced along the part of the marginal cost curve which is upward sloping and lies above the average cost curve.

The following are the assumptions of the perfect competition model:

1 U-shaped or upward-sloping marginal cost curves in the short run (and also in the long run, see below);
2 profit-maximising firms;
3 no barriers to entry or exit from the market;
4 perfect mobility of factors of production;
5 the product being sold must be 'homogeneous' (consumers cannot differentiate between the products of different suppliers);
6 large numbers of buyers and sellers;
7 perfect knowledge of market conditions on the parts of buyers and sellers;
8 no government intervention.

The firm operating in this environment has perfect knowledge and therefore knows its

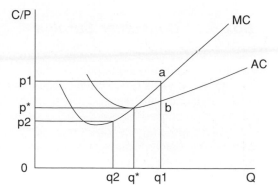

Figure 6.2 The firm under perfect competition

cost curves, and the prevailing price on the market. As explained above, it will choose to produce where price equals marginal cost. Consumers have perfect knowledge, are purchasing a homogeneous product (identical in every respect including ease of access to each supplier) and will purchase from any supplier, up to the point where they equate price and marginal value. There is no opportunity for an individual supplier to sell goods at higher than the prevailing price – consumers would all desert and go to other suppliers. There is no possibility of an advantage by undercutting the price because the firm can sell whatever volume it wants at the prevailing price. These assumptions produce 'price-taking' behaviour. The market can only reach equilibrium through the entry and exit of buyers and sellers to and from the market in response to price movements (which are generated by the market, independently of individual buyers and sellers).

Figure 6.2 describes the process of reaching equilibrium from the perspective of any 'efficient' (in the technical and economic senses – see Chapters 4 and 5) firm in this market. Firms expect to make 'normal' profit which can be considered as the minimum return to capital necessary to induce the firm's entrepreneur to remain in the market. This

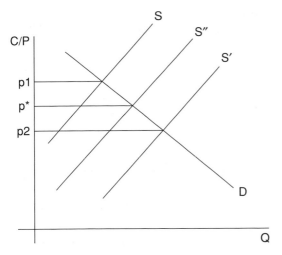

Figure 6.3 The industry under perfect competition

'normal' profit is usually considered to be part of the cost of capital, included in the cost curves. Profits above normal profits are made on each unit of production for which price (equal to marginal revenue) exceeds marginal cost. For example, at p1 the firm will choose to produce at q1, above normal profit is made on each unit of production between q* and q1. Above normal profit can be measured by distance ab per unit which is the difference between price (also equal to average revenue) and average cost.

The availability of this abnormal profit attracts new firms to the market and shifts the market supply curve from S to S′ (Figure 6.3). This produces downward pressure on price, implying a new equilibrium at p2. The efficient firm will choose to produce at q2 (Figure 6.2) but now makes a loss. These losses drive firms out of the market, shifting the market supply curve back towards the left again. Equilibrium is implied at S″ and p* (Figure 6.3), where p* is equal to the minimum point on the efficient firm's average cost curve (Figure 6.2). At this point, all inefficient firms are driven out of

business and only efficient ones can remain, earning only normal profit.

In this type of market, a number of conditions for efficiency have been met:

1 *Allocative efficiency*. Productive activity has been allocated to those products which consumers value in excess of their cost (marginal cost has been equated to marginal value).
2 *Technical efficiency*. Technically inefficient firms have cost curves above those of the efficient firm in the example and have been driven out of business. All those remaining must be operating on isoquants (not above).
3 *Economic efficiency*. Economically inefficient firms have cost curves above those of the efficient firm in the example and have been driven out of business. All those remaining must be equating the marginal rate of substitution of inputs in the production process with the price ratios of those inputs.
4 *Scale efficiency*. Production has been divided between firms in such a way that each produces that proportion of total output consistent with operation at the minimum point of a short run average cost curve.[1]

If these conditions are met across the whole economy in a 'general equilibrium analysis', still further claims for efficiency can be made. Box 6.2 provides some further discussion of this.

6.3 *The Monopolistic Market Model*

At the opposite extreme to perfect competition characterised by many sellers and price taking is monopoly, characterised by only one seller and price setting. Under the perfect

Box 6.2   *Perfect Competition and General Equilibrium Analysis*

The perfect competition model was based on a *partial equilibrium analysis*. It considered only one market in the economy, and the efficiency conditions listed at the end of section 6.2 would apply to that market only. If all markets in the economy are assumed to work on the same basis we can move from a partial to a *general equilibrium analysis*.

A general equilibrium analysis enables the analyst to focus on the linkages between markets. For example, each output uses inputs in its production, and these inputs are themselves traded in markets which for the purpose of this analysis are assumed also to be perfect. Review the efficiency conditions which conclude section 6.2. If they can be assumed true of input markets as well as of the market for the final product, we can conclude that inputs have also been produced at minimum cost, their production has earned their manufacturer only normal profit, and their price reflects the marginal cost of the last unit produced.

Now consider linkages between markets for substitute and complement goods which affect allocative efficiency. If substitute and complement goods are produced in perfect markets, they will also be sold at the marginal cost of technically efficient production including only normal profit.

Putting all this together, at the margin, consumers are choosing between goods which are all valued at marginal cost – to the manufacturer of the specific good, and to the whole economy because each input has also been priced at marginal cost. The resulting equilibrium is Pareto efficient (see Chapter 9). There is no reallocation of resources which could increase the welfare of one consumer without a cost to the welfare of another. This is often known as the *first fundamental theorem of welfare economics*.

In such a perfectly competitive economy, a number of marginal conditions are shown to hold, including:

1 *Consumption.* Consumers will consume at the point where their marginal rate of substitution between two goods is equal to the price ratio between those goods.
2 *Production.* Firms will produce at the point where the marginal rate of technical substitution between the two factors is equal to the ratio of the prices of those factors.
3 *Production sector* plans are brought into line with the plans of consumers through the price signals of the market – which always indicate the marginal costs of production. Thus the market is co-ordinated as if by an 'invisible hand' (a term coined by Adam Smith in his treatise *An Inquiry into the Nature and Causes of the Wealth of Nations* (1776) which is seen by many as the foundation of the discipline of economics).

However, conditions for perfect competition rarely prevail and in many cases are unlikely ever to prevail. In these circumstances it is important to understand the *theory of the second best* which states that if there is an unavoidable distortion somewhere in the economy, then perfect competition in any one market may not be efficient. Consider again the market linkages discussed above. Suppose that one market which provides a substitute good to that under analysis is produced by a monopolist (review the monopolistic market model in section 6.3). This implies that the price is above marginal cost. In choosing between the good produced in the perfectly competitive market, and that produced in the monopolistic market, consumers will equate marginal utility per rupee spent across the two goods. From the

Continued

perspective of efficiency, they will buy 'too much' of the good produced at marginal cost under perfect competition, because the underlying costs of production have not been equated at the margin across the two goods. It would cost society less to achieve the same levels of utility for consumers by switching production towards the good produced by the monopolist where the marginal costs of production are lower. The result is no longer Pareto efficient – a different allocation of resources could increase the welfare of at least one member of society without reducing the welfare of anyone else.

The same conclusion could be linked to a deviation from perfect competition in an input market, which distorts both the efficiency of choices made in production, and the prices which determine choices in consumption. One distortion creates a series of further distortions throughout the economy, and Pareto efficiency can no longer be claimed, even for perfect competition, in any one market.

The implications of this are profound, from the perspective of the debate over the rights and wrongs of *laissez-faire* and interventionist approaches to market regulation. If there is an unavoidable distortion somewhere in the economy, it follows that it may be efficient to introduce other distortions to help counterbalance the original one. Note that this conclusion is independent of any concern for equity in market allocations, which, as discussed in Chapter 9, is not a component of the Pareto criterion.

For example, if nurses are underpaid owing to monopsonistic (single buyer) purchasing arrangements, this will have implications for production choices which (if made efficiently from any individual provider's perspective) will use more of the services of nurses relative to other cadres of staff or of labour-substituting equipment than is efficient. If prices were then generated at marginal cost by the provider, they would be lower than without the nurse wage distortion leading to demand for more health services than efficient. Thus it may be appropriate, for example, to set 'norms' for the inputs of different staff cadres which constrain providers from acting efficiently from their own perspective but aim to lead to efficient allocations from the perspective of the economy as a whole. In consumption markets, health services might be taxed to realign marginal costs so that consumers make efficient consumption decisions.

Given the wide range and number of deviations from perfect competition existing in any economy, precise measurement of the degree and implications of individual deviations within their own or related markets is not a feasible objective of economic policy. Rather, a more general point might be carried from this discussion to the debate over *laissez-faire* versus interventionist approaches to health policy. The introduction of deliberate distortions in the form of government interventions can be justified on grounds of efficiency, as a means to compensate for unavoidable market distortions elsewhere, as well as on other grounds, for example those of equity. We explore this point further in the context of regulation in Chapter 17.

competition model, the firm, as a price taker, effectively faced a perfectly elastic demand curve: a tiny price increase would cause demand to fall to zero. Under monopoly, the firm's demand curve and the market demand curve are the same. The decision of the profit-maximising monopolist is represented graphically in Figure 6.4.

Under monopoly there is no supply curve because the supplier dictates price and sets price and output together. There is also no distinction between firm and market – the firm is the market. If all units of the good produced by the monopolist are sold at the same price (an assumption of this model), price equals average revenue. Marginal revenue can

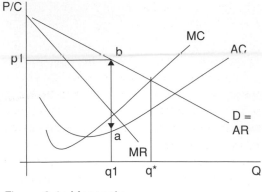

Figure 6.4 Monopoly

be derived from the demand curve, but is always less than average revenue because in order to sell one more unit of the good, the monopolist must reduce the price charged for all the units sold. Just as did the firm under perfect competition, the monopolist maximises profit where marginal revenue equals marginal cost, and prices and produces at p1q1. However, this results in abnormal profit (average abnormal profit can be measured by the distance ab between the average revenue and average cost at the chosen production level).

In comparison with the perfectly competitive outcome, the monopolistic output can be deemed 'inefficient'. A technically or economically inefficient monopolist will not be driven out of business. Profit maximisation implies a search for the most efficient ways of doing things but failure to achieve efficiency will not usually be catastrophic for the monopolist. Allocative efficiency is not achieved: units of output between q^1 and q^* are not produced, even though the marginal cost of doing so is less than the marginal utility placed by consumers on the additional units. The monopolist may operate at the minimum point of the short-run average cost curve, but only if this happened to coincide with the output level associated with equating marginal revenue and marginal cost.

6.4 From Analytical Models to Policy

The reader may at this point be feeling a little detached from reality. Almost every assumption of the perfect market model is a rare or non-existent phenomenon. In some respects, the models themselves help to explain why that should be. Firms seek to make 'abnormal profit'. Homogeneous products are a rare phenomenon precisely because it is in the interests of manufacturers to seek to differentiate their corn flake or cola from everybody else's. Suppliers collude in order to avoid price-taking. Information is jealously guarded rather than freely shared, and barriers are constructed against movement into markets in which abnormal profit is being earned by those benefiting. What are your expectations of the attitude of medical associations to the expansion of medical student numbers? No supplier wants to operate in a perfect market and earn only normal profit and so suppliers seek ingenious ways to 'get ahead of the game' and more closely resemble monopolists. In their ability to cast light on these phenomena the models are already revealing their ability to perform as analytical tools – rather than to describe reality.

Nevertheless, some markets look a lot more like perfect ones, and others a lot more monopolistic. Within the health sector, the market for surgery might be concluded to be less perfect than the market for over-the-counter pharmaceuticals. We will explore the different ways in which markets 'fail' or depart from the perfect model (see Chapter 8) – but already we can see that retailing pharmaceuticals involves many buyers and small firms competing with each other whereas much surgery takes place only in a few hospitals which are sometimes monopolies at local level; that on most estimations it is easier to become a pharmacist than a surgeon (and thus enter the market); that pharmaceutical products are more homogeneous (for example, you can buy generic aspirin or particular brands of aspirin at any pharmacy store) than surgical operations which are tailored to individual consumers, and so on.

If perfect markets are perfectly efficient, must it be true that few sellers are less efficient than many sellers in a market? Must it be true that attempts by government to intervene in markets are misguided? Such ideas seem to contradict common sense in health markets where government intervention is popular and intuitively useful, and encouraging 'free entry' to medical services – allowing anyone to practise medicine or as a nurse, regardless of their training – appears foolhardy. Fortunately, such ideas contradict economic theory too.

It is easy to fall into the trap of assuming that because perfect markets are efficient, and monopoly is inefficient, more perfect markets are more efficient than less perfect markets, and any move to impose measures which move a market closer to the set of conditions for perfect markets must increase efficiency. This leads to a great deal of confusion as to the purpose of the perfect market model. To repeat, it is not an attempt to describe reality, and it is not in itself capable of prescription. The 'theory of the second best' provides a path through this morass.

Quite simply, the theory of the second best states that once there is a single imperfection in a market, the introduction of a second imperfection may increase rather than reduce efficiency. Once knowledge is not perfect, for example if consumers cannot judge which medical practitioners are competent and which not, it may well increase efficiency to restrict entry into the market only to those who have achieved a minimal level of competence. If there are economies of scale which are exhausted only in the context of a few large producers (see note 1), this may be more efficient than many small firms. It follows that the conditions for perfect markets have no normative implications. Box 6.2 provides a slightly more formal treatment of the theory of the second best.

Before converse confusions abound, it is equally important to point out that the theory of the second best does not imply that moving away from market perfection will necessarily increase efficiency either. Perfect government intervention is as rare as a perfect market. It is as important to be aware of 'government failure' as of 'market failure'. The model is a tool of analysis which cannot produce policy prescription in itself. There is no short cut to studying real conditions in a specific market and judging opportunities to increase efficiency (and other goals of health policy) in that light.

Note

1. In the long run the same logic applies – abnormal profit will be available if price does not fall to the minimum point of U-shaped long-run average cost curves and firms will enter or leave the industry accordingly. If economies of scale are exhausted at levels of output consistent with large enough numbers of sellers to ensure price-taking behaviour, the model continues to work. However, economies of scale are usually assumed to be exhausted at higher levels of production than this, and to be one of the factors which explain the existence of markets characterised by one or a few sellers. If so, perfect competition can be assumed to imply the absence of economies of scale in the long run.

Chapter 7

Supplier-induced Demand and Agency

....

7.1 The Information Problem

This chapter focuses on what is probably the most important deviation found in health markets and some other markets, from the standard set of assumptions of the demand model proposed in Chapter 2 – the 'information problem'. The standard model assumes that consumers are 'sovereign', or are the best judges of their own interests. This point may have passed unnoticed in thinking about the health economist's decision to phone his mother or surf the net. While his mother might be an exception, most people will not believe they understand the economist's interests better than he does himself in this respect. As soon as we enter health markets, a range of objections to this perspective, implicitly and explicitly, arise.

Consumer sovereignty is challenged by widespread ideas that consumers should not be left to suffer the consequences of poor investment decisions in health, and should be required to make provision for likely health service needs. Hence, almost all countries require citizens to purchase insurance, or do so for them through the tax system (see Part IV). Similarly, a range of health-risking behaviours are usually proscribed by law – some

drugs are almost universally outlawed for recreational use, and diving into the sea from Brighton pier is prohibited; some health-promoting behaviours are required such as immunisation in some countries. These rules can be interpreted as requiring socially responsible behaviour (protecting society from the self-interested behaviour of individuals), a standard explanation of rules in any society, but they seem also to contain an element of policy makers 'knowing best'. This 'knowing best' may involve a belief in superiority of judgement in some cases (you may well understand the risk of recreational use of heroin but we still will not allow you to damage yourself), an attitude termed 'paternalism'. More commonly, it involves the belief that the information held by the rule maker is superior to that of the ruled (you do not understand the risks of recreational use of heroin and must be protected from your ignorance).

This is one type of 'information problem' encountered in health markets. More generally, there are many important areas of specialised knowledge involved in the seeking of health status improvement which are not involved in the seeking of a banana.[1] As a result, it is inefficient for each consumer (the 'principal') to seek out all the relevant information and understanding herself, and we observe the widespread use of 'agents' such as doctors, physiotherapists, pharmacists, opticians and nutritionists, employed (directly or indirectly) by the consumer to make purchasing decisions on her behalf. This phenomenon is known as 'agency', and occurs to different degrees in many fields: law, car mechanics, financial investment, education and numerous others. Almost everywhere there is a 'professional', there is an agent in disguise.

In some cases of agency including much but not all of its occurrence in health markets, the agent is also the supplier of the service. This means that demand and supply are not completely separable and gives rise to the possibility that agent-suppliers will abuse their role as agents in order to pursue their profit-seeking role as suppliers. The combination of *information asymmetry* (one party to a transaction has more information than the other), *bounded rationality* (not all contingencies can be foreseen and accounted for) and potential for *opportunism* ('self-interest seeking with guile') is a problematic combination for standard economic organisational forms to handle (Williamson 1975) and no doubt contributes to an explanation of some of the unusual institutions which arise in health markets such as medical ethics and self-regulatory bodies. It also gives rise to the *potential* for the much debated phenomenon in health economics: 'supplier-induced demand'.

7.2 Perfect Agency

Before turning to discuss whether or not we can establish that health professionals[2] 'induce' demand, or exploit their role as agents, it is useful to consider exactly what we might expect of a medical practitioner who is working as a 'perfect' agent. What would the objectives of a doctor acting as a perfect agent in recommending and supplying health services be? Possible candidates include:

1 To maximise the health status of the patient.
2 To maximise the utility of the patient.
3 To maximise the health status or utility of the whole society.

Lack of clarity in this is expressed in a wider debate about the role of doctors in society which pervades much more than health economics text books. The first option, maximising the health status of the patient, confines the doctor to her appropriate professional sphere, but risks paternalism which may not be the intention. For example, it suggests that were it to be effective, doctors should browbeat patients to give up smoking, rather than just ensure they are well informed of the risks.

The second option, maximising the utility of the patient, might suggest that the primary role of doctors should be to provide information to patients and, as far as possible, leave patients to make their own decisions. This seems to accord with many current ideas. Objections to this definition of role are more likely to relate to patients not wanting (or, in our terms, losing utility from) the making of fateful decisions than to argue that patients might in turn maximise the wrong thing (for example, give insufficient weight to health status).

The third option, maximising the health status or utility of the whole society, responds to the growing awareness of the inevitability of rationing in health markets – awareness that to provide a service to one patient may entail denial of another patient. Attitudes to this objective are likely to be health system dependent. Doctors employed privately by the patient have a much clearer duty to that individual patient, and any rationing implications for others are at least indirect and may not arise if it is simply a question of that patient deciding to spend less of their own resources on other goods. Doctors employed in a public system are potentially the agent of both the state and the individual patient. Some health systems impose this role on doctors much more than others. If drugs are in very short supply, the doctor cannot but consider those given to one patient as lost to another – perhaps an hour later in the same clinic. In less constrained circumstances, budget constraints may operate at hospital level which at least imply use of resources by one doctor in the hospital at the beginning of the year may mean their unavailability to another doctor's patient at the end of the year. In other situations, the 'down the line' implications of a decision made by one doctor may only ever be understood in the abstract – an unknown patient in another part of the system who might benefit from a budget surplus at year end is affected.

This leaves even the best intentioned doctor in an unenviable position in attempting to clarify their own role. It also leaves health economists with some, perhaps easier to live with, difficulties. If we cannot clearly define 'perfect agency', we are in a difficult position when it comes to identifying departures from that standard.

7.3 *Supplier-induced Demand*

Supplier-induced demand (SID) refers to a specific type of agency imperfection and implies that in order to promote her own interests, the doctor recommends care the perfect agent would not recommend. The idea therefore implies a definition of perfect agency and also the identification of motivation. Inappropriate advice motivated by imperfect information, for example, is usually not considered supplier-induced demand. Concern with supplier-induced demand can be traced to early contributions to the health economics literature, most famously 'Roemer's law': 'a built bed is a filled bed' (Roemer 1961). Correlations between supply and utilisation are not difficult to establish across health services but are not in themselves evidence of causal effect. Patients may cross borders to where services are more plentiful, hospitals and doctors may choose to locate in areas where demand is high, unmet demands may be high where fewer services are provided, markets may simply find equilibria! The explanation that demand is induced where supply exceeds the level it would otherwise attain requires a stronger test.

Supplier-induced demand implies the shifting of the demand curve. A doctor who aims to encourage more patients to visit her surgery by reducing her fees (in other words is aiming to produce movement *along* the demand curve) is acting only as any other supplier of goods may act. If profit maximisation is her goal, she may equate marginal revenue and marginal cost in setting her price without being said to have 'induced' demand. The problem with attempting to observe the shift of the curve is that demand curves themselves cannot be observed, only equilibrium points. This makes it very difficult to distinguish between normal market demand and supply movements, and market behaviour which implies that suppliers have shifted the demand curve.

Consider Figure 7.1. One way of looking for supplier-induced demand is to follow what happens in a health services market when the supply of doctors increases. In a standard market (Chapter 6.1), we would expect a shift in the supply curve to result in a new equilibrium at lower fee per visit and higher number of doctor visits provided (Figure 7.1a). However, if doctors are able to shift the demand

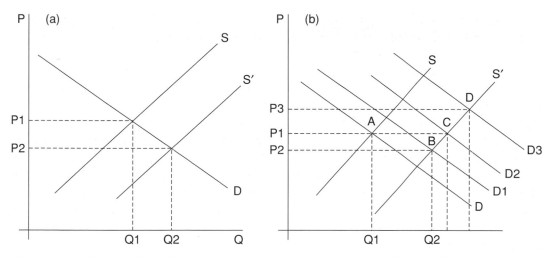

Figure 7.1 Difficulty of identifying supplier inducement: (a) no inducement, (b) inducement

curve, they will be able to protect themselves against lower fees. They may be able to do so partially, by shifting demand curve D to D1; wholly, by shifting the demand curve to D2; or may even shift the demand curve as far as D3 in which case fees would increase (Figure 7.1b). However, the observer can only observe point A, and alternative points B, C, and D and not whole demand curves. If points A and B are observed, the pattern is consistent with the normal market behaviour of Figure 7.1a: fees per visit have reduced and number of visits has increased. Only if a point to the left of point C is observed, such as D, is it clear that the market is not 'normal': supply of doctors increased but so did fees per visit.

Looking for situations in which a movement from A to D seems to have been caused by an increase in the supply of doctors is known as the 'fee test of inducement' attributed to Reinhardt (1978). It should be noted that the test is a specific rather than sensitive one: many cases in which demand is induced will fail the test, but when the test is passed, there is at least something odd about the market and inducement is a strong candidate to provide the explanation.

It will not surprise you to learn that the evidence about inducement is mixed and that most reviewers of this literature conclude that supplier-induced demand is an unproven hypothesis (McGuire *et al.* 1988; Mooney 1994; Folland *et al.* 1997). Two attempts to identify presence of SID are discussed in Box 7.1.

7.4 Imperfect Agency

Perhaps the issue need not be as complicated as these attempts to prove that demand curves shift. Much depends on the source of our concern. Most of us are likely to believe that medical advice should be given on the basis of the best scientific evidence available and may in recent years have reluctantly come to accept that expenditure control or reasonable budget limits imply rationing and the need for the use of cost-effectiveness criteria rather than effectiveness evidence alone. In public health systems, this focus on demand rather than on need may also seem peculiar. From either perspective, we do not want our doctors to be influenced by the profit motive when they give us advice.

Box 7.1   *Trying to find Supplier-induced Demand*

There are many difficulties in identifying supplier-induced demand. Many studies have attempted the identification by looking for association between the supplier to population ratio, and levels of utilisation. As discussed in the text, there are many alternative explanations of association besides supplier-induced demand.

Wilensky and Rossiter (1983) try to resolve some of these identification problems by separating physician- and patient-initiated visits within total utilisation. Many explanations of association between demand and supply – felt need, cross-boundary flow, supply responding to demand levels – are associated with patient decision making. If demand is induced, it would therefore be expected that the proportion of physician-initiated visits would be higher than if it is not.

For the population within this study (14,000 households interviewed across the US between 1977 and 1978), 39 per cent of all ambulatory visits were physician initiated and 52 per cent patient initiated (the remaining 9 per cent were referrals from elsewhere, or of unknown initiation); however, by defining all diagnostic tests, prescription drugs, surgical procedures and hospitalisations as being physician initiated, about 90 per cent of expenditure was physician initiated.

Wilensky and Rossiter applied regression analysis to these data, and data relating to the supply of physicians (the physicians or surgeons per 100,000 population in the county or small area in which the patient resides). The likelihood that a visit would be physician initiated, the number of physician-initiated visits and the expenditure on such visits were significantly positively correlated with physician supply, which would seem to support the inducement hypothesis. However, evidence of inducement in relation to surgery, total physician-initiated expenditures and physician fees was absent.

Most studies of supplier-induced demand, like that of Wilensky and Rossiter, have focused on the situation in the US, where fee-for-service reimbursement is an important mechanism for paying for services, especially at ambulatory level. In most other countries the problem is less likely to arise. For example, in the UK, medical care is not reimbursed on a fee-for-service basis, and the preconditions for supplier-induced demand are absent. Some have argued that the incentives in the UK system favour 'supplier-reduced demand' (e.g. Roberts 1993). However, dentists are reimbursed on a fee-for-service basis under a fixed-price system, and a study of dental practice (Birch 1988) suggests that similar problems can be identified.

Birch (1988) identifies another problem with trying to identify inducement in data relating to undifferentiated visit numbers. As the number of suppliers increases, the 'shadow price' (or real cost to users) of access to care falls because a larger number of suppliers is likely to reduce distances to the nearest supplier, and queues and waiting times are likely to fall. This can be represented as a shift in the demand curve. In these circumstances, Reinhardt's fee test of inducement (see text) fails. A shift in the demand curve caused by a falling shadow price cannot be distinguished from a shift caused by inducement.

However, it is the shadow price of the visit which has fallen, and not of the services provided during the visit. Therefore, inducement can be tested by considering the 'content per visit': the volume of treatments recommended per visit. If no inducement takes place, content per visit should decline as shadow price falls since marginal attenders would be likely to require a lower volume of treatment. Birch's finding that cost per course of treatment (given fixed prices) is correlated negatively (and highly significantly) with population per dentist therefore suggests inducement.

Box 7.2 *Provider Reimbursement*

Changing the Remuneration System of General Practitioners in Copenhagen

Mooney (1994) reports a study of a change to the remuneration system of general practitioners in Copenhagen from capitation to fee-for-service, which took place in October 1987 and brought these general practitioners into line with the reimbursement system in the rest of the country. Fees were paid for all types of contacts with patients and for diagnostic and certain curative services.

The table shows the results of a survey of the activity of a group of doctors affected, in March 1987 (before the change) and in March 1988 and November 1988 (after the change). The table shows dramatic responses in terms of the provision of additional services for which fees were paid, and reduction in referral which not only did not pay but would in some cases have substituted for paying services.

Number of contacts and activities in a week and number of enlisted patients in March 1987, March 1988 and November 1988 for seventy-one doctors in Copenhagen city

Activity	March 1987	March 1988	November 1988
Contacts	9,942	11,387	10,618
Diagnostic services[a]	536	768	896
Curative services[a]	99	201	203
Referrals to specialist	1,276	1,176	1,002
Referrals to hospital	251	226	176
Number of enlisted patients	122,223	125,412	125,536

Source: Mooney (1994).
Note:
[a] Services for which additional fee is paid.

This evidence suggests that while fee-for-service is associated with higher levels of provision of services by those receiving fees, it also reduces their referral of patients elsewhere. Mooney draws attention to the fact that over 20 per cent of referrals to specialists and nearly 30 per cent of referrals to hospital made under capitation appear to have been unnecessary, at least according to the implicit criteria adopted after the change.

Changing Reimbursement Mechanisms in Brazilian Hospitals

Rodrigues (1989) studied the effect of a change in the hospital reimbursement system by Brazil's main payer, the national social security programme: INAMPS. Until 1983 hospitals were reimbursed by INAMPS on a per-day basis. After that date, a per-case basis of reimbursement was introduced where the cost per case was calculated according to the average bill for a defined case or procedure group.

The intention of the new payment method was to slow the rate of increase in hospital admissions and expenditures which had contributed to financial crisis in 1981. Rodrigues shows that the method of reimbursement had no effect on the number of admissions, a result which would be expected. Instead, he concludes, private hospitals altered their case mix in favour of less complicated patients.

It is clear enough from much less complex studies, that doctors are human, and fall short of this ideal. All that needs to be tested is whether advice or interventions change when the economic rewards associated with different types of advice and interventions change. There is an abundance of evidence from many different parts of the world that this is the case. When 'fee for service' reimbursement is used, more services are provided than when systems of reimbursement that reward on a per-case or per-patient covered basis are used (see Box 7.2).

All this implies that we have a situation of 'imperfect agency'. Medical science is imprecise but this is not the source of the problem or at least not the whole source. When advice responds to economic incentives, doctors cannot be applying their best guess about the best possible treatment all of the time. It may be that uncertainty is exploited to play safe when incentives are set to reward higher levels of activity. Doctors might order multiple diagnostic tests with low likelihood of important findings, or to operate now when a 'wait and see' policy has a low risk of exacerbating the problem. The opposite might be decided and slight risks taken when incentives lean the other way. The right decisions are difficult to identify, but it is clear that if economic incentives intervene, best guesses, consideration of the risk–intervention trade-off the patient prefers, and trading off risk, effectiveness and cost are not the only considerations in the decision-making process.

This is not all bad. Recognition of imperfect agency gives policy makers important opportunities to influence the behaviour of doctors, especially where doctors identify their role in terms of the first two definitions of 'perfect agency' (concerned only with the individual patient), and policy makers are concerned to bring influence on behalf of society as a whole. The same evidence relating reimbursement method to doctor behaviour shows how powerful a tool the reimbursement system provides to seek improvements in the cost-effectiveness of the treatment pattern recommended and provided. Few health policy makers now ignore this opportunity.

Notes

1. Although we might again emphasise here that health services may not be as 'special' as they think they are. After all, the banana may be sought for its health-status-inducing effects. To this extent, the material of this chapter is as relevant to bananas as to health care.
2. The discussion of the rest of this chapter applies to most health professionals with respect to many of their duties. The term 'doctor' is used throughout, as a simplification and because most attention has been given to the doctor's role.

Chapter 8

Market Failure and Government

....

8.1 Introduction

In Chapter 6 the perfect competition model was explained, and it was emphasised that the model aspired to be a tool of analysis rather than a description of reality. In this chapter, that tool will be used further. Some of the major ways in which health markets diverge from the model will be explored and the model will be used to address the efficiency implications of these divergences. Mostly, the analysis involves only demand and supply curves, but it is important to remember that in a perfect market, demand curves are marginal value curves and supply curves are marginal cost curves (review sections 6.2 and 6.4 if necessary).

It is also important to remember that divergences from perfect markets are not necessarily bad things in themselves – positive externality is a good example (see section 8.2 below). Divergences merely imply that efficient outcomes will not be forthcoming if the market is left to freely determine price, output and the allocation of consumption and production. Of course, perfectly efficient outcomes are likely to be out of our reach by any means. Once a divergence is identified, the challenge is to find a strategy which responds to the resulting inefficiency and will perform better than leaving the market to its own devices. In many cases, there may be no such strategy, especially if the resulting inefficiency is not great. Government intervention is only recommended if likely government failure to intervene perfectly is less than the market failure under assessment.

8.2 Externality

Externality has been defined as 'a side-effect of either consumption or production which is not traded on the market or taken into account in setting a price' (Knapp 1984). In other words, consumers and producers either are not affected or do not bear the full brunt of the effects of their consumption or production.

The standard example of *negative* externality is pollution, usually (but not always) a side effect of production. A producer, such as a manufacturer of clothing, releases dyestuffs into a river. This results in tangible costs. The water company has to use additional filtering procedures to produce water of drinkable quality. The ecosystem of the river is damaged and fishing is affected. None of these costs automatically impact on the clothing manufacturer – his marginal cost curve is not affected and the costs imposed are not internalised in transactions between the clothing manufacturer and those who buy from him.

Externalities can be negative or positive and can arise in production or consumption. On the consumption side, the consumer of a radio programme in the garden on a sunny afternoon does not internalise the annoyance costs experienced by his neighbour who wished to read quietly. However, the neighbour on the other side enjoyed the programme – a positive externality on the consumption side!

There are many externalities affecting health markets. The ones which are likely to be most important are positive ones. There are clear externalities in the treatment and prevention of infectious disease. If one person's tuberculosis is treated and cured, others are not infected. If vaccination is received by the majority, the unvaccinated minority may also be protected.

The second type of positive externality which may be important in health is known as the 'caring externality'. It would appear that we are far more likely to care whether others receive health care or not, than we are to care whether others drive prestigious cars or eat out at restaurants regularly. Newspapers respond to their readers' concerns with accounts of those needing health care who are unable to access it, and often mount related appeals. Charitable institutions in the health field abound. The good Samaritan provided health care to a stranger. All this implies that there are positive externalities on the consumption side for some when others receive health services.

Both of these types of externality occur in consumption, or on the demand side. They imply that the individual purchaser of health care does not consider all the benefits associ-

Figure 8.1 Positive externality on the demand side

ated with the purchase, only those received by himself personally. His demand curve captures his personal marginal utility, but not all the marginal utilities in society as a whole which are affected by his purchase decision. We can imagine that besides the individual's personal demand curve, there is a marginal utility curve for the whole of society which lies everywhere to the right of the individual's curve.

In Figure 8.1 the individual (Mr Pink) is willing to trade a certain amount of other goods represented by a price, for a doctor's visit (for example) and in the rest of society, others would also be willing to trade some amount for Mr Pink's visits too. We assume that there is an upward-sloping supply curve equal to marginal cost. At point A, the free market solution is described – the equilibrium between the supply curve (MC) and Mr Pink's demand curve (Di). The price is $10 and the number of doctor visits purchased is four per year. However, the *efficient* solution is at B, where Mr Pink continues to make doctors' visits up to the point where all the values in society become equal to its cost (six visits per year). To see why this is so, consider the fifth visit. The marginal cost of this visit is $11 (from the marginal cost curve), but Mr Pink's marginal value for the visit is only $8. He will therefore not purchase it. However, in society as a whole there is an additional value of $6 for Mr Pink making the visit – in total (adding Mr Pink's and others' values for the visit as is done in the societal MV curve Ds), $14. From this perspective, the visit is a good buy, but the purchase will not be made in a free market. Only if institutions are created which distort the free market, can the efficient solution be made possible.

At this point, we can consider strategies which aim to move the market towards the efficient solution. The problem is the presence of values which are not translated into willingness to pay in the market. We might use charitable institutions to solicit from the public money to subsidise doctor visits. We might impose such subsidy through a tax system. These solutions are also beset by inefficiencies. Both involve administrative 'transactions' costs. Charity encounters 'free rider' problems – although the Samaritan cared about the stranger, he might have waited to see if someone else would pick him up. Tax systems may involve compulsorily extracting payment from those who do not care subtracting more from their utility functions than they gain.[1]

Uncertainties apply to both strategies. Either charities or government might over-subsidise relative to the extent of the inefficiency and too many doctor visits might be utilised. In the example, free doctors' visits would result in over-utilisation relative to the efficient point, at eight visits per year for Mr Pink (he would 'purchase' all visits for which he had a marginal value greater than $0). If we

are going to provide free services, we should try to estimate how many visits, or how much health education, is 'appropriate' in the sense that social values are higher than cost. In the case of the doctor visits, we would have to ration Mr Pink to that number of visits and set up rationing systems which try to ensure that visits made are the most 'appropriate' ones. Ultimately, we must estimate the areas of inefficiency involved, estimate whether intervention of any sort is likely to improve on or make worse the market outcome and if we believe that intervention can increase efficiency, plan the strategy likely to maximise the impact. Economic evaluation (see Part II) offers one set of methods for tackling this complex task. In many circumstances, it is impossible to apply such methods and a more intuitive way of tackling the problem is needed. A policy maker's guess at what is 'affordable' may be an implicit judgement of society's values.

Equivalently, negative externalities might be addressed by banning or taxing the relevant activity. However, zero activity will only by coincidence equate to the efficient level of activity, and even in principle a ban may therefore create more inefficiency than it solves. Policing bans may also be expensive and poorly policed bans may be most expensive of all – potentially giving rise to criminal modes of behaviour and inability to exert any controls whatsoever.

In principle, taxes can be assessed by asking what is the appropriate tax to ensure that external costs are imposed on the producer so that she then equalises social marginal cost with social benefit. A tax which tries precisely to 'internalise' a negative externality (i.e. is at every level of production equal to the relevant external cost) is known as a 'Pigovian' tax after the economist A. C. Pigou (1877–1959). Setting taxes at the appropriate level

involves the same difficulties as setting subsidies – can the external costs be measured
and allocated to the appropriate producers?

With respect to all these strategies 'market
failure' has to be balanced against 'government failure' and an assessment of whether
or not the best intervention improves on the
market outcome has to be made.

8.3 *Public Goods*

When I eat a banana, I use it up – nobody
else can ever eat that banana. It is 'rival'. If
I am selling bananas, I can give them to those
who pay, and refuse them to those who
don't. Bananas are 'excludable'. Public goods
are characterised by *non-rivalness* and *non-
excludability*.

'Non-rivalness' means that one person's
consumption of a good does not prevent
another also consuming it. A theatrical performance is 'non-rival' to the extent that once
provided for one person, it costs nothing to
provide it to others up to the seating capacity of the theatre. 'Non-excludability' means
that it is not possible to exclude non-payers
from consuming. Once a street has been
cleaned, it is not possible to prevent anyone
who uses the street from enjoying the benefits.
Non-excludable goods are also usually non-
rival, but non-rival goods are quite often
excludable. It is quite easy, and indeed usual,
to exclude non-payers from a theatrical
production.

Environmental health services and public
health education campaigns are examples
of goods which are both non-rival and non-
excludable and are therefore close to being
'pure' public goods. Positive externality in
consumption implies a degree of non-rivalness
and although the two types of market failure
are usually separated, it may be more useful
to identify degrees of public goods characteristic from the 'pure' to the 'positive externality' type to pure private goods.

Figure 8.2 suggests a representation of
degree of public goods characteristics of a

			PURE PRIVATE GOOD
Desirability of exclusion		♦ cancer treatment ♦ water connection to household ♦ immunisation	
	vector control through ♦ environmental management ♦ mass health education	♦ water standpipe	
PURE PUBLIC GOOD	Ease of exclusion		

Figure 8.2 The public–private good continuum
Source: Bennett (1991).

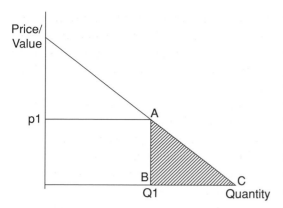

Figure 8.3 Welfare loss from setting a price for a public good

few health-related interventions on a two-dimensional map of non-rivalness and non-excludability. Cancer treatment is both rival and excludable and therefore a private good. Immunisation is also relatively easily excludable (although there are advantages to providing the service to groups of people at once moving it slightly to the left in comparison with cancer treatment on the 'ease of exclusion' axis). Much of the benefit of immunisation is captured by the immunised individual, but to the extent that benefits are captured by others, non-rivalness is implied.

Non-rivalness creates market failure because it causes the marginal cost of supply of the good to drop to zero for each additional person provided with it, after the first. Although it is possible to exclude non-payers, it is inefficient to do so. Consider Figure 8.3 which might represent the situation of a theatrical production. The marginal cost curve coincides with the x axis because after the first person, the marginal cost of additional provision is zero. The private demand curve for tickets (Dp), as usual, can be used to estimate individuals' values of tickets. If the price is greater than zero (for example, p1), there

will always be some people who would value a ticket (would pay more than zero price) but would not pay the price charged. Providing free tickets to these people would create more value in society than it would cost. There is therefore an opportunity to increase social utility which is not seized. The inefficiency in comparison with a perfect market can be represented by shaded triangle ABC. (Theatre companies try to capture some of this lost efficiency by pricing differentially in the form of student and pensioner discounts and same-day tickets – students, pensioners and those not determined to book in advance may have lower values for tickets than average – but the attempt is inevitably imperfect and some areas of inefficiency remain.)

Non-excludability implies severe difficulties in organising a market in the good concerned. In many cases, the total cost of providing the good will exceed the willingness to pay even of the individual with the highest value of it. No one person may have a value of mosquito control sufficient to be willing to fund a whole area's programme. Under these circumstances, the good will not be provided at all by the market.

Since non-rivalness is an extreme form of positive externality on the demand side, health policy strategies, responding to a recognition of public goods characteristics, echo those discussed to deal with positive externality in section 8.2. However, if marginal costs are truly zero, there is a stronger likelihood that free provision of the good in question, as opposed to a limited subsidy, is the appropriate strategy, and if non-excludability also applies, this is the only feasible course. It should be remembered that public provision implies taxation and uncompensated losses to those who do not value the public good. Overall, the total benefit to be derived from the service in question must exceed the total value to the society before there is even a potential gain from public provision.[2]

A non-government option in the case of non-excludable public goods is for individuals to voluntarily club together to purchase the good. However, 'free riders' will wait for others to do so, and may falsely claim zero values in the hope of avoiding payment – the expressed willingness to pay cannot be relied upon to reflect the true willingness to pay of the society, and at the margin, provision of the amount of the good which would equate marginal value and marginal cost cannot be attained.

Public provision might answer both non-rival and non-excludable characteristics of public goods.

Where values are more difficult to measure, a recourse to criteria such as whether the public good benefits are non-trivial and the costs of provision relatively 'affordable' may be the best judgement possible as to whether public provision is likely to be warranted. Even if it were in theory possible to eliminate a disease agent such as the rat population, if enough resources were directed to the problem, it is not necessarily efficient to do so. The conclusion that it is 'impossible' to do so might be read as meaning that the opportunity costs of doing so would be unreasonably high.

8.4 Monopoly and Oligopoly

Many components of the health sector are 'natural monopolies' – they exhibit features which tend to limit the number of suppliers in the market. Competitive markets require the entry of small contenders for a share of the market's business, and opportunity for such small firms to become established. A number of factors militate against this. High

fixed costs imply that only those firms which can call on substantial resources from capital markets will be able to make the initial investments necessary to start in business (in contrast if variable costs are relatively high, a business can start small and expand as its business does). 'Sunk' costs – investments in specific assets which cannot be moved from one market to another – are a particularly off-putting type of investment for a market entrant: if entry proves to have been a mistake, very little of the investment is likely to be recoupable, especially if the entrant's own failure in the market suggests limited capacity for market expansion. These arguments are especially relevant to more sophisticated and high-technology services which require large capital investments, often of a 'sunk' nature – for example, diagnostic services such as x-ray and CT scan; and operating theatres and equipment. More generally, the provision of hospital services as a whole encounters this constraint. Only very large markets (larger cities) offer the possibility for more than a few hospitals to compete.

Economies of scale also militate against the entry of many firms to a market. If the 'minimum efficient scale' is large in relation to the total demand for the service, only a firm which captures a high proportion of market business will be able to operate at that scale. This acts as a barrier to entry to other firms. Even if the dominant firm's price is high, reflecting its profit level, it can always reduce the price for long enough to drive a new contender out of the business again. Unless the new contender can immediately start to operate at the same scale as the dominant firm, it will be unable to enter. The barrier to entry is similar to that presented by high fixed costs.

Chapter 6 explored the inefficiency implicit in the abnormal profit levels associated with monopolistic markets. Strategies to deal with the inefficiencies caused by monopoly and oligopoly are unlikely to focus on trying to increase the number of providers since the causes of monopoly and oligopoly often suggest that larger numbers of providers would be even more inefficient. Rather, strategies are likely to focus on public provision and regulation. The latter subject is discussed in Chapter 17.

8.5 Other Sources of Market Failure

Considerable attention has already been given to imperfect knowledge and agency, which as suggested in Chapter 7 are possibly the most important sources of market failure. In addition to failure resulting from agency itself, Chapter 7 suggested that imperfect knowledge causes the relationship between the demand curve and marginal value to be questioned. We can still rely on the demand curve to indicate the patient's best guesses as to her marginal values of different services, but we can no longer rely on those best guesses to be her 'true' marginal value. For example, in the early 1960s there was a high demand for the drug thalidomide in pregnancy. Later information as to its link with certain congenital malformations reduced this demand to zero. The 'true' marginal values (presumably highly negative) of antenatal thalidomide use were not represented by 'ignorant' demand curves. For types of services for which imperfect knowledge is likely to be greatest, demand curves may have little relevant information from an efficiency perspective.

A different type of uncertainty, with different implications, arises from the individual's inability to predict her demands. Health service costs can be large and time-concentrated. From the individual's perspective they should therefore be planned and saved for, but the added complication that they are uncertain means that savings may still be inadequate. Health insurance ensures that contribution levels will prove adequate, even where costs for health service needs prove to be above average. However, health insurance also causes the market to fail. The two main ways in which it does so are through 'moral hazard' and 'adverse selection'. Moral hazard arises when consumers face zero prices at the time of use: their utilisation decision does not take account of marginal cost. Adverse selection arises where low-risk individuals are able to opt out of the risk pool. As a result, average risk rises causing the cost of insurance to rise and further lower-risk individuals to opt out. Ultimately, it may be impossible to organise a market in health insurance, or at least one which does not exclude a large proportion of those needing to access health services.

As with monopoly and oligopoly, insurance arrangements arise in response to an underlying inefficiency. Sensible strategies do not therefore try to imitate perfect markets by trying to remove insurance arrangements but are more likely to regulate the insurance market. Compulsory insurance or 'social insurance' is a regulated arrangement which addresses adverse selection for example (see Chapter 23). Insurance agencies themselves can address some of the problems through specific contract forms. For example, the 'no claims bonus' is an attempt to mitigate moral hazard (see Chapter 14 on contracts).

8.6 Merit Goods and Equity

Many believe that health services are special, or 'merit', in other words, that those in need have a basic right to medical care and that 'rights' imply that no one should face financial or other barriers to use of health services.

This argument can be seen as an absolutist one – not amenable to consideration of degrees of efficiency and equity implicit in different market arrangements but leading directly to the policy prescription that health services must be offered free at the point of use.

Absolutist arguments are always difficult to sustain, however. If not all goods are merit, it is difficult to identify the boundaries without recourse to relative standards. If health services are 'merit' because they relieve pain or even extend life, perhaps those health services which do neither (some types of plastic surgery might provide an example) should be excluded. Recognition that even the most prosperous societies could allocate their entire GNP to health interventions with life-extending and pain-relieving potential (however minute or unlikely) suggests that scale and likeliness of such potential have to be taken into account. These considerations tend to suggest that more relativist rationales for health policy are required.

For example, some would argue that the principal objective in organising a market for health services is not efficiency but equity. Hence markets 'fail' in that even perfect markets make no special claims with respect to equity. This is a very persuasive argument, but it warrants some further examination.

First, it is not sensible to exclude efficiency considerations altogether. Production of health services has to take place, or there is nothing to share round equitably. *Ceteris paribus*, even the most avid egalitarian would prefer more to share round than less. Concerns that productive resources are not just wasted, and in fact are used to produce the most health care possible, for any given distribution, must be important in any schema.

Second, a set of misunderstandings can arise from the normative rather than analytic use of the perfect market model. If we be-

lieve that efficiency dictates that the perfect market should be imitated as closely as possible – in other words, if we don't understand the 'theory of the second best' (see Chapter 6.4 and Box 6.2) – there are clear conflicts with equity. This can leave some to intuit a fundamental conflict between equity and efficiency: a 'zero-sum game' in which every unit of equity gained is at the expense of efficiency and vice versa. In this case, a choice between efficiency and equity must be made which is ideological rather than technical.

Once the theory of the second best is admitted, however, there may be substantial overlap between the dictates of efficiency and equity. The concepts of allocative efficiency and equity can in practice, and even conceptually, be difficult to unravel. Concern that resources should be allocated according to where they can most efficiently produce health will direct those resources to the greatest need (at least where need is defined as the 'capacity to benefit').

On a specific set of definitions allocative efficiency and equity may be almost identical. For example, Mooney (1983) suggests a list of possible definitions of equity. According to this list, equity might imply equality of: (1) expenditure *per capita*; (2) inputs *per capita*; (3) inputs for equal need; (4) access for equal need; (5) utilisation for equal need; (6) marginal met need; (7) health. If need is defined as 'capacity to benefit', definitions 3–5 coincide with allocative efficiency (if 'capacity to benefit' is per unit of input, unit of access or unit of utilisation respectively).

Between these extreme viewpoints, situations in which allocative efficiency and some definitions of equity conflict can be identified. If need is defined in terms of extent of health problem rather than capacity to benefit, the productivity of health resources then varies in situations of equal 'need'. For example, if Mr Pink responds better to a health intervention for the same health problem than Ms Brown, allocative efficiency would allocate more resources to Mr Pink, whereas equity would indicate an equal allocation.

Notes

1. This implies that *Pareto optimality* cannot be inferred – see Chapter 9.
2. Or a 'potential Pareto improvement' – see Chapter 9.3.

Part II

Economic Evaluation

Chapter 9

The Theoretical Bases of Economic Evaluation

....

9.1 Adding up Costs and Benefits: the Need for a Conceptual Basis

We all personally make decisions on how to allocate our limited resources for our families and ourselves. If we are 'utility maximisers' (see Chapter 2) we aim to maximise our expected welfare by choosing to buy the goods and services that should achieve this end. To do this we check that there is no alternative mix of goods we could consume that would increase our welfare. Once this is achieved we cannot increase our welfare simply by changing the mix of goods and services we consume. For the formal treatments of efficiency in production and exchange see Boxes 9.1–3. By analogy, when a decision is made on behalf of society to provide some services collectively, the aim may be to maximise the welfare of the whole of society, and in a similar way to ensure that no change in the mix and pattern of consumption of goods and services would increase overall welfare.

But what works easily for the individual does not so obviously work for collective decisions. If we try simply to compare different options by adding up the costs and the benefits we immediately run into the problem of comparing benefits to different individuals. Does a cataract operation to restore my sight offer more benefits than one that restores the sight of a keen reader, an artist, a farmer or a mother? Are benefits greater from supplementing iodine in the diet (and avoiding damage to intellectual skills) or from measures to control the transmission of malaria? How much extra is it worth paying for a new treatment with no additional impact on survival but fewer side effects? Should we give priority to life-extending treatments over those that enhance quality of life? An individual can, in principle, answer these questions for herself, and decide on priorities for her treatment. But as soon as there are two or more people involved, we face the difficulty in comparing different people, with different likes, wants and needs.

In some senses this dilemma cannot be resolved – there will always be differences between individuals, and it is likely that views on what should be the priority will depend in part on personal circumstances. However, it is important that some principles be applied to the issue of how we make decisions on the use of resources. One obvious starting point is the body of theory on the economics of welfare.

Box 9.1   Efficiency in Exchange

In a world of two individuals and two goods, individuals will trade the goods in order to maximise utility. They will do this until the marginal rate at which they are willing to substitute the goods (the *marginal rate of substitution*, MRS) is equal to the ratio of the prices of the goods. Thus, for efficient exchange, for any two individuals and any two goods:

$$MRSa,b^{n,m} = Pa/Pb \; \forall a,b, \forall n,m$$

where a, b are goods, n, m are individuals, Pa and Pb are the prices of goods a, b and $\forall$ means 'all'.

What this is saying is that for all pairs of goods, and all pairs of individuals, the marginal rate of substitution is the same.

Box 9.2   Efficiency in Production

In a world of two factors of production, say equipment (K) and labour (L), production is efficient when the cost of the inputs is the lowest possible. Keeping output constant, we can vary the proportions of equipment and labour. The rate at which we can substitute K for L for a given output is the *marginal rate of technical substitution* (MRTS) between K and L. The lowest cost of production will be when no further substitution leads to a reduction in cost, that is, when the MRTS is equal to the ratio of input prices.

This principle applies to all inputs. For production at minimum cost, the MRTS for all pairs of inputs should be equal to the ratio of the input prices.

Formally the marginal rate of technical substitution between inputs x and y is equal to the ratio of the prices of x and y for all pairs of inputs:

$$MRTSx,y = Px/Py \; \forall x,y$$

where inputs are x and y; prices of inputs are Px and Py.

Box 9.3   Efficiency in Production and Exchange

Where production takes place in an economy, the rate at which it is possible to switch production between any two goods a and b (the *marginal rate of transformation*, MRT) must equal the ratio of the prices of goods for efficient production and exchange:

$$MRTa,b = Pa/Pb$$

Thus for efficiency in production and exchange:

$$MRSa,b^{n,m} = MRTa,b = Pa/Pb \; \forall a,b, \forall n,m$$

9.2 Markets, Microeconomics and Paretian Welfare Economics

In most societies most goods and services are allocated through market processes. Some markets work well, and can be very efficient mechanisms to match available goods and services to those that need them and want them (see Chapter 6). Using market mechanisms may remain the best available option even when the conditions for perfect markets are violated (Chapters 7 and 8). The great strength of markets is the way they use information. There is no need to gather and analyse the data on who wants what, and who wants to provide what services. Buyers and sellers bring the necessary information with them to the market, so it is available when and where it is needed. But when markets fail badly, for example due to problems of monopoly, limited information or externalities, we need to find other ways to make collective choices. What happens in a well-functioning market can give us some guide to how this should be done.

To achieve the aim of obtaining the greatest benefits to society from health interventions, certain conditions must prevail. An important one is that the processes of production of services must be efficient. There are two main ways in which production can be inefficient – using unnecessarily large amounts of all inputs, and using inefficient combinations of inputs. For example, if we employ ten people to do a job that can easily be done by six, then this is just wasteful. Technically, under these circumstances production is at a point off the cost curve (sometimes known as X-inefficiency: Leibenstein 1966). More subtly, if highly paid and expensively trained doctors do work that could be done by other staff, that is inefficient. If we use expensively equipped facilities for work requiring only basic equipment, that is also likely to be wasteful. There

may also be cases where production is inefficient because the technology used is not the one with lowest costs. If three individual vaccines are used where a combination vaccine is available (costing slightly more), it may be more efficient to pay more for the drugs, but less for staff. Conversely, it may be more efficient to employ a larger number of staff who are equipped with bicycles than to employ fewer that drive cars.

There are really two steps in finding the lowest-cost process of production (see Chapters 4 and 5). First we need to identify technically feasible ways of producing the desired outcomes. Second, we apply information on the cost of the different inputs in order to find the lowest-cost method. In a country where staff are relatively cheap, but equipment expensive, it is likely to be most efficient to use relatively labour-intensive processes (for example, in laboratory work we might choose processes involving examination of slides by skilled staff rather than automated processes or use of pattern-recognition equipment). The process of searching for the best combination of inputs should continue until no further changes can be found that would lower the production cost. Formally this is when *the marginal rate of technical substitution* between any pair of inputs equals the ratio of the costs of the inputs (see Box 9.2 and Chapters 4 and 5).

Having ensured that services are being produced efficiently, a second requirement for efficiency is to choose to provide those services that will maximise welfare. This again involves comparing the benefits of different services and their relative cost. For example, consider the available life-extending interventions in the field of HIV. There are options for primary prevention, either personal health promotion activities or by reducing the risk of transmission by the treatment of other sexually transmitted diseases. There are potential interventions, which can improve the health and extend life for people who are already seropositive, such as treatment of tuberculosis. There are treatments that aim to control the virus directly using combinations of drugs. Unless we assemble detailed information about the effectiveness of each of these in a particular country it is not self-evident which should be given priority. In a simple case we might define output of health services as years of life gained. We could then choose the combination of these interventions that would maximise this for any given overall expenditure. At that point, no further changes in the mix of interventions will increase output. More formally, the marginal rate of transformation between all pairs of interventions is the same (see Box 9.3).

But we are not interested only in interventions that extend life for people with or at risk of HIV. We need to choose not only the best ways of achieving health gain for this disease, but also how to achieve the maximum health gain overall. Again a useful starting point is the likely choices we each make. An individual chooses to consume combinations of goods and services that maximise her welfare. In principle she will switch between different services until further switching cannot increase her welfare. Imagine she has a range of chronic conditions (such as arthritis, coronary heart disease, diabetes and asthma) and has access to only limited funds to buy services. She would choose the combination of surgery, physiotherapy, occupational therapy, drug treatments, assistance with personal care and home modifications that she would expect to have the greatest overall impact on her health and quality of life (within her limited resources). She would choose more of a service if this extra would have a bigger impact on her health than any other use of the resources.

Formally this means that her marginal rate of substitution between any pair of goods is equal to the ratio of the prices of the goods (see Box 9.3 and Chapter 2).

Finally, we have to choose the extent to which we allocate our limited resources to health compared to other goods. Although it is tempting to believe that health care is always the most important good, we can observe that people do not act as if this were so. People take risks with their health by smoking; mountain climbing; driving faster than necessary and even crossing roads they could avoid. In so doing they are indicating that they value the associated benefits more than the cost of the associated risk. At this level too, the rational utility-maximising individual would choose to equate the marginal rate of substitution between health goods and other goods.

When people interact in a market they trade until no further trades increase their welfare. They will take their income and the goods they already own (their *initial endowments*), and buy and sell till they have maximum benefits from what they consume. In a perfect market, with all individuals aiming to maximise their welfare, we see the best use of resources *for any given initial distribution of wealth and incomes.* At prevailing prices all individuals have their chosen combination of goods and services. No one can be made any better off without someone else being made worse off. Formally we have a situation where the *marginal rates of substitution* between all pairs of goods for all pairs of individuals are equal and are equal to the *marginal rate of transformation* between all pairs of goods and the *ratios of prices*. In production the *marginal rate of technical substitution* between all pairs of inputs for all goods and services is equal and is the *ratio of the prices of inputs* (see Box 9.3).

In one sense we can describe this state of affairs as optimal. If we accept the initial income distribution, then we have a situation in which all individuals have maximum welfare. Simply by carrying out voluntary trades people convert their initial endowments, which may include many goods they do not like, into their desired consumption. Those who like holidays spend more on holidays; those who want transport buy bicycles or cars; those who want more housing or food choose these. No one can be made better off without someone becoming worse off. This circumstance is described as a *Pareto optimum*, after the Italian sociologist and economist Vilfredo Pareto (1848–1923) who first formalised the concept.

It is easy to see the limitation of the notion of a Pareto optimum, since in many instances it may not seem like a very nice state of affairs. If one person starts off owning half of the assets in a country, and all others live in grinding poverty, there can still be a Pareto optimum, despite the hardship and misery. But before being too dismissive it is interesting to think about situations that are not Pareto optimal. If further voluntary trade would give people more preferred combinations of goods and services, then their welfare will be improved when they trade. If I am a vegetarian, I gain no welfare from meat, and would be better off selling the meat and buying more or better vegetables. Voluntary trades of this kind make at least one person better off, and no one worse off. This is known as a *Pareto improvement*. There is a strong intuitive appeal to the suggestion that if one person is better off, and no one worse off, then society as a whole is better off.

Perfectly functioning markets move us automatically towards a Pareto optimum. Collective decisions are normally taken in circumstances where markets have for some reason failed. When making these collective decisions a possible choice rule is to seek out Pareto improvements. This will increase welfare, in the Paretian sense, for any starting point (in terms of income distribution). Many economists argue that if we do not like the current income distribution we can change it by tax or subsidy, but once that is done we will act only when we spot an opportunity to effect a Pareto improvement. To many economists this forms a conceptual justification of cost–benefit analysis, the underlying framework in economic evaluation.

9.3 Developments in Welfare Economics, Social Welfare Functions and Cost–Benefit Analysis

In the real world of collective decision making it is not always easy to find Pareto improvements. When we build a road, there are winners who benefit from better transport, and those who lose from pollution and danger. When we develop a vaccination programme there are many that are saved from disease, but some that are harmed (and a few who may be killed) by the vaccine. When we develop computing skills in teenagers some will help solve problems of world poverty and some will become hackers or write viruses. Almost no activity can be guaranteed to be without losers. Strictly applied, the criterion that no one may be worse off means that almost no decisions can be made. Taking this to *reductio ad absurdum*, if eradication of malaria could be achieved only if Bill Gates had to pay €20 in taxes against his will, we could not justify doing it on Paretian grounds. When taxes are used to pay for services, then there are likely to be losers, since few people enjoy paying taxes. In this strict interpretation, any programme that uses any tax finance cannot constitute a Pareto improvement.

Most people would judge that it is reasonable for there to be some losers if the gains to

Box 9.4   Scitovsky Paradox

By definition a Pareto improvement occurs when at least one person is made better off, and no one is made worse off. By extension it is argued that a potential Pareto improvement occurs when it would be possible to make at least one person better off with no one worse off, but the compensation to the losers is not actually paid.

What Scitovsky was able to show was that there are circumstances in which the potential Pareto improvement criterion could be used to argue both for a change and conversely for a return to the original position. This is clearly worrying if the potential Pareto improvement is used as a rule for resource allocation.

A simple example illustrates how this can happen. For a fuller account of why this occurs see Quirk and Saposnik (1968). Imagine the hypothetical case of two people who have hypertension, but the supply of drugs to control it are very scarce. In their cases both thiazide diuretics and beta blockers have some effects. For these patients combination therapy has proved more effective at controlling their hypertension than either drug alone. Given the severity of their problems they are both recommended to take one standard dose of each, and failing that to take double the standard dose of one.

Suppose an intervention enabled a change in the world so that scenario 2 applied rather than scenario 1:

Scenario 1	Juan	Maria
Thiazide diuretics	Two standard doses	None
Beta blockers	None	One standard dose

Scenario 2		
Thiazide diuretics	One standard dose	None
Beta blockers	None	Two standard doses

Juan would lose from the intervention and Maria would gain. However, Maria could compensate Juan for his loss by giving him one of her beta blocker doses and still being as well off as she was under scenario 1. On this basis the compensation criterion would approve the intervention.

However, suppose the intervention instead enabled a change in the world so that scenario 1 applied rather than scenario 2. Now Juan would be better off and Maria worse off – but this time Juan could compensate Maria for her loss by giving her one dose of thiazide diuretics, maintaining his own welfare at the scenario 2 level while improving Maria's.

This hypothetical example shows that, unless the compensation is actually paid, there is a risk that a change in either direction can be justified on the basis of offering a potential Pareto improvement. To ensure that the change is really equivalent to a Pareto improvement we need additionally to check that this 'reversal' will not occur.

those who benefit are sufficiently large. We need some basis for judging the relative importance of the gains to the gainers and the losses to the losers. One approach is to ask those who gain to compensate those who lose. If they do this, and are still better off, then it shows that their gains exceed the losses to those who lost. In effect the compensation means that there are no longer any losers, so there is a Pareto improvement.

An apparently small step is to argue that even if they do not compensate the losers, if they *could* do so and still be better off, then there is a *potential* Pareto improvement, and this justifies a decision. Sadly there is a problem with this argument. Since there are losers, some sections of the population now have lower incomes. It was demonstrated by Scitovsky (1941) that there can be cases where the changes in incomes from doing a project lead to a paradox – the potential Pareto improvement can be used to justify a change, and also to return to the starting point (see Box 9.4). This is most likely to happen when the project has a large effect on the distribution of incomes. It is not clear how likely it is that this will happen, but it is a warning that the apparently modest development of the idea of a Pareto improvement to a potential Pareto improvement may undermine the welfare economics basis for the analysis. In practice, most economists are aware of this problem, and are concerned if the effect of a project is to harm some people significantly. Most of the time the Scitovsky paradox is treated as a theoretical nicety.

The cost–benefit framework can be justified as the application of the idea of the potential Pareto improvement. When the gains to those who gain exceed the losses to those who lose, then the benefits exceed the costs. The justification does not require decision makers to compare the welfare of individuals, but only to ensure that the winners *could* compensate the losers fully and still be better off than before the change.

The Paretian framework tries to avoid the need to make direct comparison of the welfare of different individuals. However, many of us are willing to do this. A case can be made that it is more important to provide treatment for mothers, people who are working and supporting families, medical scientists on the brink of important new insights, film stars who bring pleasure to millions or Presidents and Prime Ministers rather than for people who are single, childless, unimaginative and lack political ambition. In a shipwreck the tradition is that the first priority for scarce lifeboat places goes to women and children. In preparations for nuclear war, priority is to be given to senior politicians and leaders. It is interesting to think about our feelings about these types of priority. Many people would agree with the priority for children and those with dependants, but perhaps fewer would put film stars and politicians above others (see Box 9.5).

The potential Pareto improvement criterion is based on individuals and their welfare. In effect the approach is to define the welfare of the community as being made up of the welfare of individuals. The perspective does not rule out the possibility of people gaining utility from benefits to others – their utility functions might well include welfare gains to others as arguments, but it does rule out the possibility that the welfare of society is different from the sum of individual utilities. Other perspectives are possible, involving notions of a common good that are more than simply the sum of welfare of individuals (see Box 9.6). If the utility of any individual rises (with no fall for anyone else) this increases social welfare in the Paretian sense, but this framework does not allow us to quantify the change. In other words, we can say a little about the direction of change of social welfare if particular individuals are better off, but we can say nothing about the extent of the change. More technically, the Pareto framework specifies a social welfare function where social welfare depends on individual utilities. Social welfare increases with increases in the welfare of individuals, but otherwise the shape of the function is not determined. This has two limitations. First,

Box 9.5 Welfare Economics and Income Distribution

Paretian welfare economics aims to answer questions about how to maximise welfare from a given income and wealth distribution starting point. In thinking about health care priorities decisions on use of resources may change the distribution of income and wealth.

It is possible to argue that economic efficiency (in the Paretian sense) and issues of distribution should be considered separately. Many economists argue that if we do not like the current distribution of income we can take measures to change it, such as taxing the relatively rich or subsidising the poor. The advantage of this approach is that it allows us to use information about people's demands and choices as measures of their welfare.

In all situations, redistributing income and wealth is not as simple as issuing edicts, since tax and subsidy regimes affect incentives. In the case of health interventions there are still further problems. A particular issue is that, in general, ill health is concentrated in parts of the population that are relatively poor. This might mean that the greater health needs of the poor would be assessed as relatively unimportant, since their ability, and therefore willingness to pay, are lower than for (fitter) richer people.

Also, the willingness of richer people to subsidise poorer ones may depend on what is being provided. They may be willing to pay taxes to help people restore their health, but not to allow them to increase spending on gambling. Rich people might be willing to subsidise decent housing for poor people but not to allow more smoking. Thus the availability of tax funds to provide subsidies may depend on the use to which they are to be put. This can make it even more difficult to use the general tax system to sort out issues of income and equality.

See Chapter 12 for discussion of how issues of income and equity are sometimes taken into account in economic evaluation.

we have no clear basis on which to compare the effects on social welfare of utility gains to different individuals. Second, even if we are able to derive ordinal rankings of welfare implications of different population health profiles, we cannot value them.

A society may wish to be more specific in valuing different health profiles. For example, we may wish to impose the condition that particular gains to any individual will be considered of equal value. In this case we are saying that for the purposes of analysis we assume that the utility of an additional year of life, or of a year of good eyesight, or of a year without pain from angina, are given the same value, regardless of who is the individual. In this case, for any category of treatment or care, we would maximise welfare by maximising

the health gain (measured as years gained, years of good sight, etc.).

In principle there is no reason to choose any particular social welfare function. Some people argue for equal access to care regardless of, for example, age. In effect they argue that the welfare gain depends only on how many treatments were provided for people who have any treatable problem. There is an obvious disadvantage in specifying social welfare in this way. A procedure to remove a cataract would produce ten more years of good eyesight in an average seventy-year-old than in an average eighty-year-old. By taking age into account in setting priorities, assuming all other factors are the same, we increase the output if this is specified in terms of years of enjoyment of the improvement. At least in

Box 9.6   Social Welfare Functions

'Social welfare' has been defined as 'whatever is good, or whatever ought to be maximised' (Ng 1983). A social welfare function (SWF) implies that a single set of welfare values can be assigned to any specified state of the world.

We have already encountered the Paretian social welfare function which is based on a vector of individual welfare values (or 'utilities'), and applies the criterion that social welfare improves only if each value changes in a non-negative direction. The compensation criterion amends the Paretian social welfare function and implies the ability to *aggregate* the individual welfare values in the social welfare function. Both approaches are 'individualist' and 'utilitarian' in that they base their estimation of the well-being of society on utilities from individuals' perspectives.

However, aggregation presents complex issues which are avoided by the Paretian social welfare function. Suspicion of interpersonal comparisons of utility are long-standing and characterise the 'new welfare economics' (in comparison with the 'old welfare economics' of Pigou). Many believe that while it is possible to order an individual's utilities, it is not possible to measure them 'cardinally' (against a natural zero) or to compare them between individuals. If this is the case, aggregation is impossible.

The 'revealed preference' approach, proposed by Samuelson (1938), seems to offer a way forward. This approach argues that, in making choices between goods, individuals reveal their marginal valuations of each. Although unlabelled, the approach has already appeared in this volume – for example, underpinning the notion of 'consumer surplus' in Box 7.1. It is tempting to conclude that consumer surpluses can be aggregated to produce a measure of total utility – or a social welfare function.

Economic evaluation, when it uses 'willingness to pay' measures, or seeks equivalents to perfect market prices, adopts this approach – but in doing so, as in the case of the Paretian social welfare function, it has ignored issues of income distribution and the underlying problem of inter-personal comparison of utility. Proposals to 'weight' the results according to income level cannot be derived from the underlying rationale of 'revealed preference' on which the social welfare function is based. They can only effectively be arbitrary judgements of how 'society' might want to re-weight those preferences.

Some argue that the attempt to derive the social welfare function from the aggregation of individual welfares is misguided. Social welfare is more than the sum of its parts. A 'communitarian approach' claims the existence of an explicit or implicit 'social contract' and a community-based notion of the common good (for example, see Reich 1995). This notion provides a standard by which to order alternative states of the world.

In contrast a Marxist approach rejects the existence of a unique social welfare function. Stewart (1975), for example, argues that individuals do differ not just in their tastes but in their interests, which are embedded in class. These cannot be reconciled, averaged or substituted: 'To select projects in such a way that net benefits are maximised is meaningless until we have defined whose benefits we are talking about.'

extreme cases we would normally find this argument compelling. Most people would choose twenty years of extended life in preference to twenty days, or ten years of better

eyesight over ten days. It is common for the measurement of benefits to take account of duration of effect, but to assume that any given benefit is of equal value regardless of who is receiving it. Thus it is not age *per se* that is being used as a criterion, but rather duration of benefit, which is likely to be associated with age in treatment of non-life-threatening conditions.

A liberal 'Rawlsian' approach suggests that only improvement in the welfare of the member with the worst starting position constitutes an increase in the social welfare function. This also implies the ability to make interpersonal comparisons. This philosophy might be judged to underpin Robert Chambers's approach to decision making in rural development projects of 'putting the last first' (Chambers 1983).

9.4 Limits of Welfare Economics: the Extra-welfarist Approach

This brief discussion of the framework of theoretical welfare economics has demonstrated that Paretian welfare economics can provide a theoretical framework for economic evaluation, but also that there are problems in deriving clear rules from this framework. To many economists it is absurd to agonise over the application of a framework that in any case offers limited guidance for many real world decisions and for judging the merits of different choices. In many countries there is a clear consensus in favour of policies and changes that have winners and losers, and it may be more fruitful to spend time eliciting values in the population that can then set the rules for economic evaluation.

Dissatisfaction with conventional welfare economics has led some leading researchers to reject Paretian ideas as a basis for economic evaluation. The main drive to develop alternative frameworks is normally associated with Amartya Sen (1979). Culyer and others (e.g. Culyer 1989) have vigorously promoted

these alternative 'extra-welfarist' ideas and approaches in application to health.

Some important implications follow from a move away from a welfarist basis for economic evaluation. Culyer argues that the objective to be maximised should be health rather than utility. Instead of attempting to devise measures of changes in utility, we have the (slightly simpler) task of measuring changes in health. He proposed the use of quality-adjusted life years as the measure of health. On the face of it this may not seem very different from taking a welfarist approach – many welfarists would also advocate this measure of outcome. In practice, many of the problems associated with utility and revealed preference (see Box 9.6) remain unsolved. The debate around the question of age (see above) has many dimensions in common with the debate around income weights in relation to revealed preference-based measurements. Nevertheless, without the constraints of attempts to remain within a welfare economics framework, a wider range of information might be considered to be legitimate. Hurley (1998) offers a useful discussion of the similarities and differences between welfarist and extrawelfarist approaches, and how these may be important in application to economic evaluation in the health sector.

Existing guidance on the application of economic evaluation has always emphasised strongly the importance of making assumptions and judgements explicit, and this is stressed strongly in the development of extrawelfarists' approaches. For example, we may wish to give higher weighting to benefits to women with children, or to people who have uniquely valuable skills. A case can be made for favouring workers over non-workers, or, as happens in many countries, those who have been injured in the service of their country. It is perhaps poignant that both the US and

Vietnam give former soldiers special access to health care. This can be interpreted as saying that benefits should be allocated partly on the basis of former contributions to national defence. There is nothing necessarily right or wrong in such judgements, but it is important to know what they are if we are to make sense of the results of any analysis. For example, in assessing antenatal screening programmes it is important to know if termination of pregnancy is thought of as a legitimate clinical intervention or is considered to be murder. The same framework can be applied, but the criteria for assessing benefits would be very different.

Economists often assert that the two important dimensions of health care outcomes are length of life and quality of life. But many people would argue that there are other important issues, such as previous behaviour, previous suffering or religious belief. So long as the judgements are clear and explicit, then they can be included in the analysis, and any recommendations can be shown to depend on these values.

It can be argued that the practice of economic evaluation is not significantly affected by whether its justification is derived from the body of theory in Paretian welfare economics, or is based on a set of values and criteria taken from outside this framework. However, the interpretation of the results, and the acceptability of some criteria, may depend on the approach taken. Theoretical debates are not best resolved by voting or numbers. However, it is probably the case that the majority of health economists believe that economic evaluation has its foundations in Paretian welfare economics, and that this offers a justification for the measurement of cost and benefits. It can be helpful to understand how much and how little we can say is based on Paretian principles, since this helps in interpretation of the results of any evaluation.

9.5 Time Value of Money and Discounting

The discussion on the theory that supports economic evaluation has focused on choices between individuals and between services. Another important dimension is time. It is widely asserted that the value of a cost or benefit is not the same if it occurs at different times, and we need therefore to take this into account.

Try an experiment with your colleagues. Ask one of them to buy you a bicycle now. In exchange, in twenty years' time you will give that person a bicycle of the same quality. It is unlikely that anyone will agree to this (apparently fair) deal, and it is interesting to think why. Several factors may come into play. First, your colleague (or indeed you) may not be around in twenty years, and she may not be fit enough to cycle. She may refuse because she expects to be richer in twenty years' time, and would therefore prefer to borrow from you. She may just prefer things now to getting them later. The exact reasons for refusing this offer may be complex, but the general preference for now rather than later is found in all countries.

Given that we give a different value to goods and service today or in the future, we cannot add up costs and benefits that occur at different points in time *without adjusting them to take into account this time value of money.*

9.6 Interest Rates, Time Preference and Discount Rates

The time value of money is reflected in the existence of positive interest rates. When

---

Box 9.7 *Five Ways of paying for a Vehicle: an Illustration of the Time Value of Money*

The effects of interest payments and discounting can be seen clearly in the decision about how to finance a new vehicle. If a new van costs €10,000, we can in principle pay for it in at least five ways. First, we can simply pay today, and the funds paid will be €10,000. Four other options have very different 'headline' prices. In all these examples the interest rate is taken to be 10 per cent.

The first option is to set aside funds ten years before the purchase, and allow them to accumulate. At 10 per cent we would need to set aside €3,855.

The second option is to save a certain amount each year for ten years, allowing interest to accumulate on the saved amount and the van to be bought at the end. In that case we would need to save €570 per year (a total of €5,700).

The third option is to pay in instalments over ten years after the purchase. In this case the amount payable per year would be €1,627 (a total of €16,270).

Finally, in the fourth option we might agree to pay ten years from now, and we would be charged €25,937.

What is important to note is that in an important sense all these sums of money have the same value – in all cases they describe the cost of a new van to be delivered today. However, in terms of the number of euros paid, there is a difference of over €22,000. When interest has to be paid, or when it is received on balances held, it matters significantly when the money is paid over.

---

borrowing money we have to pay back the original sum, and also pay interest to compensate the lender for having to wait for the use of the money. Interest rates may vary depending also on other factors, such as risk. Looking at the level of interest rates over time there is tendency for rates in real terms (i.e. after allowing for any inflation) to be around 3–4 per cent for low-risk loans.

If we know the interest rate (say 5 per cent) we can make comparisons of sums of money in different periods. €100 today would be worth €105 in one year and around €128 in five years. The important point is that these different sums of money have the same value at the start. We can show this more formally, that the value of one euro after n years at y per cent interest is:

$$€(1 + y/100)^n$$

Normally we replace the description of interest in percentage terms with the equivalent decimal, so that 10 per cent is 0.1. We can then write the formula as:

$$€(1 + r)^n$$

where r is the interest rate expressed as a decimal. This is just the working of compound interest. We can easily reverse the process. The value today of €100 in five years' time is €100/128, which is just over €78. So we can say that the present value of €1 in n years' time at interest r is:

$$€1/(1 + r)^n$$

Box 9.7 illustrates five different ways of financing a new vehicle.

In economic evaluation some costs or benefits often occur at the same level for several years. Instead of calculating the present value for each year, we can use an annuity factor, which is just the sum of the different present values. The present value of €1 per year for N years, starting next year, is calculated as:

$$PV = \sum_{n=1}^{N} 1/(1 + r)^n$$

This is also known as the annuity factor for N years at interest r.

Tables of values of discount rates are available, and it is easy to set up programs on computer to calculate present values. In economic evaluation we must identify the year in which costs or benefits fall, and then discount to ensure that all sums are in present value. It is sometimes also convenient to calculate the costs of a project in terms of *annual equivalent cost*. The best way to think about this is to consider it as the rent that would be charged by an efficient not-for-profit supplier. A present value sum can be converted into an annual equivalent cost by dividing by the annuity factor.

9.7 Choice of Discount Rates for Costs and Benefits

Discounting of costs and benefits aims to make them comparable over different years. There has been some controversy as to whether it is appropriate to discount all costs and benefits (Parsonage and Neuberger 1992; Cairns 1992). Part of the concern comes from the fact that discounting of health benefits can produce some surprising results. The discounted value of benefits in fifty years' time can be almost zero, which means that many health-promotion interventions seem very poor value. For example, if we discount benefits in year 50 at 5 per cent, the value is reduced by about 90 per cent. It is interesting

to consider why we accept the principle of time value of money, but do not always feel comfortable with the results of it.

Economic theory would suggest that, in equilibrium, we would adjust our lending and borrowing so as to have the optimal flow over time of costs and benefits (within the constraint of our wealth and income). This implies that at any given interest rate we choose how much to save and how much to borrow. Since interest rates are positive, over a lifetime we consume more if we consume later. It has been observed that our behaviour is not always consistent with discounting costs and benefits at the same rate. We may have a different view of discounting benefits in terms of better health and less pain than we do of a need to pay money at different times.

There are several reasons why we might not be consistent (in addition to the possibility that we are just stupid). Markets, which deal with rights over time, are often distorted in various ways, and may therefore not be in equilibrium. Also it is possible that we do not treat benefits in different years as independent events. A schoolchild may enjoy the prospect of a long summer holiday and the apparently infinite period of happiness before returning to the drudgery of school work. This is in some ways separate from the actual enjoyment of each week of holiday. Similarly, we may get reassurance and pleasure now from the knowledge that we are likely to have a healthy old age, or that we will receive palliative care if close to death or that we are protected from the risk of hepatitis and its effects. In a technical sense, what seems to be happening is that the individual's utility in the current year is affected by the expected utility in future years, and that knowledge about future events and health influence the quality of life today. In the simple formulations of outputs of health services the benefits of an intervention change quality of life in particular years, and these gains are summed to derive the overall benefit. In principle there is no reason why we should not take into account effects of knowledge about future health states on utility – it just is not normally done. There is a need for more work to gain a better understanding of the effects of knowledge and anticipation on the utility gains from health interventions. There is a fairly clear consensus that both costs and benefits should be discounted in economic evaluation, and that the discounting should be at a common rate.

There is less consensus about the rate that should be used to discount costs and benefits. In principle the rate chosen should reflect the social opportunity cost. In a well-functioning capital market that will be the same as the rate of interest for low-risk borrowing. In most countries this would be around 3–5 per cent. Many countries specify the discount rate to be used in public or quasi-public economic evaluation. For example, in the UK the recommended rate was for many years 5 per cent, and was increased to 6 per cent. The World Bank has generally used a higher rate. In order to ensure some consistency in the reporting of economic evaluations, the guidelines in the *Journal of the American Medical Association* recommend reporting results with costs and benefits discounted at 3 per cent as well as any other (nationally recommended) rate. The effect of using a higher rate is to give relatively little weight to costs and benefits in the distant future, so it can significantly affect the choices made.

9.8 Do these Theoretical Disputes undermine Economic Evaluation?

In judging the merits of the different possible theoretical bases for economic evaluation it is worth distinguishing between unresolved debates about theory, and proceeding without a theoretical basis. All good science is based on clear and explicit theory. For example, most clinical research (and almost all good clinical research) draws heavily on statistical theory, and theoretical models of biological processes, which are crucial to understanding disease processes. These theoretical frameworks are not true in any absolute sense, any more than quantum physics or postmodernism is true, but they provide useful frameworks for understanding the problems and designing the empirical work. In a similar way, it is important that economic evaluation is carried out and interpreted within clear and explicit theoretical frameworks, which guide the conduct of the research, and assist in its interpretation. The existence of disputes over the theoretical basis of economic evaluation is similar to disputes between classical and Bayesian statisticians. The position adopted by the analyst may affect in detail how the evaluation is carried out and interpreted, but adherents of the different schools of thought can accept the legitimacy of the alternative approaches.

An understanding of the theoretical issues can be useful in understanding what the results of economic evaluation mean, and the extent to which there remains a need for policy judgements to be made. Since we have no absolute basis for making interpersonal comparisons of welfare, it can be quite legitimate to specify some groups for whom benefits should be more heavily weighted. In this sense economic evaluation provides guidance to decision makers, but does not remove the need for interpretation and judgement. However, economic evaluation should not be seen as just another argument to feed into the decision-making process. The reason for this is that the evaluation attempts to assemble all (or at least most) of the relevant information. If we are not careful, some arguments will be counted twice. If the cost–effectiveness ratio already includes a valuation of a benefit this same benefit should not be counted again when decision makers are making political judgements.

Consideration of the difficulty in agreeing a clear theoretical framework for economic evaluation reminds us of how difficult the choices really are. It is unusual for any development or change to have no losers. Careful thought needs to be given to the losers and the losses. Is it likely that the overall benefits outweigh them? It is common for there to be groups with needs who will not have these met, and we need to be confident that we have done our best to prioritise services that will yield the greatest benefits. The fact that the theoretical issues are difficult is not a reason to run away from them.

Chapter 10

Issues in the Measurement of Costs

10.1 How should Costs be Measured?

There are really only two practical problems in economic evaluation – measuring costs and measuring benefits. Superficially, measuring costs appears to be easier than measuring benefits. In almost all organisations there are some attempts to measure costs, if only for the purposes of financial control and accountability. But measuring costs accurately is often very difficult, and there are important conceptual and practical problems to overcome.

All good students of economics know that cost is the opportunity foregone, and in economic evaluation the aim is to measure *opportunity cost* (see Chapter 5). This implies that cost estimates produced for the purpose of economic evaluation will not be applicable to all possible other purposes that cost estimates might serve. For example, if a health service manager is interested in the financial implications of the introduction of a new service; or even the maximum effect (in health or welfare terms) achievable for a given expenditure *by the health service*, a separate analysis of this would need to be commissioned.

The justification for the choice of opportunity cost is that it takes into account the costs of all members of society, as they impinge on the social welfare function (see Chapter 9), and so is consistent with the attempt to measure benefits in the same way. Alternative conceptions of cost, which are not consistent with benefit measurement, can lead to illogical conclusions. Box 10.1 provides some examples. Nevertheless, if we believe that health services are 'under-funded' relative to other parts of the economy (see Chapter 21 for further discussion of this idea), we might mean that money in health service hands has a higher value than elsewhere. This might provide a justification for analysing the costs to the health service only, of achieving health improvement (for example). Before making this tempting judgement, it is worth bearing in mind that 'under-funding' is hard to demonstrate and that Box 10.1 contains a powerful argument for consistent treatment of costs and benefits. On that basis, this chapter will largely focus on opportunity-cost-based analysis, but will make occasional points relevant to a greater focus on health service costs.

To measure opportunity cost, we need to know the context in which choices are made. Good costing exercises start from a clear understanding of how current or potential services operate, what resources are used solely for particular groups of patients, which are

Box 10.1 *Opportunity Costs or Health Service Costs?*

Suppose we are interested in maximising the health effects achievable from the health service budget. This implies that we are not interested in costs to patients, or in adjusting financial costs to reflect underlying social costs. We are interested in whether or not AIDS treatment is better carried out in patients' homes or in hospitals and we discover that the following matrix of costs and benefits applies.

Costs and benefits of home-based versus hospital-based AIDS treatment (000 pesos per patient per month)

Cost or benefit	Home-based care	Hospital-based care
Costs to the health service	10,000	10,000
Costs to patients	5,000	8,000
Value of health benefits to patients	18,000	20,000

The analyst who ignores patient costs will conclude that hospital-based care is producing health benefits from the health service budget more efficiently than home-based care. This is concluded on the basis that although costs to the health service are the same, patient benefits are higher under hospital-based care. However, not only is hospital-based care less efficient from a societal perspective than home-based care, but patients' *net* benefits are lower (12 million pesos compared with 13 million pesos). This means that despite better health effects from the hospital-based programme, patients would prefer the home-based one – they would choose to sacrifice the marginal health effect to avoid the costs associated with hospital stays. It should be remembered that these might be extreme, perhaps involving inability to work and support a family.

Furthermore, considering costs and benefits inconsistently can sometimes produce an analysis that can be interpreted in multiple ways, undermining the objective stance which is the goal of the approach. For example, immunisation imposes financial costs on the health service. In rare cases, it also imposes serious health costs on patients. If we treat these as costs in this framework, we will ignore them – the only costs we are interested in are financial costs to the health service. If we treat them as a reduction in health benefits, they will be included. Clearly, it is possible that the results of our evaluation will be affected by which we do.

Most would argue in this case for accounting for these effects as reductions in benefit. But if we include these patient costs in our analysis, what about other possible patient costs? Milder but more common immunisation side effects? The burden on home carers and the associated stress? The financial losses associated with a long absence from work, which may have implications for a family's health status? It becomes clear that what is apparently a simple framework is prone to serious problems. Drawing a line between health and non-health effects is not straightforward. Justifying why only those items on one side of the line should count is even less so.

Adjusting financial costs for social costs has the same logic as including patient costs. We are trying to enquire after the impact on the whole of society, not just a particular budget. The potentially illogical results of trying to avoid this step are equivalent.

shared, and how the staff actually spend their time. For example, in one study that was assessing the cost of a long-stay mental health facility, it was found that the staff actually spent most of their time caring for a small group of patients with the most serious problems. This meant that very little direct support was provided for the majority of residents. The actual use of the staff resources, and therefore the way in which costs varied between different groups of residents, would not have been observed if costs had been calculated only from accounting data. It is likely that costs would have been assessed as being the same for all residents in the facility.

A good understanding of current provision can also help to identify if there is any spare capacity, which would allow the service to be expanded at low cost. It can be important to assemble information about the choices of technology and organisational structure available at different scales of provision. It is unusual for it to be possible to assess the costs of new developments accurately without quite detailed knowledge of the technology, management and human skills needed.

Some costs are fixed, some can be changed but only slowly. Some elements of cost can be easily observed and are obviously related to a particular activity, but others, especially buildings and land, senior staff, equipment and administration, may not vary directly with the level of activity, and it may be difficult to apportion these costs.

The simplest approach to calculating costs looks in detail at all the inputs into a service, multiplies by the unit cost of each, and thereby calculates total cost. This can present an accurate account of the direct costs of a particular service, although overhead costs may be hard to apportion. A drawback of this approach is that it does not demonstrate clearly how costs are likely to behave in the event of changes in scale, case mix or technology. There is therefore an argument for trying to estimate cost functions from information on costs and outputs in a larger number of service providers (see Chapter 5). These data are analysed using statistical methods to identify how costs vary with the level and mix of output, and to identify the factors that affect costs.

It is quite common for costing exercises to use a mixture of approaches, since there are usually constraints on access to appropriate data. In some studies a cost-function approach is used to calculate the unit costs to be applied to activity data.

Costing is not a simple technical exercise – it is too important to leave to accountants alone. Understanding the services provided as well as the financial data and analysis are important. Some examples may help. Many health interventions exhibit economies of scale, so that increasing the output may allow a lower cost service to be developed. In these circumstances the average cost based on current services will overestimate the costs of an expansion. Most emergency services exhibit economies of scale due to the possibility of using the capacity more intensively. An example is neonatal care (O'Neill *et al.* 2000). Since the need for such services is inherently unpredictable, most centres aim to keep at least one cot free at any time. The proportion of empty cots is therefore lower when there are fewer, larger centres. In cases like these it would be very misleading to cost services at the average if changes in the scale of provision were being contemplated. Other services are less likely to show significant scale economies, such as palliative care for people dying of cancer, and many parts of primary and secondary care. In such examples, the advantages of centralisation are often balanced by the disadvantages to patients of greater geographical distance between home and facility.

It may take time to adapt to higher levels of output, so scale economies may not be realised instantly. The technology used may be lumpy (e.g. bits of equipment come only in certain sizes, so that expansion beyond a certain threshold requires a large additional investment). New approaches to provision of certain services may involve a large change in scale of provision.

Tradition plays a large part in how services are organised. Many patterns of care owe more to historical accident than careful and rational planning. This means that it is important to understand what inputs are really necessary. For example, immunisation schedules may be rationalised, grouping a number of vaccines within a single administered dose. Among the reasons for doing this might be a more efficient use of staff time, but it is unlikely that staffing levels of an immunisation programme will be immediately adjusted. After some time, it might be apparent that there is a little more slack in the immunisation programme than in another programme, and staff might be reallocated.

There are several reasons why costs of care for different patients may vary. First, there may be characteristics of the patient that lead to longer hospital stays or more interventions, and therefore higher costs. Second, habits and traditions in different hospitals can differ, and this can lead to variation in cost. For example, the policy may be to keep all emergency admissions in hospital for at least one day, or alternatively it could be to review all patients admitted and discharge those not receiving active investigation or treatment. Given the somewhat limited evidence about the outcomes related to different patterns of care, it can be difficult to impose lower cost (but possibly lower quality) approaches to care. Third, the providers may have different levels of technical efficiency, and so any given service will have a different unit cost.

If we are seeking the opportunity cost, in principle we should be interested in identifying the lowest feasible cost of providing a given service. Differences that are explained by patient characteristics must be taken into account. It is less obvious how we should treat different clinical policies – normally they vary most where the evidence is weakest, and we often do not know if lower-cost practices reflect greater efficiency or lower quality. In principle the opportunity costs should not allow any X-inefficiency (technical inefficiency), so we should try to identify the cost in an efficient care provider.

Technically, cost that results from inefficiency is not a part of opportunity cost. Simply by using the resources efficiently it is possible to increase welfare. However, if we are convinced that it is impossible to eliminate X-inefficiency within a particular time scale, then it may be appropriate to include some element of inefficiency in the estimates of cost. What we are saying in this case, is that in practice these are the minimum costs of providing the programme, in the short term at least.

Identifying the appropriate concept and measure of cost can be particularly difficult when economic evaluation is carried out as part of clinical trials and studies. Patients recruited into a study are normally heterogeneous, and some variation in costs is likely. Normally they are not completely typical of patients who are likely to receive the treatment. Large trials normally recruit patients from many centres, and clinical policies and efficiency will also be important. To assess the cost-effectiveness of a new intervention we need to calculate the costs for those patients likely to be provided with the service, in the ways and places they are likely to receive the service. It is important therefore to know how costs vary with such factors as age, sex, disease severity, co-morbidities, case mix and scale of provision. To do this properly we need large enough samples of patients for variations to be understood, and for it to be possible to calculate confidence intervals for the estimates of cost. Since little is currently understood about the patterns of costs and these factors, it is not yet easy to estimate *ex ante* the sample sizes needed for costing studies, but it is clear that in some cases the variations are large. There has been widespread criticism of the lack of data on confidence intervals in economic evaluation studies (Barber and Thompson 1998), and a range of methods is often applied to estimate these. Issues in estimation of confidence intervals are considered in section 10.2.

Ideally costing studies calculate unit costs of services from a range of settings, but this is not always feasible. Where a range of different providers show very different unit costs, and these are not explained by characteristics of patients or effectiveness of treatment, there is an interesting issue of which estimate should be used. Since opportunity cost is the objective, there is a case for choosing the lowest observed estimate of unit costs, as discussed above. However, differences in unit costs by institution may not only reflect differences in technical efficiency as this perspective suggests. Since interventions are administered through a given infrastructure, there is a need to match the ideal infrastructure for this particular intervention and the ideal infrastructure for the health system as a whole. This intervention may be most efficiently delivered in medium-sized health centres, whereas others are most efficiently delivered in small or large ones. Additionally, health infrastructure as a whole has to balance technical efficiency questions from a health service

perspective with patient access costs. Patterns of human settlement do not present standard problems capable of producing a single 'best' solution to health unit size.

On the assumption that the most important determinant of cost variation between units is technical efficiency, some costing studies use data envelopment analysis (DEA) or stochastic frontier techniques, which aim to show costs of the most efficient care providers (Vitaliano and Toren 1994). Both these approaches aim to estimate cost functions in terms of the lowest observed costs rather than as the average of those observed. DEA is a non-parametric technique, and simply joins up the lowest cost observations to describe the function. Since there is likely to be measurement error there are advantages in using a method that takes this into account. Stochastic frontier analysis aims to do this.

Using these techniques the relative efficiency of different hospitals can be estimated by comparing observed cost with the lowest observed cost for a comparable provider. A typical measure of relative efficiency is the ratio of the cost of a service and the cost of the lowest cost observed service.

As with all statistical methods of estimating costs, the concern must be to ensure that differences in case mix are properly controlled for, so that the lowest observed cost is genuinely an example of greater efficiency and not simply the result of easier cases. With that proviso, there are many advantages in frontier methods to estimate cost. The estimate of cost is the lowest for a comparable provider and should therefore contain less X-inefficiency than the average provider. Thus, the frontier estimate can be viewed as being closer to opportunity cost than the average unit cost for all providers. Of course, such techniques can only identify relative efficiency, since the comparison is with the most efficient observed provider, and not with one that is necessarily efficient in absolute terms.

The costs we are aiming to estimate will usually be associated with adding a new service, or expanding an existing service. Where we are expanding an existing service, whether increasing the level of activity within a unit, or expanding the service from one set of units to others, information derived from cost functions can be very helpful. When a cost function is estimated it can be used to identify costs at higher or lower levels of output, and with different mixes of cases. By comparing the costs at the present level of activity with the costs at the level after implementation of an expanded service, we can obtain estimates of additional (or *incremental*) cost. The incremental cost is a similar concept to *marginal* cost, but in this case the change in service volume may not be small.

Where we are adding a new service – which is not yet provided anywhere in the health system – existing cost data are probably not very useful, and we are likely to be evaluating experimental provision (as where the economic evaluation is attached to a clinical trial – see below), or building up a hypothetical picture of costs. Nevertheless, our interest is still in incremental cost. Whereas, when we are expanding an existing programme, economies of scale cause divergence between average and incremental cost, when we are introducing a new programme, economies of scope cause this divergence (see Chapter 5).

In principle a focus on incremental cost is useful since in assessing options we really want to compare differences in costs and benefits between options. When costs are estimated using measures of changes in activity and a vector of (average) unit costs, the estimated costs or savings are likely to be over or under estimates of incremental cost. It is, of course, possible to make adjustments to the unit cost

vector to reflect any economies of scale or scope, and therefore to derive estimates that are closer to incremental cost. If we know the change in output associated with a development, the incremental cost (calculated from a cost function or from a hypothetical model of a new activity) can be used in the cost vector in place of average cost.

There is continuing controversy about the best estimates of incremental costs. In the short run capital costs are not relevant to measuring incremental costs, since there will be no change in capital (and other fixed) costs. If the current service has excess capacity, then there may be little or no need to invest in new facilities and equipment, and there may be no need for additional staff. Under these circumstances the incremental cost will only include consumables. However, in the long run all efficient services will adapt capacity to that which is most efficient. Changing the volume of a service will therefore mean that the fixed costs will change in the long run. For this reason, many economists argue that the correct basis for calculating incremental costs includes any changes in capital and other fixed costs. In many cases this means that the short-run average cost is a better proxy for long-run incremental cost than the short run incremental cost.

In circumstances of economies of scale and scope, divergence between average and marginal or incremental cost applies to the long term. For example, where the underlying cause is 'lumpy' investment requirements, or 'indivisibilities' (units of investment are large), there will be no long-term reconciliation between the two measures of cost. In these circumstances, it is clearer that adjustments for incremental cost have to be made, although there is debate over the extent to which long-run economies of scale and scope exist.

When average cost is being used as an estimate of long-run incremental cost, it is important to check that the change in activity is unlikely to lead to a major change in the most efficient technology of provision. For example, if a new universal vaccination programme replaces a smaller selective one, the whole organisation of the service, and probably the equipment and staff in use, will change. Average costs are unlikely in these circumstances to be a useful basis for estimating the incremental costs of the additional services. In general, for small changes in the volume of a service it is safe to use short-run average cost as a proxy for long-run incremental cost unless the technology is such that there is spare capacity in the current provision, and the service can be efficiently expanded without additional investment.

10.2 Sources of Variation in Cost Measures, Confidence Intervals and Assessing Sample Sizes for Costing

There are many reasons why costs vary for the same service in different locations, and some of these were discussed in section 10.1. There is a useful analogy here with the measurement of the effectiveness of different treatments in clinical trials and studies. The statistical principles for judging the comparative effectiveness of different interventions are widely accepted (if not completely uncontroversial). Before the start of a clinical trial there is a calculation of the sample that will be needed to give a particular probability of demonstrating a given difference of effect with a given level of statistical significance. Clearly this calculation is dependent on assumptions about the likely distribution of effects, and this assumed variability in effect for any given

treatment is one factor in determining the sample size needed.

In the case of clinical trials it is normal for the basic unit to be the patient. In most studies patients are allocated to different treatments (using random allocation if feasible), and variations coming from different facilities or staff skills matter little since in each site the patients are allocated at random. A problem arises in cases where randomisation has to be by hospital or district rather than by patient, since local facilities or skills may play important roles. There can be similar problems in assessing costs. Since costs for a particular patient depend on disease severity, co-morbidity, hospital size, location and efficiency, it is not clear whether we need a large sample of patients or hospitals in order to assess the range within which costs are likely to lie.

There is a growing understanding of the ways costs vary as a result of differences in patient characteristics. Many costing studies, particularly in clinical trials, calculate costs for each patient, and this gives data on the degree of variability. Such evidence can give a basis for the calculation of sample size that will allow costs for each category of patient to be assessed with reasonable reliability. When economic evaluation is being carried out alongside clinical trials or studies, this should be done. Some studies have shown that the distribution of service use is highly skewed in certain patient groups, especially in mental health and in cases where some patients receive treatment involving high-technology equipment (Gray *et al.* 1997).

It is usually desirable, but not always feasible, to assess unit costs of services from many different hospitals. In terms of interpreting the results of economic evaluation there are two reasons to be interested in understanding variation in cost between facilities. First, it may be that a particular service or intervention is cost-effective only if provided in a low-cost facility. Knowledge of the structure of costs can allow judgements to be made about where such developments should be located. A good example could be haemoglobinopathy screening. Given the large economies of scale in testing, the service is only likely to be cost-effective if testing can be centralised. Second, unless we know the variation in unit costs in different facilities, there is a risk that the assessment of cost-effectiveness reflects the chance that the evaluation was done at a low- or at a high-cost location. This is somewhat analogous to drawing conclusions about the efficacy of a new treatment from case reports or small studies.

Since it is often not possible to calculate unit costs for services in more than a few centres, it can be impossible to explore the range of likely costs using conventional statistical methods. It is still useful to present evidence of variation in unit costs, but confidence intervals for cost variation are only possible if it is possible to include in the study data from a large enough range of providers to allow the distribution to be analysed. But we should remain interested in the consequences of any errors in estimates of cost, and we should try to ensure that strong recommendations reflect our level of confidence in the estimates.

10.3 Using Sensitivity Analysis on Costs

While it is desirable where possible to calculate mean costs and confidence intervals around the mean, since variability may be related to location of services, it is often impossible to do this. In these circumstances it is still desirable to explore the consequences of variation in costs. This is best done by sensitivity analysis. There are two ways in which sensitivity analysis can be used. First, a range of plausible assumptions can be tested out (such as plus or minus 15 per cent), to see if this is likely to affect the conclusions of the analysis. If there is some basis for judging plausible levels of variation this is appropriate. An alternative is to start from the other end, and ask the question 'What size of variation in cost would be needed to change the conclusions?' If the conclusion remains the same with even quite large variations in cost, then this may be grounds for accepting the results as robust.

10.4 Costing in Economic Evaluation

The normal approach to calculating costs in economic evaluation is to estimate the number of cost-generating events for each patient, and to multiply this matrix of different events for different patients by a vector of unit costs. As suggested above, this unit cost vector may be calculated using a range of methods, from accounting or budget data or estimates of cost functions. In many cases simple approaches have been considered to be adequate, and most studies do not take into account changes in costs with time or technical progress. It was argued at the start of this chapter that costing requires understanding of circumstance as well as technique. It may be quite acceptable to assume that costs for a particular service will remain stable over time. Equally, there are some instances in which such an assumption leads to serious errors. For example, in most surgery in industrialised countries, the length of hospital stays has fallen consistently, and this trend seems likely to continue and to be capable of exploitation in other countries. Failing to take this into account may lead to overestimates of the costs of surgical options in the future. New technologies

Box 10.2   *Economic Evaluation of Renal Services for Older People (I)*

You are in charge of policy on acute health services development for older people in your region. Recent press comment has been highly critical of the current policy of rationing access to certain renal services for older people. At present haemodialysis (HD) and peritoneal dialysis (PD) are available only to people who develop end stage renal failure before the age of seventy-five. In order to make a better choice on what, if anything, to do about this situation you commission an economic evaluation. The stages of this evaluation are considered here in Chapter 10, and in Chapters 11–14.

Since this service exists only in other districts you have to use information from elsewhere to estimate costs. You have found three districts that provide a service for older people, but in two cases this is in the context of a trial of a new form of peritoneal dialysis.

What follows is extracts from the report by the economic evaluation team and questions you have raised for discussion with them. Brief responses from the consultants are also given.

Costs of dialysis were calculated on the basis of a detailed assessment of the use of resources by each patient in three dialysis services. Details of service use were collected from the hospitals providing the services, and from interviews with the patients to find out more about use of services in other hospitals, use of primary care and social care.

Question. I can see that the information from the dialysis centre is likely to be quite accurate, but what about data from patients? Can they really be relied upon to give accurate information about other services used?

Consultant. This is a good point. Studies have shown that patient recall can be quite accurate over a relatively short period – indeed, in this study we compared what patients said about their use of the hospital (where we also had information from medical records), and we found that there was close correlation between data from patients and data from the medical records.

Costs to patients, families and friends were also assessed. In principle costs were included regardless of who paid. In the case of the clinical trials, the makers provided some equipment free, but a cost was nevertheless included for this. As instructed we tried to assess the full opportunity cost.

Question. I don't quite understand this point – if the equipment is free then surely it is free!
Consultant. No. All resources have an opportunity cost. The fact that it is paid in this case by the equipment manufacturers makes no difference. The decision to develop a service should depend on the balance between opportunity cost and the benefits of the new service.

Once a full list of services used had been gathered the next step was to calculate unit costs. For equipment the unit cost was assessed by assessing the cost of new equipment, its likely useful life, and from this imputed a rental equivalent cost (the *annual equivalent cost*). The assumption was made that equipment would be used to 90 per cent of its capacity, allowing for servicing and repairs.

Question. I can understand that to add up capital costs and running costs it is useful to treat equipment as if it were hired – this allows you to add capital costs and running costs all

Continued

in terms of cost per year or cost per patient treated. I'm more worried about the assumption of 90 per cent usage. Is this realistic?

Consultant. This is always difficult. My advice is always to work closely with professionals who actually understand using the equipment. In addition to needing to account for maintenance, there is also some variability in needs of patients. We got round this by doing a sensitivity analysis on the level of use – you'll remember, this appears later in the report.

It was decided to calculate the unit costs of dialysis from information from the three hospitals. Information on whole-time equivalent staff by grade was collected, taking account of the sharing of staff with other services. In one case we were able to compare staff costs before and after an expansion of the service, so it was possible to calculate the incremental cost of providing services for the additional patients. This gave a lower estimate than that from those hospitals that had no records of previous staffing levels. An attempt was also made to count only staff actually needed to provide the service, and to exclude those that are needed to support the research projects.

Question. What difference did you find between the three centres, and how do we know which is right?

Consultant. Ideally data on unit costs would be available from more centres, and it would then be possible to calculate costs using statistical methods. In this case we just had to use our judgement. One centre seemed more expensive, and it looks as if this was due to a long tradition of weak management and overstaffing, so we used staffing levels from the average of the other two. Not very scientific, perhaps! However, we did carry out a sensitivity analysis on the staffing costs. We were more concerned that one centre was much larger, and we expected to find lower staffing due to economies of scale, but there was no sign of this.

The pattern of costs differs greatly between haemodialysis and peritoneal dialysis. In the former case there is expensive capital equipment, but the consumable costs are relatively low. Staff costs for haemodialysis are also higher than for peritoneal dialysis, since peritoneal dialysis is mainly delivered at home by the patient and family. Family time off work was costed at the average national wage, but for non-working family members half of this was used. Peritoneal dialysis patients have high costs early in their dialysis as they were being prepared and trained. Prices (net of discounts) for consumables were used as a proxy for costs.

Question. This makes it likely that the choice of haemodialysis or peritoneal dialysis will to be quite sensitive to wage levels and costs of consumables. Should we really make these decisions on cost grounds?

Consultant. See the comments later in the report. Yes, since the cost of consumables is so high for peritoneal dialysis it is likely that the choice will be sensitive to this and wage costs. There is some evidence that consumables are priced so as to leave the overall cost of the two technologies the same.

Two important findings about costs emerged. First, dialysis patients are very low users of primary care services – perhaps not surprising, since they see doctors and nurses regularly. It was also found that patients requiring nursing home care cost nearly twice as much in total as those living at home. The full cost of their care has been included.

Continued

Question. Surely we should include only those costs directly related to dialysis and related treatment? People get primary care because they need it, and the same could be said of nursing home care.

Consultant. It is always difficult to decide the boundaries. In our view both these costs should be included. The benefit side of the equation is years of life (of whatever quality) gained. The full cost of this benefit is the overall cost of all services. The low cost of primary care means that the difference in cost between those with and those without renal failure is less than the cost of dialysis, but really we should be asking how much we get for how much. Some of these issues are taken up later in the report.

may reduce in price over time, and may be the subject of learning, suggesting that health workers' skills may develop in such a way that they use the technology more efficiently. Patients and potential patients learn more about the service and how to use it, contributing to reduced costs. For example, a new technology such as the treatment of bed nets with insecticide to combat malaria may require aggressive marketing at first, but rely on word of mouth later once its uptake has reached high levels. Drugs normally become much cheaper when patents expire. Costing studies should take all these factors into account.

Costing cannot be an exact science, but costs estimated using sensible approaches by people who are well informed about context are more likely to reflect the true foregone opportunities.

Chapter 11

Measuring Benefits in Economic Evaluation

....

11.1 The Different Types of Economic Evaluation

The practice of economic evaluation in health care takes a number of forms, and most of these are defined in terms of the ways in which benefits are measured. It is easy to be confused by the terminology used. Drummond *et al.* (1997) did their best to make things clear with detailed definitions of the hierarchy of types of evaluation from those comparing costs alone to full cost–benefit analysis, where all costs and benefits are measured in money terms (see Further Reading section on p. 94). Several problems result from this attempt at standardisation. First, since practitioners normally ignore the suggested classification, terminology is normally used 'incorrectly'. For example, the *Journal of the American Medical Association* published guidelines for economic evaluation that use the term cost-effectiveness analysis for what the Drummond classification would describe as cost-utility analysis. Second, the enthusiastic amateur has a tendency to see the different ways of measuring benefits as being different types of analysis, when in reality they are variants on a theme. Benefit measurement is normally difficult and placing a value on benefit is very difficult.

The choice of type of evaluation to use is normally made on the basis of how difficult it is to obtain data that will allow benefits to be measured or valued.

When benefits are traded in the market a value is put on them automatically, since the buyer must consider that they are worth at least what she paid. Sometimes it is possible indirectly to assess the value people place on benefits from their behaviour. For instance, even when they do not pay directly for a service, they may be willing to take time off work and travel, so there is a 'price' on the service. But often it is really not feasible to put any sensible money value on the outputs of health interventions. It may however be possible to compare them in some standard unit, such as years of healthy life gained or improvement in activity of daily living scores. Sometimes it is difficult even to find proxies for output or outcomes, and all that can be compared is the volume of services, but this type of measure is difficult to interpret.

The best way to think of the different economic evaluation techniques is as a spectrum, with cost–benefit analysis at one extreme, where benefits are valued, through cost-utility studies with benefits measured in some standard unit, to cost-effectiveness analysis, where outcomes are defined in natural units. If the outcome is assumed the same for all options, then the analysis simply seeks to identify the lowest-cost delivery of the service. The decision on what type of analysis to use may depend mainly on the resources available for the study. Assessing values and utilities is expensive and controversial, and many people prefer to leave the benefits in years of life gained or some specified improvement in health status.

Further Reading – Drummond *et al.* Classification of Economic Evaluation Methods

It is a great mistake to think of the different methods of economic evaluation as different approaches. Rather, they should be seen as variations in what is desirable and feasible. All methods have their logic in the cost–benefit approach, and the differences come mainly from the judgement about how best to assess benefits.

In *Cost–benefit* analysis costs and benefits are assessed in money terms. This allows all types of service to be (in principle) compared, but it is often difficult to measure benefits in this way.

Cost–utility analysis adopts an index of benefit that is common across different types of service. The most commonly used is the *quality-adjusted life year* (QALY).

Where the units of outcome can be described and measured, in natural units only, the approach is *cost-effectiveness* analysis. Outcomes might be measured as (for example) years of life gained, number of children immunised or days of palliative care.

Cost-minimisation analysis is appropriate if the outcome is the same for all options, and the question is simply what is the lowest-cost way of achieving the outcome.

Rather than a free choice as to what technique to use, it is better to think of the problem as being 'How constrained are we in the measurement of outputs?' Often the desirable analysis would use outcomes measured in money terms or utility scores, but the data that would allow this cannot be accessed. Source: Drummond *et al.* (1997).

11.2 Measuring and Valuing Outputs

Advocates of attempts to assess benefits in financial or utility measures stress that without a standard and comparable system of measurement, it is difficult to compare outcomes of different types of intervention. For example, comparing life-extending interventions, such as dialysis or ORT, with (mainly) quality-of-life-improving ones, such as cataract surgery, normally involves comparison of outcomes that are in different dimensions. Somehow the value of the different benefits must be compared if evaluation is to be used for setting priorities. This can be done as part of the political decision-making process, and many would argue that this is how it should be done (Carr-Hill 1991). However, it is also argued that it is much better to set in advance the way in which benefits will be compared (Williams 1991). As a society we might agree in advance on the relative value of, say, thirty additional years of life for one person and better vision for 300 people who will expect to live for another five years.

Specialists in quality-of-life measurement understand that there are many dimensions of quality, and some measurement instruments deliberately avoid having a single overall score. Even on the different domains (such as physical abilities, pain or psychological well being) it is possible to argue against overall scores. For example, whether improved mobility is more or less important than continence depends in part on the lifestyle of the person involved. And attitudes to a given set of circumstances may not be stable over time. Tolerance of disability can increase with experience and adaptation. It is inevitable that any system that derives single-figure scores for complex effects will ignore important subtleties, and will destroy some important detail in the data. But no simple way exists for making comparisons of multiple dimensions.

Measures of quality of life can be designed to meet the needs of a particular patient group, or can attempt to be more generic. Disease or patient group specific measures have apparent advantages of deriving more detailed and sensitive data on those dimensions of health that are most affected by a particular disease. For example, instruments used in palliative care will emphasise pain control, and a range of objectives in terms of psychological and spiritual well being. They are also likely to take into account the impact of an intervention on informal carers. Outcomes measured in this way have a lot of meaning in terms of the particular service, but are of little use in making comparisons between disparate services. In general there is a trade-off between using measures with meaning in a particular context and using ones that allow comparisons to be made. The ideal for comparisons is a single index number, which can be applied to health gains of all types. Such an instrument is less sensitive for making detailed comparisons within a particular service. However, implicitly or explicitly, comparing a malaria-control programme and cataract surgery involves judgements about their relative importance, and this may be helped by the use of a common system of measuring benefits.

Measuring benefits in money terms has particular attractions for decision making. There are two main advantages. First, since the same unit of measurement is used in all cases, all potential developments can be compared on the same basis. Second, it is in principle possible to make judgements not only on relative priority, but also on whether or not something is worth doing at all. On the basis of the 'potential Pareto improvement' rationale, if the costs exceed the benefits, a project should not go ahead, even if it is the best of the projects under consideration in the analysis.

11.3 Valuing Benefits in Money Terms

The demand curve for any good or service is the schedule of *willingness to pay*. This can be interpreted as the self-assessed benefits to consumers (after all you would not buy something if you did not value it at least at the price). At the margin, the last unit consumed will be valued by the consumer at what she had to pay for it (i.e. the benefit is equal to the price for the marginal user). Of course there are objections to using estimates of willingness to pay as measures of benefit, not least because willingness to pay is closely related to *ability* to pay. But in a well-functioning market, for any given distribution of income, we can say that the willingness to pay represents the users' own measure of benefits.

A feature of most circumstances in which economic evaluation is used is that there is an element of market failure. Under these circumstances the benefit to the marginal user may not be equal to the marginal social cost. Also, since consumers are not fully informed, their willingness to pay may not reflect their preferences fully. Observed prices for those who do pay for services may also be misleading as a guide to willingness to pay. Often only a small proportion of the provision of a service is traded, so that observed trading may be only by an unrepresentative sub-group in the

Box 11.1 *Willingness to Pay and Measurement of Benefits*

The analysis of demand for health and health care in Chapter 2 showed that the quantity of a good demanded depends on price. In Box 7.1 we extended that concept to argue that consumers 'reveal their preferences' through the demand curve, and outlined the concept of consumer surplus. That concept relied on the idea in the diagram.

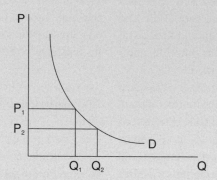

When the price is P_1 the individual chooses Q_1. This means that the person assessed that the benefit to herself of the last unit of consumption was exactly equal to the price P_1. The demand curve can be interpreted as a schedule of willingness to pay for individuals. To maximise their utility, each person equates the marginal willingness to pay to the additional cost of buying the service. If price falls to P_2, the individual will buy more, not because the willingness to pay has changed, but because of additional units which are valued above P_2 but below P_1.

Just as the individual should equate marginal willingness to pay (marginal benefit) to marginal cost to maximise her welfare, so too should a society with this objective equate willingness to pay for a service with the marginal cost.

population. In practice it is therefore seldom reliable to use information on prices paid for services to estimate willingness to pay (see Box 11.1).

An alternative to observing directly the willingness of individuals to pay for health care is to ask them how much hypothetically they would be willing to pay for treatment or for a defined improvement in health. There are many ways in which this can be done, and many studies have attempted to derive estimates. Although in principle information on people's declared willingness to pay is very valuable, there are several reasons for doubting if the estimates will be robust. First, it is difficult for people to detach themselves from existing institutional arrangements – if a service is currently available without charge to the user, she may say she is willing to pay nothing, since she believes she should get it free. Second, if the respondent knows that the information will be used to set priorities for service development, she has an incentive to overstate the willingness to pay, and if it is to be used to set fees, to understate it. As with other methods of assessing benefits, there is the problem that if the respondent needs the service she will naturally want the assessed willingness to pay to be high, and if she has no need it may be difficult to think about what would be the willingness to pay for treatment of a hypothetical need.

Willingness-to-pay-calculations currently play only a small part in the practice of economic evaluation, but the inherent attraction of the approach keeps researchers interested in developing it (Donaldson *et al.* 1995). There has been some recent interest in eliciting views on preferences using techniques from marketing and applied psychology, especially discrete choice modelling (Ryan and Hughes 1997). This approach can be interpreted as being based on the theoretical work of Kelvin Lancaster (1966), that suggested that demand for goods is a function of their characteristics. By observing a large number of choices between services with different characteristics (including price) we can potentially assess the value placed on each characteristic. Early evidence suggests this approach will have uses mainly in understanding better the value patients place on details of how services are delivered, but it may come to be used more widely in assessing willingness to pay.

11.4 Standardised Measures of Outcome and Utility Scores

If it is not feasible to measure benefits in money terms, it may still be possible to compare very different health gains related to treatment for different needs. If a common system of measuring outcomes can be used, then the costs and benefits of different interventions can be compared. This is the reason why attempts have been made to devise measures that combine the different dimensions of health gains into a single score. This allows comparison between the costs and health gains of different interventions, although it cannot

directly help us to assess whether or not an intervention should be provided.

The economic theory of demand uses the concept of utility (see Chapter 2). Rational consumers spend their income so as to gain the maximum utility from it. The task is made more difficult by the fact that some benefits are uncertain. Spending on a health care intervention may or may not effect the desired health gain, and in some circumstances may actually lead to a deterioration of health status. This is common in other sectors, and there is a well-established body of theory on the problems of choice in the face of uncertainty or risk.

The general expectation in economics is that a person's utility rises with consumption, but probably at a decreasing rate. In other words, as someone consumes more of a service, her utility rises, but each subsequent unit of consumption has less and less impact on utility. This is known as 'diminishing marginal utility'. It is interesting to consider this against a number of possible measures of health gains. If we give equal value to a year of life gained, irrespective of to whom, and the circumstances of the recipient, then we are implicitly saying that the value of that gain in terms of utility is constant. More formally the utility function of all individuals is identical, and is a linear function of the number of years lived. This conflicts with the usual expectation of diminishing marginal utility.

Further, to argue that years of life should be weighted according to their quality, appears at first sight an uncontroversial technical improvement. For any individual, it is clear that a year of life at high quality is better than a year at low quality; any intervention which produces the first will be preferred to one which only produces the second. However, the proposal when applied as a means of determining priorities between individuals is more contentious. It implies, for example, that it is a lower priority to extend the life of a disabled person than it is a fully able-bodied person. This type of problem does not arise in most economic evaluations because the beneficiaries are anonymous at the time of evaluation. They can be assumed all to be in perfect physical condition other than with respect to the need under evaluation. However, where an intervention is specifically designed to extend life of those suffering from a quality of life affecting disability (for example, cystic fibrosis), the question cannot be avoided and requires an explicit judgement to be made. More generally, the issue arises for services for the elderly who are more likely to have coexisting pathologies and disabilities.

The commonly used measures of health gain in economic evaluation are the *quality-adjusted life year* (QALY) and the *disability-adjusted life year* (DALY). They both make some adjustment for the different circumstances of different individuals, but otherwise assume that gains are of equal value. There is no direct adjustment to account for diminishing marginal utility of health gains. In effect they assign equal value to measured improvements in health.

Interpreting the meaning of these measures is not straightforward. There is a fuller discussion below about the ways in which the adjustments are made to allow for diminished quality of life in these measures, but at this stage the interesting question is what a QALY means – how we interpret the unit we have constructed. If it is used as the basis of setting priorities, then implicitly the QALY score is used as if it is a measure of social welfare, and it is common for this to be the interpretation. We have already seen that the extra-welfarists reject this interpretation of the QALY and it can be argued that such measures are interpretable only as utility or welfare on some rather restrictive assumptions.

A simple illustration is the issue of risk. Since the effect of treatment for an individual is not known, what is being chosen is at best a known mean and distribution of gains, and is at worst uncertain (i.e. we do not know the mean and distribution of the likely gains). The degree of risk may significantly affect the attitude of people to a likely but risky gain. In principle it is possible to derive QALYs that are adjusted for risk aversion, and to allow for diminishing marginal utility of health status improvement, but this is complex and costly. In most cases the data simply do not exist to do this. The important point to bear in mind is that more QALYs can be interpreted unambiguously as a welfare gain only if we accept certain assumptions about the relationship between health status, risk, distribution of gains and utility. Attempts to negotiate the problems of interpreting QALYs and to remain more closely rooted in utility theory have generated a continuing debate.

The debate about the meaning and interpretation of QALYs is important, especially when they are used to inform important priority setting issues. There are also important practical issues in how the weighting of years for quality of life is best done. Some hypothetical questions are easier to answer than others. If people are asked to choose which they would prefer, a longer spell in a state of diminished health, or a shorter one in good health, then most could answer. This allows at least an ordinal ranking to be derived.

11.5 Measuring Health Gains and Utilities

Tools for measuring health gains and utilities attempt to take into account the size of potential benefits, the likelihood that benefits will be realised and when they will occur. In economics it is normally assumed that consumers maximise utility. In a world of certainty this is relatively straightforward, but when faced with risky alternatives (as will always be the case in health interventions), it is more complicated. If the distribution of possible outcomes is known, then the patient can maximise expected utility. However, other strategies may be adopted when outcomes are genuinely uncertain (such as adopting a maximin strategy, where the person takes steps to ensure that the worst conceivable outcome is as good as possible).

There is much debate about the extent to which the different approaches to measuring health gains do or do not represent maximisation of expected utility in the sense of the formal Neumann–Morgenstern formulation. Von Neumann and Morgenstern's proposition is:

Consider three events, C, A, B, for which the order of the individual's preferences is the one stated. Let α be a real number between 0 and 1 such that A is exactly equally desirable with the combined event consisting of a chance of probability $1 - \alpha$ for B and the remaining chance of α for C. Then we suggest the use of α as a numerical estimate for the ratio of the preference of A over B to that of C over B.

(Neumann and Morgenstern 1947)

QALYs and Healthy Years Equivalents (HYEs) are both attempts to measure outcomes that reflect benefits of longer life and better quality of life, but proponents of the HYE approach claim the two-stage procedure proposed for HYEs gets closer to being a representation of expected utility maximisation (Gafni and Birch 1997). Several contributors to the debate have demonstrated that under certain conditions the two measures can be shown to be identical (Morrison 1997).

Various methods are used to combine length of life and health-related quality of life to form health gain or utility scores. In some cases a combination of methods is used, first to describe the different outcomes in more generic ways, and then to value these. For example, we can describe the outcome of cataract surgery in terms of visual acuity or in terms of months of ability to undertake certain tasks. The latter has the effect that it is easier to compare this to benefits from quite different interventions, such as accident prevention or supply of hearing aids. The trade-off between greater complexity with more sensitivity, and simplicity with less power to discriminate, was discussed above (section 11.2). Box 11.2 shows the classifications of one of the simplest systems, the EUROQOL EQ-5D. Users of this instrument convert different states of health into scores on these five dimensions, and then apply weights for these different combinations that have been derived separately.

Deriving a weight for quality of life can be done by asking people directly to assess the value of a year in a state of diminished health or by asking them to choose between periods in different health states using time-trade-off questions. For example, I might put the same value on four years of life in full health and eight years with severe pain. In doing this I would be saying that the value of a year with severe pain was approximately half that of a year of full-quality life.

Valuing health states has been done using visual analogue scales, where people are asked to rate their quality of life by choosing a point on a scale that most nearly describes how they feel about their health. A general problem that always occurs in these situations is interpreting what people really understand by the different points on a scale. However, it does at least provide an ordinal ranking of health states.

Box 11.2 EUROQOL EQ-5D

This is one of the simpler systems of classifying health states, and is intended mainly to be used as a standard instrument alongside other measures. Combinations of the five dimensions have been valued using a number of methods. The health states are defined not in terms of a single score, but rather as the different combinations.

Mobility
1 No problem with walking.
2 Some problem walking about.
3 Confined to bed.

Self-care
1 No problem with self-care.
2 Some problems washing or dressing self.
3 Unable to wash or dress self.

Usual activities
1 No problems with performing usual activities (e.g. work, study, housework, family or leisure activities).
2 Some problems with performing usual activities.
3 Unable to perform usual activities.

Pain/discomfort
1 No pain or discomfort.
2 Moderate pain or discomfort.
3 Extreme pain or discomfort.

Anxiety/depression
1 Not anxious or depressed.
2 Moderately anxious or depressed.
3 Extremely anxious or depressed.

Attempts to derive weights for the different combinations have come both from population surveys and from the use of a visual analogue scale for self-reported quality of life alongside the five dimensions. Time trade-off has been used to rate the different profiles.

If we wish to rate the change from cataract surgery we might find changes in mobility, self-care, usual activities and possibly anxiety and depression. For example, the profile might change from 22212 to 11111. This might improve the quality of life from say 0.8 to 1.0.

Economists have often argued for the use of the standard gamble technique to value health states, mainly in the belief that it comes closest to applying Neumann–Morgenstern expected utility theory. The method is conceptually simple. A given health state which will persist for t years is compared with a gamble between perfect health for t years and certain death. The perfect health occurs with a probability p, and death with a probability $(1 - p)$. The experiment is to vary the values of p until the person is indifferent between the health state and the gamble. The value of the probability is the measure of how the health state is valued as compared to perfect health.

In practice it is not always straightforward to carry out standard gamble experiments, since it is not easy for people to understand and think in terms of probabilities. In addition to coming closest to applying Neumann–Morgenstern expected utility theory, the standard gamble approach has been argued to introduce risk into the evaluation, since the comparison is made between certain and uncertain outcomes.

There have been several attempts recently to derive quality-of-life weights for use in economic evaluation from health status measured using generic instruments such as SF36 (Brazier *et al.* 1998). SF36 is a commonly used questionnaire that assesses both physical and psychological dimensions of health-related quality of life. It has thirty-six questions, and was developed from the longer Medical Outcomes Study quality-of-life measure (Ware and Sherbourne 1992). It has the advantage that it has been used in many different circumstances, and benchmarking data are available for many diseases. Most such tools are designed to rank health states, but not normally to produce a cardinal score. However, since health states can be ranked, it is then possible to ask people to place a value on each. In most cases the aim is to place health status and the related quality of life on a scale running from zero for death to one representing full health-related quality of life. The advantage of this approach is that these instruments are widely used, and thus comparison with other evaluations may be possible (if other features of the two evaluations are sufficiently similar).

Time-trade-off approaches ask a person to indicate indifference between longer periods in poorer health and shorter ones in full health. An advantage of such approaches is that the questions asked directly address the relationship between the two main objectives of most health interventions – to extend life and to improve its quality. Standard gamble approaches have the advantage that they also put the decision about trade-offs into the context of the riskiness associated with different patterns of interventions. Respondents are asked to choose between different combinations of likely outcomes and the risk associated with these.

Of course it is possible to argue endlessly about what is meant by full quality of life, especially as many aspects of health status are affected by ageing. It is also possible to argue that factors other than health status are important, since some people are unable to convert healthy life into good quality of life. However, it is normal to consider quality of life in the context of what health status a reasonably fit person of that age might hope for, and to ignore all aspects of quality of life that are not caused by illness and/or modified by treatment and care.

Although many advocates of QALYs question if they really measure utility, their use tends to imply this is the case. An alternative interpretation is that the QALY is simply a standardised measure of outcome that can usefully be used to compare different interventions with very different types of effect. On this interpretation its use to guide decision making is to provide quasi-objective information about the patterns of outcomes and their impact, but not necessarily to provide a basis for recommending particular priorities.

The *disability-adjusted life year* (DALY) is a more modest attempt to weight years for quality, where the main adjustment is for the effects of illness on disability. (See Further Reading on p. 102 for a more detailed description of the composition of the DALY.) DALYs have been widely used in assessing the global burden of diseases and in identifying priorities in low- and middle-income countries. Different diseases were compared in terms of their effects on DALYs lost, and in terms of the cost-effectiveness of treatments in terms of DALYs gained.

The most obvious criticism of the DALY is the bias against health improvements that reduce pain, improve survival and quality of life but do not significantly affect disability. The calculation of the DALY also builds in adjustment for the social value of time lived at different ages, and the timing of benefits from discounting both of which reduce the transparency of the measure. DALYs have been widely used in comparison of health programmes for poor countries, and there must be some concern that they lead to a bias against interventions of benefit to old and very young people. This reflects a judgement that members of these age groups also benefit from health benefits to those of working age, owing to their dependent status. Those involved in the development of DALYs claim that they do not aspire to be a measure of utility, but their use in setting priorities means that they are used in ways that imply correspondence with social welfare.

Further Reading – The Composition of a DALY

The disability-adjusted life year (DALY) is used in two ways – to calculate the 'global burden of disease' by estimating the extent to which disease causes loss of life and disability in geographically defined populations; and as a generic measure for use in cost-effectiveness analyses. The measure combines an estimate of the duration of time lost due to premature death; a weight representing the social value of time lived at different ages; a weight for disability; and a discount rate.

Treating all these components together, the DALY formula is complex, but it consists of a series of relatively simple stages:

1 The duration of time lost owing to premature death is calculated using the 'standard expected years of life lost'. This uses a standard mortality table approximating life expectancy in rich Western economies which produces a life expectancy for each age cohort. Deaths in each age cohort are deemed responsible for the loss of this amount of life expectancy. Mortality tables associated with rich Western economies are deemed appropriate for all countries because they are argued to measure the potential length of life, rather than the actual one, and therefore to be a better indicator of the gap between potential and actual life which global burden of disease measurement aims to capture. It is admitted by the authors of the measure that a different approach would be more suitable for use in economic evaluation.

2 A weight representing the social value of time lived at different ages is calculated so as to reflect different social roles of different age groups, and the dependence of some age groups on others. It is argued that 'The concept of dependence and social role is broader than formal sector wage productivity and is not linked to total income levels.' Nevertheless, many interpret this weight as a productivity weight, and although it is not used to discriminate between individuals of different income levels, it is otherwise not dissimilar.

3 Disability is weighted according to the table. The classes of disability were defined without reference to empirically based description of disability states, and weights were calculated on the basis of the opinions of a group of 'independent experts'. Note that,

Disability weightings

Class	Description	Weight
1	Limited ability to perform at least one activity in one of the following areas: recreation, education, procreation or occupation	0.096
2	Limited ability to perform most activities in one of the following areas: recreation, education, procreation or occupation	0.220
3	Limited ability to perform activities in two or more of the following areas: recreation, education, procreation or occupation	0.400
4	Limited ability to perform most activities in all of the following areas: recreation, education, procreation or occupation	0.600
5	Needs assistance with instrumental activities of daily living such as meal preparation, shopping or housework	0.810
6	Needs assistance with activities of daily living such as eating, personal hygiene or toilet use	0.920

in contrast to the QALY, these weights work negatively – the higher the score, the worse the health state.

4 Finally, discounting is conducted for all components of the calculation at 3 per cent on the basis that this is 'consistent with the long-term yield on investments'.

The authors of the DALY do not claim to be consistent with any specific conception of a Social Welfare Function, rather, they argue that the four components 'have enjoyed wide consensus with the groups involved in the study'. Source: Murray and Acharya (1997).

11.6 Whose Views should Count?

A general problem with any system of valuing health states for the purpose of setting priorities is to determine whose views should count. It is not really possible to understand fully the impact of a disease or disability without having experienced it. However, those with a disability are interested parties, and may not be expected to take a fully detached view. An interesting example of why this might matter is the weighting given by different groups to disability that requires use of a

wheelchair. Those with direct experience may consider the problems to be less severe than those who simply observe – although the reverse is also possible.

Similar issues arise in giving information to people who are asked to score or weight health states. It is difficult to give such information in sufficiently neutral ways that the information does not also encourage a particular interpretation. Democratic principles might suggest that elected politicians, who in other contexts are the decision makers, should do the scoring. This is not always a popular suggestion. When opinions are sought from the general population there are several typical findings (Bowling *et al.* 1993). In general low priority is given to services for older people, and to certain groups of people deemed to have brought problems on themselves, but this is not entirely consistent. Low priority is normally indicated for HIV and other mainly drug-related or sexually transmitted diseases, but the same prejudice does not seem to prevail against smokers who develop smoking-related diseases. There is also typically an enthusiasm for children's services and those treatments that use high technology. Some studies have found that the public favour using health-gain information for setting priorities, but like also to have other criteria for rationing. It is important to understand that the weightings given to health states and therefore the priorities for interventions will depend in part on whose views are sought, and how the views are aggregated.

11.7 Measuring and Describing Outputs in Natural Units

The advantage of using utility scores as measures of outcome is that this allows comparisons between programmes with different types of outcome. However, it may not always be helpful to do this, and the conversion of information on outcomes into utility scores involves losing some of the meaning. It is therefore often sensible to compare options only in terms of the costs and outcomes measured in natural units. For example, if we are considering TT vaccination we can assess the number of cases averted, and would have a picture of the significance of this achievement in terms of treatments and ultimately deaths avoided. In screening for congenital dislocation of the hip we can (in principle) measure numbers of cases averted. It is also easy to interpret a case averted, since it leads fairly directly to less disability, fewer operations later in life and less pain. In either case, the cost per case averted at the margin could be used to inform policy on what service, if any, to provide. However, if we measure the outcome as number of suspect cases identified, or numbers of doses of vaccine administered, this is more difficult to interpret, given that only a small proportion of cases testing positive will in fact become disabling, even with no treatment, that a small proportion of those vaccinated will be exposed to the disease, and that some of those vaccinated will not be protected.

In general we should avoid using measures of process unless these can easily be interpreted in terms of useful health gains, or there really is no possibility of data to provide a better basis of outcome measurement.

An advantage of using natural units to measure outputs can be the greater ease of making judgements about the value of such effects. QALYs allow comparison between interventions, but lose some of the richness of the full description of benefits. In areas such as continuing care, where the objective might be to provide better quality of life for elderly people, or in palliative care when dignity and spiritual well-being are important, it may be difficult to convert the complex descriptions of the outcomes into measures of utility without losing important details. In this case measuring in natural units may be preferable. In cases of infectious diseases there may be particular interest in numbers of cases since an objective may be to achieve herd immunity. Cases averted may therefore be a sensible objective for a cost-effectiveness analysis.

A good rule is to try to use measures that as far as possible reflect outputs and not just processes of care. It should not be an objective to provide care, but really to improve quality of life. If we take the analogy of an airline, it could describe its output as happy holidays enjoyed, passengers carried or aircraft kilometres flown. The first is hard to measure, but is the real output. The second may be a good proxy if data on the first are not available, but the third is clearly not an objective in itself.

11.8 Comparing Costs when Outcomes are the Same

There are some occasions when the objective of a programme is clearly identified, and the question is only how best to do this. Under these circumstances the appropriate analysis is simply to compare costs. No additional useful insights are gained from looking at the benefit side. The danger of this approach is that the objective may not, in fact, be so easy to specify. Policy makers may believe that the objective is to ensure universal vaccination against a particular disease, but their real objective should be to avoid cases of the disease, and universal coverage may not be a cost-effective option. Clearly this approach does not require the analyst to worry about measurement of outcomes or benefits, but it is important to worry about the assertion that the outcome is determined, and that the only remaining question is the method of achieving it.

11.9 Taking into Account Income and Equity

Measures of outcome or health gain do not normally take distribution and equity explicitly into account. Gains are normally assessed as being of equal value regardless of who receives them (although quality of life of individuals may be used in assessing benefits). Several approaches to taking distribution into account explicitly have been proposed. One option is to weight benefits to give greater importance to those for poorer people. Another is to add a rule such as not supporting any change that makes distribution less equal, or that makes poorer people worse off.

It is difficult to think clearly about issues of equality and fairness in health care. The effect of a rule on special treatment of poorer people might be to lower the average level of health. To what extent are we willing to have worse health on average in order to have it more equally distributed? Would we accept a higher infant mortality rate in order to have

it equal between urban and rural areas? Are we concerned mainly with reducing deaths in childhood, or do we also care about which deaths we avert?

Since poorer people have more disease, in some cases this means that they also have the greatest opportunities for health gains. Many simple and highly effective interventions reduce disease burden in poor people, many of whom have worse health and lower use of health services than richer people. A policy of supporting interventions with the largest benefits might in this case also be weighted towards poorer people. Unfortunately, although richer people are often less sick, they sometimes have more capacity for improved health, so this argument may not hold. This may be because richer people comply more fully with the treatment, or it may be because their general level of health is better, and they therefore are more likely to respond well to and recover quickly from treatment. Additionally, rich people can be easier to reach. At least in some contexts, the poorest live in the most remote areas and interventions reach them only at high cost.

There is a large literature on appropriate ways of defining equity, equality and justice. A common principle is 'do to others as you would have them do to you'. Perhaps the most elegant formulation of this idea is that associated with John Rawls (1971). A feature of his analysis is that it does not require that people care about each other – his approach works even when people are selfish. His analysis started from how people would rate different distributions of income when they know the different possible distributions, but do not know which share they would get. This 'justice as fairness' is a reflection therefore of what people consider just when behind a 'veil of ignorance' about how they would fare. When faced with this situation people tend

Box 11.3   *Economic Evaluation of Renal Services for Older People (II)*

For the first part of this case study see Box 10.2.

Measuring benefits in services for ESRF

The framework for analysis in this report is cost-effectiveness. The costs of dialysis are compared to years of life gained in this group. As can be seen from the early results from the clinical trials, survival was over 90 per cent in each year for those selected for dialysis. Since those denied dialysis die quite quickly, we can use years on dialysis (adjusted to account for expected survival without treatment) as a proxy for survival. The main results are presented as cost per year of life gained.

In addition there was an assessment of quality of life using two instruments – a renal services measure known as KDQOL and a generic measure (SF36). This allowed some assessment of the quality of the life years that were gained.

Question. Why did you not combine these two dimensions – if you know life extension and quality of life, surely you can calculate QALYs?

Consultant. Yes, in principle that is possible. The particular instruments were not designed for this, and perhaps in retrospect it would have been good to use also a measure designed for calculating QALYs. The attempts to use SF36 to calculate QALYs have been only partially successful. I can see that for the purpose of comparing expansion of renal services with other priorities it would have been helpful to have an estimate of QALYs. The role of KDQOL is a bit different – it may be more useful for comparing the different dialysis modes.

No attempt was made to measure willingness to pay or other monetary measure of benefit. This would have required more work, and many people find the idea offensive.

Question. But surely this is in principle the best way to measure benefits? In this case it's pretty clear that people would be willing to pay a lot – after all, just look at the alternative!

Consultant. You have a point, but we would be more likely to measure ability to pay than willingness to pay. Few older people could afford the full cost of dialysis. The doctors would have refused to co-operate with the study if they thought we were assessing benefits in money terms. However, I can see that there would be interesting results.

to opt for treating people in some sense according to their needs.

A common issue in discussing equity and fairness is the extent to which account is taken of differences in needs and differences in likely capacity to benefit. An attractive (if not very operational) principle is to treat equals equally, and unequals unequally. If someone has much greater problems most fairness prin-ciples would give them more than those with lesser problems. However, there is no con-sensus about how to define fairness when different people, with similar problems, have very different capacities to benefit. For ex-ample, two people with angina would both benefit from surgery, but the non-smoker would benefit more. It may be that the symp-toms of the smoker are worse. The utilitarian response is to make priorities of services that maximise health gain, and this is the usual perspective in economic evaluation. This perspective may maximise improvements in health, but it does not mean that the scale of the suffering *per se* is a criterion.

A further set of issues in equity is whether we should strive for equality in health, or only some measure of equity in health care or in access to health care. Many would argue that we cannot force people to be healthy or to consume care, and we should not strive for equity in use, but only in access to services. There is a lot of evidence that people are uncomfortable about seeing people with serious ill-health being denied treatment that will help them. This is particularly the case when they have other problems or deprivations. There is no simple way of incorporating equity weightings into economic evaluation. One approach is simply to describe in some detail the distributional consequences of different options and allow decision makers to apply their judgements.

Chapter 12

Practical Steps in Economic Evaluation

....

12.1 Asking the Right Questions

The discussion of problems in the measurement of costs and benefits aims to make people cautious in the use and interpretation of economic evaluation studies. However, much can be learned from careful and sensible use of economic evaluation of health interventions. The most important starting point is to ensure that the evaluation is concerned with the right, or at least sensible, questions. Several principles are important. First, the objective should normally be defined in terms of achievement that matters rather than well-intentioned effort. The objective should always be to get as close as possible to 'output' while recognising that that is often difficult. Different ways of reducing infant mortality can reasonably be compared. Different ways of providing continuing care to terminally ill people may be subjected to evaluation. The point is that we can be clear about the objectives. In the first case we want low infant mortality, and in the second we want good-quality care. In contrast, we can only set the number of appendicectomies as an objective if we are sure that more would be better – in other words, that the current rate of the procedure means people are suffering or dying

for want of this treatment. If this is not the case, one can still evaluate whether or not there are lower-cost methods of achieving the same rate of appendicectomy but need to be very careful not to fall into the 'more is better' way of thinking.

It has been argued that the best way of describing objectives is in terms of achievement. It is also important that evaluation be carried out without a clear prior view about the answer. It is common for economists to be asked to carry out an economic evaluation study to show that a service is cost-effective. Often attempts are made to avoid even considering options that are considered by clinicians or managers to be unacceptable. While being realistic about what can be achieved in the highly political context of much decision making in health, it is important to try to ensure that a wide range of alternatives is considered in the evaluation exercise.

12.2 Choosing the Perspective for Economic Evaluation

Economists usually argue that the appropriate perspective for economic evaluation is societal.

The argument is that a cost is a cost whoever pays, and similarly benefits should be included regardless of who receives them. It is inappropriate to choose an option simply because it shifts costs from formal health services to families, or because the harm done is not taken into account. A societal perspective means that the evaluation tries to include all costs and benefits, whoever pays or receives them.

It is difficult to make a coherent argument in principle against this perspective. Any serious case for looking only from the point of view of a government, insurance company or hospital has to be on practical or pragmatic grounds. For example, it may be shown that the spillover of costs to other parties is small, and it makes no sense to spend resources on costly calculations that are unlikely to affect the outcomes. It is less clear that it makes sense to take a more restricted perspective (say that of the government or insurance fund) if there are significant shifts of costs to patients and families, and these have not been taken into account (see Box 10.1).

Managers in commercial organisations typically are concerned to pursue commercial goals, and this means that they do their best to make profit for shareholders (and in most countries are legally obliged to do this). Any evaluation carried out by such organisations is likely to take the perspective of the best interest of the shareholders. But in the context of government-mandated systems of health care the best outcomes will come from evaluation of options for change from a broader societal perspective.

12.3 *Measuring Costs in Economic Evaluation*

The most common approach to measurement of costs is to record all services provided for each patient, and then to convert this into cost by multiplying by the unit cost of each service. If the economic evaluation is alongside a clinical trial, this allows both point estimates and standard deviation of costs to be assessed. In turn this means that cost-effectiveness ratios can be quoted with confidence intervals. It is not always easy to record all events, and it is sometimes necessary to use a range of sources of data. For example, it may be necessary to draw on data from deployment of staff, clinical records, patient diaries, direct observation or published sources to assess the number and type of services. It can be an exercise in detective work to find all the relevant information.

Deriving a list of unit costs can also be a difficult task. Financial data are often poor in the health sector, and the observed prices (if any) may not be good indicators of opportunity cost. The normal starting point is financial accounts and budgets. These are devised for purposes of planning and accountability, but may nevertheless be suitable sources of information. If these data are provided at an aggregate level (for example, hospital ward or health centre), and are to be used to compute unit costs, it is important to be clear that:

1 The services delivered are similar for different patients.
2 Overhead costs are presented in a sensible way.
3 Apportionment of shared costs is appropriate.

It is also very important to be confident that using a single measure of unit cost is reasonable. In particular it is worth checking that there are no significant economies of scale or scope. If there are it may be necessary to adjust the unit costs for different levels or volumes of service. Unit costs may change over time, and it is important to use recent data if they are available.

Although it is common for a single set of unit costs to be used, it may be better to develop a separate cost vector for each care provider if there are reasons why they may differ. Also, it may be important to explore the combined variability of use of services and unit cost of services, so that costs can be quoted in terms of means and confidence intervals taking all relevant variation into account. If a study involves many different sites it may be best to derive the set of cost weights from data on costs in the participating providers. Cost functions may be estimated to give a better understanding of the level and pattern of unit costs. Although many early economic evaluation studies have estimated costs based on averages for all patients at a single centre, this is no longer considered best practice, and results of such studies are now often treated with caution. Nevertheless, cost-effectiveness analysis, like other technologies, has to be practised 'appropriately' in context. Where data and research funding are scarce, basic cost-effectiveness measures based on limited data and simplifying assumptions can provide a better basis for decision making than no data whatsoever. The important consideration is that the analyst is aware of the limitations of estimates produced in that way, and communicates a suitable level of caution in interpreting findings to decision makers.

12.4 Measuring Benefits in Economic Evaluation

The first step in assessing benefits is to ask two related questions – what approach to measuring benefits would be desirable, and what is feasible? In most cases there will be more than one dimension of benefits – longer

life, better health, higher productivity or reduced risk. It is useful in the first instance to identify the main objectives of the intervention, and what implications these have for measurement. For example, a malaria-control programme may aim to reduce deaths and the harmful effects of disease, and this may justify assessing benefits in some detail. On the other hand, if the service is cataract surgery in older people, then the outcome may be adequately described in terms of years of eyesight restored.

When the benefits are defined in terms of simple natural units they may need no substantial economic work. However, if utility scores are used, there is a need to ensure that the necessary data are collected, normally using a standard method, as discussed in Chapter 11. It is common for there to be gains in life years and gains in quality of life. The example in Box 12.1 illustrates how the two can be combined.

12.5 Presenting the Results of Economic Evaluation Studies

The most common format for presenting the outcome of economic evaluation is to show the *incremental cost-effectiveness ratios* (ICERs) of moves from the *status quo* (do nothing option) through better but more expensive options. The ICER is the extra cost of the additional service divided by the extra outcome of effectiveness. Where an option costs more and achieves less than another, then it is said to be dominated. Since the ICER would be negative it is not presented in the table of ICERs. Box 12.2 gives an example.

Transferring the results of an economic evaluation. Results of economic evaluation are dependent on a wide range of highly localised factors and, as we have discussed quite

Box 12.1 Calculating QALYs from Data on Longer Life and Better Quality of Life

In this group of patients percutaneous transluminal coronary angioplasty (PTCA) has the effect of extending life by one year, and improving quality of life from an average of 70 per cent to 90 per cent. The life expectancy of the patients in the absence of PTCA is five years.

QALYs are gained in the following ways. First, for each of the next five years the quality of life is improved by twenty percentage points. Without treatment the person would have 3.5 QALYs (that is, 0.7 × 5 years). With treatment there is an addition of one QALY (0.2 × 5 years). In addition there is one year at 90 per cent of full quality of life, which gives a further 0.9 QALYs.

Therefore the total effect of the intervention is to produce 1.9 QALYs.

If benefits are to be measured in terms of money, some method must be used to identify either willingness to pay or some other appropriate monetary valuation of benefit.

It is important to present the outcomes measured in terms of both means and the confidence intervals around measures of benefits as well as costs.

Box 12.2 Presenting Options in Terms of ICERs

Three options are being considered for developing an eye service. In the table they are shown in comparison with the current provision. Clearly we should not choose option 2, since it is dominated by option 1. Two questions arise. Should we do option 1? If yes, should we go further and do option 3?

Option	Cost (€)	Additional years of sight
1	2,000	100
2	3,000	90
3	4,000	160

The ICER for a move from the *status quo* to option 1 is 20. For the further move to option 3 it is 33.3 (that is, 2,000/60, the additional cost of 3 compared with 1, divided by the additional gains).

In some senses option 1 is more cost-effective, since the ICER is 20 compared with 33.3. However, we might still consider that it is good value to pay €33.3 for each additional year of sight. This raises an important point. The ICER is a picture of the relative cost-effectiveness, but it is not true to say that we should choose the option with the lowest ICER. For each best way of increasing benefits we ask if the ICER represents good use of resources. The question facing policy makers is how much more will be achieved for how much more? The ICER answers that question.

This contrasts with the situation where the outcomes are identical or where the costs of the intervention are identical. In these cases there is a simple decision rule – the most cost-effective option is the one with the lowest ICER.

extensively, cannot be relied upon to be similar when one unit is compared to another within the same health system, and even within the same town. Nevertheless, inside a single health system, a number of factors are more similar than outside it. There are considerable international differences in the practice of medicine itself which are often even greater than those differences inside a single system (Wennberg and Gittelsohn 1973, 1982): doctors trained in different health systems are likely to prescribe different drugs and procedures for the same condition. A hospital stay for treatment of a given condition cannot be assumed to involve the same inputs. Official laws, regulations, guidelines and 'protocols' vary from country to country.

Health systems are characterised by different levels of resource availability (see Chapter 20) which imply that components of care regimens offered within one health system will not be offered within another. Different prices apply, and this implies not only that costs differ for an identical package of care, but that the most *economically* efficient way of delivering care varies (see Chapters 4 and 5). For example, where labour is cheap, more efficient production techniques will be more labour intensive.

Health systems are organised differently, meaning that the context in which care is received varies. For example, specialist doctors take responsibility for much primary care in the US and France; generalist doctors play the same role in Canada and the UK; paramedical workers take much of this responsibility in developing countries. A procedure carried out as day surgery in one system may involve a several-day stay in hospital in another, and it may not be the result of inefficiency in the latter case. To convert in-patient surgery to day surgery may imply use of a more sophisticated technique, or rely on the availability of systems supporting patients in their homes that may not be available in some health systems. In general, day surgery may be more technology and less labour intensive, making it more appropriate for an economy with high labour costs. Similarly, mass campaign programme modes of delivery of immunisation cannot be expected to have similar costs to programmes that operate through the routine health system – but choice between the two approaches depends on various health system characteristics.

Population characteristics also affect results. An immunisation programme is more costly to deliver in the remote hill settlements of Nepal than it is in the densely populated cities of Bangladesh. Effectiveness depends on the underlying disease conditions – cost-effectiveness ratios for anti-malaria interventions cannot be transferred to Oslo! More generally, an expectation that prevalence is an important correlate of cost-effectiveness is frequently appropriate, though this may not apply to treatment of relatively rare conditions.

Since the importance of the different comparability problems briefly surveyed is likely to vary between interventions, it follows that the ordering of cost-effectiveness need not be transferable from one country to another either. Differing levels of the general price index will affect cost-effectiveness measures but not their order. Every other difference cited above is likely to affect *which* interventions are most cost-effective. As was discussed, a difference in labour costs may affect the relative cost-effectiveness of in-patient and day surgery. Differences in underlying disease patterns and in health system configurations can affect whether it is most cost-effective to combat malaria using specific treatment regimens, preventive measures such as insecticide-treated bed nets, spraying for mosquitoes or using malaria prophylactic drugs. This point is equally applicable to the choice of rehabilitative regimens following heart attacks. Both depend on the distribution of underlying aetiologies in the population; the economically efficient use of inputs in the context of divergent relative prices; the availability and cost of community-based support services and even the cultural acceptability of alternative treatments such as exercise or bed nets.

All this suggests that looking to the international literature for evidence of cost-effectiveness relevant to choices to be made in a specific country is best avoided. Where it is not feasible to expect that local cost-effectiveness estimates will be available, transferring expectations of relative cost-effectiveness needs to be done with great care, considering each of the important sources of variation discussed above and whether or not differences between the target country and the source country are likely to be sufficient to change the conclusion regarding relative cost-effectiveness levels. Clearly, the use of actual ICERs converted at current exchange rates, to make incremental choices, is likely to be highly misleading in all but extremely similar conditions.

Lastly, measures of effectiveness such as the QALY and DALY, and the health status measurement surveys they are based on, are argued by some to be culturally specific. While the EUROQOL has been adapted and translated for use in a large number of European countries, it has been argued that people's perceptions of what constitutes health varies between cultures, and therefore any instrument aiming to measure health status must also do so. The KENQOL (Fox-Rushby *et al.* 2000; Bowden 2001) is an instrument developed on the basis of research into

perceptions of health in rural Kenya. A KENQOL–EUROQOL comparison illustrates the potential extent of the problem. Even countries which consider themselves closer to those for which the EUROQOL was developed might question whether minor adaptation and translation are sufficient to capture the potentially different perception of what constitutes health, and what matters most within that. This perspective undermines the quest for internationally comparable cost-effectiveness data. The interest in making international pronouncements on health priorities underpins both the EUROQOL and the DALY. If Swedish, French or US perspectives on what constitutes health and what components of health matter most are used to identify priorities in Turkey, Thailand or Tajikistan, we have to ask the question '*Whose* priorities are identified?'

12.6 Sensitivity Analysis

The aim of economic evaluation is to support decision making. The data that are used in the analysis may be inaccurate for many reasons – there may be bias or measurement error, or the data may be taken from experimental conditions that will not be replicated in normal service conditions. Calculating confidence intervals is useful in helping decision makers to understand some elements of uncertainty. However, where this is not done, and where there are other sources of uncertainty that are not described in the confidence intervals, it can be useful to test the results of economic evaluation for their sensitivity to certain types of error.

The practical steps in sensitivity analysis are simple – the values of the relevant variables are varied by different amounts to see if the changes in the observed ICERs are likely to change the order of the options or change the decision to or from any intervention. The process requires knowledge of the services, understanding of the likely sources of error or uncertainty, and the likely size of any errors.

It is sometimes best to present the sensitivity analysis in terms of the robustness of the findings. For example, it might be found that even with an error of 30 per cent in the value of the estimated cost, the decisions would be unchanged. Equally it might be found that an error of 5 per cent would change the order of options. This type of sensitivity analysis allows the analysts and decision makers to judge if errors are likely to be in a range that would change the outcome, and in some cases is the basis of a decision to do further research with a view to improving the estimates, if the current degree of uncertainty makes decisions difficult.

12.7 Long-term Costs and Benefits

Economic evaluation can draw the data on costs and benefits from current practice, experimental evidence, observational studies and some knowledge about developments and changes in technology. However, many interventions have long-term effects on costs and benefits that cannot be adequately assessed within the current data. In these circumstances it is necessary to use modelling techniques to make the best assessments of long-term effects.

The simplest forms of modelling for long-term effects use current knowledge of events or probabilities of events, and simulate the future on this basis. A common approach is to use Markov models (which allow the probabilities associated with possible future states

to be dependent on the condition of the previous time period) to explore future scenarios. In all cases the principles are the same – current knowledge is used to make the best estimates of future costs and future benefits.

It is often objected that modelling introduces extra uncertainty, but not to look at likely future costs and benefits means that serious bias can undermine the findings of economic evaluation. Where there is great uncertainty, sensitivity analysis can be used. There are particular risks of bias if the measured benefits include long-term effects (such as additional years of life, which will be lived decades hence), but the analysis does not include estimates of the resources needed in the future to support that benefit. It is common to find economic evaluations that have included as benefits years of life gained, but have not included the corresponding long-term costs of care.

12.8 Useful Guidance on Economic Evaluation in Health Care

The aim in this chapter has been to outline the underlying theory and issues in the application of economic evaluation. It should give readers sufficient understanding to assess the meaning and quality of reports and published studies. It does not aim to be a definitive guide to the practice of economic evaluation. Several books of guidance exist (e.g. Creese and Parker 1994; Gold *et al.* 1996; Drummond *et al.* 1997). In addition, there are various sets of national guidance in many countries, which specify how studies should be carried out, and what rates should be used for discounting. It is important to ensure that any economic evaluation carried out is at least done in the knowledge of local guidance and recommendations. In addition it is useful to look at guidance provided by certain journals – in some cases it is necessary to present the results of economic evaluation studies in a particular way.

There is particular importance in following guidance on best practice when the evaluation is carried out as part of the case for licensing or reimbursement of a new drug or treatment. In these cases the evidence will be accepted only if it complies with best current practice. However, as with all techniques, the best practice is evolving, and it is important to draw on the available guidance, but not necessarily to accept it all.

Chapter 13

Economic Evaluation as a Framework for Choice

13.1 A Framework for Choice

Economic evaluation provides a framework within which a range of evidence can be assembled. In some senses this makes economics seem arrogant, since findings from many other health sciences can be brought together within the economic framework. This does not imply that the economic framework is more important, but simply that the rôle economic evaluation plays is to help to interpret diverse information and provide a framework for choice.

There are several reasons why it is useful to bring together evidence within the framework of economic evaluation. First, it helps us to ask the right questions. The issue is normally not 'Does it work?' but rather 'Should we do it?' The question should be, 'Do the benefits of this service or intervention justify the costs?' Not all costs and benefits are easy to measure. This has been a major issue in the preceding chapters. It is nevertheless useful to ensure that they are all listed, and taken into account. Similarly, it matters when costs and benefits occur, and this should be taken into account.

The concept of cost used by economists is appropriate for decision making on behalf of society – the opportunity forgone reminds us that the inefficient use of resources harms real people in real ways. Apologists for inefficient use of resources can be confronted with the full implications. For example, a decision to allow scarce health care resources to be used for low-priority uses is a decision to allow more babies to die, more people to become or remain disabled and more people to suffer avoidable pain. Third, the framework helps to ensure that measurement is consistent, and the same assumptions are used throughout. It is important that measured differences reflect real differences, and are not simply an artefact of the measurement process.

By being more explicit the perspective of the analysis should be clearer. Economists normally advocate taking a societal perspective, so that all costs and benefits are included, irrespective of who pays. Thus, a decision to close local services to save money may be shown to increase costs if patients have to travel further. Shorter hospital stays may reduce hospital costs, but may also increase costs for primary care, social services, informal carers, family, friends and the patient herself. A societal perspective considers the effects on all of these. But if another perspective is taken, then this can be clearly stated and the results interpreted accordingly.

The main argument for economic evaluation is therefore that it helps us to see the whole picture. Decisions taken on partial information are likely to be flawed, and it is important to know at least what information should have been used.

13.2 Using Economic Evaluation to assess Existing Policies

Any analysis of current health sector services will identify things that are clearly high priorities, services that were previously useful but which should now be discontinued, and some that should never have been provided in the first place.

Economic evaluation can help to distinguish these. There is considerable inertia in health service provision, not least because many people develop an interest in continued provision of particular services. It is important always to remember that there is no good reason to continue to provide a service just because it has always been there – it is just more difficult to make change. It is no less ethical to discontinue a service than it is to decide not to provide it in the first place. A careful assessment of the costs and benefits of the services can help to determine if it should be given priority over other potential uses of resources.

Measuring the costs and benefits of existing services can be relatively easy, since there are activities and outcomes to observe. This can give opportunities to measure the resources used and how they improve health. However, there are also some common difficulties. If a service has existed for a very long time, it is sometimes almost impossible to tell what would happen if it did not exist. A good example is

screening for congenital dislocation of the hip in newborn babies. There are grounds for doubting whether this programme actually reduces the number of people with disabilities in the long run, but since Western countries have been doing it for years it is difficult to assess what would happen without the service.

It is often easier to get agreement to carry out economic evaluation of possible service developments than to revisit the priority of existing programmes. There is no inherent reason why we should accept current provision, especially where technological change may have reduced the need for some services. There is marked variation in the extent to which countries have seized opportunities to use less invasive surgical techniques and reduce the need for in-patient rather than day-case surgery. While as was emphasised in Chapter 12 some of this variation may reflect differences in marginal rates of substitution between inputs, it cannot be seriously doubted that some variation reflects inertia in some of those countries that have been slower to adapt. Careful evaluation of existing practices can identify services that should no longer get priority.

13.3 Evaluation of Potential Policies and Developments

Ideas for development of health policies and services have complicated origins. Often the early developments come from an inspired (or misguided) enthusiast, and what starts as an experiment can quickly become a routine service. Recent awareness of scarcity of resources has helped to raise questions of priorities and appropriateness, but it is naive to ignore the fact that new ideas normally already have supporters among potential providers and patients.

Policy makers are not always detached and clear-thinking. Faced with demands for a new service, they may prefer positive findings in an evaluation, or may want the analysis to be negative in order to legitimise inaction. The analyst should be aware that in some cases policy makers are commissioning the evaluation in the hope of a particular outcome and not simply to inform the choice. Requests for analysts to find particular results are normally subtle, but good evaluation starts from a neutral position. Even the title of a study can be important. For example, the request may be to carry out an economic evaluation of a proposed new primary care facility in a particular town. This already restricts consideration to a particular way of expanding the service (excluding options of mobile services or services provided in the home) and alternative siting of the facility. Sometimes the initiative comes from the existence of a building, and a desire to put it to some use, rather than from the needs of people for services.

It is very common for proponents of services to try to limit the options that are considered, and for the choice of alternatives to favour their preferred option. It is normally wise to ensure that the options favoured by interest groups are included in any evaluation, but it is also wise to include options that do not have significant support, but may offer better value. Historical promises often colour the thinking of the public and policy makers, however misguided these promises may have been. It is very common for schemes for major new facilities to have been agreed many years before, with a sequence of financial crises that prevented the start. Press reports describe decisions not to proceed as cancellation, and referral for evaluation as prevarication. These are the real circumstances in which options for new services are often evaluated, and the analyst needs to be aware of such issues and context. But it is important to remember that previous mistakes, ill-considered promises and vocal advocates are not in principle reasons for making bad decisions about the future use of resources.

13.4 What the Results of an Evaluation Mean, and What they do not Mean

The results of economic evaluation can be presented in several ways, normally reflecting the ways in which it has been possible to measure benefits. In some cases this allows a single number to be presented, representing the net benefit of a particular choice. For example, if the costs of a project have a value of €2 million and the benefits a value of €1.8 million, the net benefit is €0.2 million. Each potential option can be assessed, and the one with the largest net benefits would normally be chosen. In many cases the measurement of benefits will be in terms of some non-financial measure, so that alternatives might be compared in terms of the ratio of costs to effectiveness. Thus we might compare the cost per year of life gained, or simply the cost per fully immunised child.

Care must be taken in the interpretation of cost-effectiveness ratios, since there are circumstances in which we would not choose the lowest. Take, for example, the case of screening for chlamydia in asymptomatic women in Canada. There is a choice between non-culture tests, with low cost (Ca$20) and sensitivity of around 70 per cent, and culture tests, with much higher cost (Ca$50) and sensitivity of over 80 per cent. If we compare the cost-effectiveness ratios in a high- to medium- (10 per cent) prevalence population, it costs Ca$290 per case detected for non-culture screening and Ca$630 per case for culture test screening. However, this does not mean that we should necessarily choose non-culture tests. The additional cost of detecting one additional case (in this case Ca$3,000) may be considered good value, since the disease is treatable, and successful treatment can help to reduce the spread of HIV and other sexually transmitted diseases. What this illustrates is that we need to be careful in interpreting ratios of costs and effectiveness.

Just as there is no correct level of funding for the health sector (see Chapter 19), there is no particular value of cost-effectiveness ratio that indicates that a service should be provided. What a cost-effectiveness ratio does is to indicate what can be bought with resources in a particular programme. As discussed in Chapter 12, it is also very important to look at the marginal or incremental cost-effectiveness ratio as well as the average, since the fact that a service is good value does not necessarily mean that more of it would be good value.

13.5 Double Counting, Muddled Thinking and Making Bad Decisions

Economic evaluation can help to ensure that all relevant factors are counted once, and to avoid counting anything twice. It is surprisingly difficult to avoid double counting. There are particular risks of double counting resulting from assessing benefits both as benefits and as lower costs. Sometimes when policy options are discussed informally, benefits are counted twice (for example, 'there is a reduction in mortality' and 'there is an increase in healthy years of life' are in part the same benefit). Sometimes it is more difficult to detect double counting in the complex descriptions of costs and benefits. An advantage of setting out clearly what are all the flows of

costs and benefits is that it makes it easier to detect double counting.

Equally, it is common for important costs not to be taken into account, especially when an asset is already owned. Even where a resource is not marketed, or apparently marketable, the opportunity cost of its use is still the alternative use of the resource by the owning institution. For example, a hospital might build a new wing on a car park, claiming that the land had no value, as it could not easily be sold. However, the land has alternative uses irrespective of its saleability. Where are patients and staff going to park their cars now? The hospital might find that some time later it has to spend a large sum to buy some adjacent land for car parking. Alternatively, there may be a private company interested in operating a concession using that land and willing to pay rent. The new wing may still provide the best use of resources, but that can only be established by considering the value of the land in alternative uses.

It is often not possible to place a value on, or even to give a clear description of, some costs and benefits, so that additional judgements need to be made outside the framework of the analysis. This does not mean that the economic evaluation should be taken to be just one argument, since it is in itself a framework within which we present a collection of arguments. When using economic evaluation in such circumstances it is important to remain clear about what is included and what arguments are genuinely additional. Only the latter should be allowed to supplement the economic evaluation in the decision process.

Sometimes the most effective use of economic evaluation is to confront decision makers with the implications of their potential choices. One former British government minister complained that the economic advisers

Box 13.1 *Economic Evaluation of Renal Services for Older People (III)*

For the first two parts of this case study see Boxes 10.2 and 11.3.

Some practical issues in the economic evaluation of renal services for older people

The tender document for this study asked for an economic evaluation to support the decisions on expansion of dialysis services for older people. This suggests that the answer is already known, and all that is needed is the supporting documents. The evaluation team could not accept that the answers were already known given the lack of any published studies.

In the first phase of the project it was agreed that it would be important to give more focus in the questions addressed in this report. Three questions have been addressed. First, are there any people for whom additional services would be cost-effective? Second, which groups should be included in the expanded service? Third, which mode of dialysis should be chosen, and for whom?

Question. This is useful – the original documents were unfocused. The doctors were not keen to include peritoneal dialysis – they said that it was already well known that older people do badly on peritoneal dialysis.

Consultant. Yes, it is important to agree the right questions, and to include all relevant ones. The views on peritoneal dialysis are typical – people often do not like analysis of options that seem wrong, especially when there is no evidence to support this feeling. I have often found that people are particularly reluctant to consider options if they think there is a risk that careful analysis will suggest that they are cost-effective. This is probably the case in the inclusion of peritoneal dialysis in this study. We found little evidence comparing the different dialysis modalities, and in this study we found no differences in outcomes for the majority of patients.

The calculations of the costs of dialysis took a societal perspective, including costs to patients and their families, as well as to the funders. Since all those included in the study were retired it was decided not to put in any cost for time off work for patients, but where there was a carer of working age a cost was calculated. Costs for all health services used by patients were included, since these all contribute to the person's survival and quality of life. However, the cost of pensions was not included, since they are a transfer payment.

Question. I don't understand this point at all. You say in the report that you would include the cost of lost wages, but not pension. Surely pensions are just incomes in old age, just like wages for younger people?

Consultant. Many people find the distinction between costs and transfer payments difficult, but it is important to understand. Remember we are interested in assessing opportunity cost – that is, the loss to society of using resources for a particular purpose. A pension (or indeed any welfare payments to people who are not working) is really just funds taken from one person and given to another. It is like giving your children pocket money – at the time you do that your family does not get richer or poorer – it just transfers spending power between generations.

Continued

The results of this study showed that the lowest cost per year of life gained is for those who are successfully put on to peritoneal dialysis. Costs are higher for those on haemodialysis, and are much higher for those who have generally poor health. The costs do not seem to be related to age itself, although older people in the study generally have more co-morbidity.

Question. Does that mean that we should only provide peritoneal dialysis since it is more cost-effective than haemodialysis? And should we refuse treatment to those with other health problems? Is it fair to give older people treatment in preference to those less old?

Consultant. All that this study has shown is that peritoneal dialysis is *relatively* more cost-effective than haemodialysis. Remember that we can only ever assess cost-effectiveness relative to other uses of resources. Even though haemodialysis is shown to be less cost-effective than peritoneal dialysis it may be better value than treating other diseases. The evidence does not suggest that we should never treat people with co-morbidities, but if we are setting priorities then there is a case for giving them lower priority, and increasing the overall health gain.

You raise an interesting and controversial question concerning age. There are some advocates of age discrimination on equity grounds that we should all have a chance of the same length of good quality life, but others fiercely oppose any age discrimination.

always made him feel uncomfortable about the choices he wanted to make. That was probably a sign of effective economic advice.

13.6 Use and Abuse of Economic Evaluation

The aim of these chapters on economic evaluation has been to discuss the theoretical basis for economic evaluation, to outline the methods used and the problems encountered in carrying out an evaluation, and to assist with the interpretation of evaluation results.

There are several warning signs to look out for in assessing economic evaluation results. First, it is important to look at the perspective taken by the analyst. If the evaluation is from the point of view of a provider of care or a particular interest group, this should be interpreted as such. Second, it is important to assess whether the full range of plausible options has been included. If important

options have been excluded, then the best option might be lost. Third, in assessing the costs and benefits, were appropriate techniques used? Are the cost estimates likely to reflect opportunity cost? Has a sensible approach been taken to the assessment of benefits? Fourth, have costs and benefits been brought into present value, and is the discount rate used the one that is recognised as appropriate?

There are other warning signs. It is sometimes clear that the analysis has come after the main decision to proceed with a project, and simply aims to justify existing decisions. It can be very difficult to persuade policy makers to abandon policies based on previous misunderstanding and errors.

Since economic evaluation aims to provide a framework for the inclusion of data on efficacy, effectiveness and costs, it is not 'just like any other argument'. If the premises of the evaluation are accepted it should not be possible to argue against the conclusions that follow. However, it is equally true that economic evaluation is not simply a tool for making decisions, since it is almost never possible to include all important arguments, and to measure everything that is relevant to the decision. But when the additional judgements of policy makers are added, it is important to ensure that it is only additional factors that are taken into account, to avoid double counting.

It is useful to understand the limitations of economic evaluation, both in terms of its theoretical foundations and in the practical problems in doing it. It is equally important to understand that decisions made without the help of such evaluation are likely to be worse. Thinking clearly, measuring carefully and interpreting sensibly can increase health gain, improving life expectancy and quality of life.

Part III

Further Economics of Markets and Market Intervention

Chapter 14

Contracting

....

14.1 Introduction

In Chapter 6 we developed the model of 'perfect competition' and in Chapter 7 we considered some features of health markets which cause the market to fail. One of the key features of the perfect competition model, which we have yet to consider, is that transactions are assumed to take place in a single instant. This assumption seems reasonable for the sale or purchase of a single item in a shop or market stall. However, many goods and services are not bought and sold through such one-off exchanges. Buyers and sellers may undertake an exchange of goods and services over a period of time and develop long-term relationships. Contracts are one method by which these relationships are developed. In this chapter we examine the economic rationale for a contract and issues related to the design of contracts.

For example, each time new drugs are needed, a hospital's purchaser (who might be a member of hospital staff or a purchaser for a larger group of hospitals) is unlikely to visit a pharmacy and make a series of purchases on a one-off basis. It is more likely that a long-term contract is entered into with a pharmaceutical supplier which specifies, among

other things, ordering procedures, negotiated prices associated with particular purchased quantities, quality specifications and delivery schedules. A series of purchases over a given time period are likely to be covered by the contract, and the current contract may be the latest in a series, with the expectation on both parts that the contract plays a role in a long-term relation between the supplier and hospitals. Even this is a relatively straightforward situation compared with the kind of contract that would need to be developed in relation to the maintenance of the hospital's building and equipment. In that case the services required over a given time period cannot all be specified in advance, since breakdowns are not fully predictable. It may be wise, for reasons we will explore further below, to specify a payment arrangement other than a price per service. Quality specifications are more difficult to write. A contract covering maintenance in hospitals in Bangkok is one of those considered in Box 14.1.

There has recently been interest in the use of contracts to purchase clinical services on behalf of patient populations. For example, the National Health Service of the UK has been reorganised so that purchasing groups at district or sub-district level purchase clinical

Box 14.1 *Contracting out in Bangkok Hospitals*

The Thai government has directly addressed the 'make or buy' decision in the public sector by mandating that public employment must decrease. As a result, hospitals are increasingly contracting out both non-clinical services, like cleaning, and clinical services such as diagnostic and treatment technologies.

In comparing the transaction costs associated with employment and contractual relationships, it is clear that entrenched privileges associated with public employment which are common to many developing countries adversely affect the comparison in favour of contracting out. For example, difficulties in disciplining or firing civil servants make employment contracts particularly inefficient methods of procuring goods or services. In the Thai case, it was also argued that cultural attitudes to hierarchy compounded the adverse comparison. For example, cleaners would carry out any tasks allocated by their superiors and consequently neglect the cleaning job for which they had been employed.

In contracting diagnostic and treatment technologies, other apparently inefficient characteristics of the bureaucracy also affected the transaction cost comparison. Procurement rules meant that equipment could take three years from order to installation, by which time it might be outdated. Most of the contractors were reimbursed by nominal monthly rent and an out-of-pocket patient fee. This produced an efficient service from the perspective of its smooth running, very limited 'down time' and hence availability when needed. However, it proved difficult to implement an exemption policy by which those unable to pay could still receive treatment. Contractors had no incentive to operate such a policy, and hospitals were apparently in a weak position to negotiate, monitor or enforce it.

It is interesting that contracting out the whole diagnostic or treatment service proved more successful in terms of maintenance (down time) than contracting out maintenance alone, which had been tried earlier. It is difficult to specify an efficient reimbursement mechanism for a maintenance contract which embodies appropriate incentives to make effective repairs only when they are needed. An annual payment (for example) might result in the contractor claiming that equipment needed replacement when repair would be possible but expensive. A payment per repair might result in shoddy work which would frequently need to be redone. The problem is that the underlying state of equipment (repairable or not) and the quality of repair work are inherently difficult to observe and monitor.

For non-clinical services, contracts were poorly monitored and the quality of services generally believed low, but not as low as those which prevailed under the directly provided services. Costs were slightly lower for the contracted-out service. This emphasises the importance of taking a comparative stance in the 'make or buy' debate. The contractual difficulties associated with the arrangements for non-clinical services (such as the implicit contract between superior and junior employees that orders would always be obeyed no matter how unreasonable) are considerable. In those circumstances, even unsatisfactory formal contractual arrangements may be the relatively better option.

Source: V. Tangcharoensathien, S. Nitayarumphong and S. Khongsawatt, 'Private sector involvement in public hospitals: case studies in Bangkok', in Bennett *et al.* (1997).

services from public hospitals on behalf of a defined patient population. The Zambian health system has been redesigned on similar lines. While these types of reforms will be addressed more fully in the final chapter, it is worth while at this point, and as you read this chapter, considering the following question. What kinds of contract specifications are feasible and appropriate for the purchase of clinical services? 'Spot' contracts[1] are unlikely to be indicated where a third party pays for the transaction, given the difficulty and cost of third-party attendance at every transaction. It should be clear that contracting clinical services has some features in common with, and probably surpasses the complexity of, the hospital's maintenance contract.

The concepts and ideas described in this chapter derive from the economics literature on contracting. They enable us to structure and categorise the types of complexity involved in contracting in the health sector, and to analyse its implications for appropriate contract specification.

14.2 What is a Contract?

The contract contrasts with the market transactions assumed in previous chapters in which:

1 You expect nothing more than exchanging goods at mutually satisfactory prices.
2 There are no long-term relations between buyers and sellers.
3 All parties have good information (and can walk away from the transaction if they want).
4 Transactions are costless.

Where these conditions do not apply, exchange is made possible through the use of contracts. As we have seen above, contracts can be quite simple, presenting few difficulties in their specification, execution and monitoring. However, in this chapter we are more interested in contracts which are not straightforward. Such contracts are at the heart of debates focusing on how to structure exchange in the health sector.

Contracts can be formal and explicit (written and legally binding agreements) but they can also be implicit. Milgrom and Roberts (1992) define implicit contracts as 'Shared understandings that are not legally enforceable but that the parties consider to be binding on one another's conduct.' For example, the type of clothing expected to be worn at work may not be written in a formal employment contract, but may be mutually understood by employer and employee to be part of their implicit contract. Defined this broadly, it is important to recognise that all relations are governed by contracts. It is often helpful to think about the advantages and disadvantages of more implicit and more explicit contracts in a particular context. If the question is instead framed as *whether* to contract, it is likely that difficulties in the non-contractual (or implicit contractual) relationship will be missed.

From this perspective, the debate as to whether or not to introduce formal contracts between public 'purchasers' and providers, as has been done in the UK and Zambia for example, is a debate about whether formalising the otherwise implicit contract between those who pay for and those who provide public services brings more advantages or disadvantages. The argument for greater explicitness is that formal contracts clarify purchasers' objectives, and more clearly specify distinct roles of purchasers and providers. In contrast it can be argued that flexibility and mutual goodwill are better fostered under more implicit contractual relationships, and the presence of unmeasurable dimensions to the delivery of health care. The idea that contractual difficulties can be avoided if explicit contracts are avoided is naive.

14.3 Transaction Costs

In a seminal article in 1937 Ronald Coase asked the questions 'If markets operate so efficiently, why have firms?' 'Why is everything not bought and sold through a contract?' and their corollary: 'If the organisation of economic activity in firms implies that markets don't work well, why have contracts?' 'Why not make everything in one big firm?'

Within a firm a number of economic activities are organised, and exchange between those who carry them out is made under different rules from those operating in markets. Even in a simple firm with an owner and an employee producing a single product, Coase's questions could be rephrased as 'Why does the owner choose to employ a labourer rather than buy the labourer's product on market terms?' An intuitive answer is that the owner owns the means of production and the labourer has insufficient wealth to purchase them, but that does not explain why means of production are not rented out to the labourer, or why an efficient capital market will not be able to lend the labourer the resources to purchase his own means of production. In fact the replacement of employment arrangements with market arrangements through the 'contracting out' of services in some health sectors illustrates that this choice is not purely theoretical. In some cases, for example, hospital contracts have been awarded to cleaning firms which have been established using cleaners who were previously directly employed by the health authority or hospital.

Another intuitive answer is that economies of scale may determine the choice. It may be cheaper to purchase goods from a company that is producing in bulk for several purchasers than to try to produce them yourself. However, the firm could decide to produce in bulk to cover more than its own needs, and to sell to other purchasers itself.

Coase's answer to the question is that a firm's decision to 'make or buy' (or to employ cleaners or enter into a formal contract with a cleaning company) depends on an assessment of the transaction costs associated with the two modes of procuring a good or service. At one level this is almost a tautology. Firms will organise the procurement of a good or service in the manner that costs them least. This is not particularly helpful. The value of the insight is rather in the attention that it draws to a category of cost, *transaction cost*, which lies at the centre of the 'make or buy' decision and thereby determines the pattern of economic activity. By implication, transaction costs can be defined as all those costs associated with using a particular type of exchange relationship – for example, in terms of the previous section, formal or informal contracts. This simple idea paved the way for a branch of economics known as 'transaction cost economics' which is associated with the economist Oliver Williamson, and has increasingly been informing debates on the use of formal contracts in the health sector.

14.4 Transaction Cost Economics

Williamson relies on two 'behavioural assumptions' which depart from those of neoclassical economics: opportunism and bounded rationality. Opportunism is defined as a strategy involving guile, intended to further self-interest. The term 'bounded rationality' was coined in

		Bounded rationality	
		Absent	Admitted
Opportunism	Absent	Bliss	General clause contracting
	Admitted	Comprehensive contracting	Serious contractual difficulties

Figure 14.1 Contractual difficulties under bounded rationality and opportunism
Source: Williamson (1985).

1957 by Herbert Simon, an organisational theorist. It refers to information problems, but adds limited cognitive, reasoning and computational abilities on the part of individuals. It is distinct from uncertainty, which is usually an additional assumption of Williamson's models. Given uncertainty, bounded rationality implies that individuals cannot calculate all the possible outcomes and their associated probabilities which would enable the computation of the rational price or offer of supply. The presence of bounded rationality implies that contracts are 'incomplete' – they cannot specify all relevant possibilities which affect the contracting parties from participating in the contract. Williamson uses Figure 14.1 to explain the importance of these departures.

Where neither new behavioural assumption applies, the situation is described as 'bliss': contracts can be fully specified and followed. Where there is opportunism and no bounded rationality it is possible to specify contracts completely, leaving no scope for opportunistic behaviour. Where there is bounded rationality but no opportunism, contracts can be governed by a 'general clause' such as 'parties to the contract promise to disclose all relevant information candidly and to behave in co-operative fashion during contract execution and at contract renewal intervals'. However, where both behavioural assumptions apply, contractual difficulties arise.

These problems are particularly acute in the context of 'asset specificity'. The distinction between specific and non-specific assets is whether they are redeployable or not. (Notice the distinction between a 'fixed' cost and a 'specific asset'. A building, for example, is 'fixed' but could be redeployed in many uses.) There are four types of asset specificity: site specificity (successive stages of production need to be located in close proximity to each other); physical asset specificity (assets are mobile and specificity is related to physical features); human asset specificity (skills and knowledge embedded in the labour force are specific – e.g. because of on-the-job learning, or the importance of team configurations) and dedicated asset specificity (for example, expansion of an existing plant on behalf of a particular buyer).

Asset specificity causes two types of problems. The first is the 'fundamental transformation': a situation that starts with competitive bidding *prior* to contract can become one of '*ex post* monopoly' *after* the contract. The problem is that once investment has been made, no alternative supplier will be able to match the prices of the first successful bidder – since each new successful bidder would have to invest *specifically* to fulfil the contract. The second problem is the inherent monopsony in asset specificity – the assets have a single buyer.

The resulting bilateral monopoly means that one or both parties are vulnerable to

Behavioural assumption			
Bounded rationality	Opportunism	Asset specificity	
0	+	+	Planning
+	0	+	Promise
+	+	0	Competition
+	+	+	Governance

Figure 14.2 Contractual difficulties under bounded rationality, opportunism and asset specificity. Key: + present to a considerable degree, 0 absent. Uncertainty is assumed in all cases
Source: Williamson (1985).

appropriation. If one party pulls out of the contract, behaves unreasonably, or announces a sudden change of price, the other has the choice of complying or pulling out of the contract. Opportunism implies that such behaviour must be expected. Bounded rationality implies that such behaviour will not always be resolvable by recourse to a law and the explicit, formal agreement of the written contract. Asset specificity implies that the option of responding by pulling out of the contract is highly costly to the investor in the specific asset.

Suppose a company negotiates with a hospital to build a disposal unit for hospital waste at a hospital-convenient site and agrees a contract specifying an annual fee for the disposal of all hospital waste. The waste-disposal unit is a specific asset and the company may be exposed to risks of appropriation of the value of its investment by the hospital. If the hospital increases the volume of waste the company's costs increase but it is in a weak position to renegotiate the contract because it cannot redeploy the asset. It might be argued that the contract was not very well specified at the outset. The example is deliberately crude for simplicity's sake, but bounded rationality implies that there will be holes in contracts which opportunistic contracting parties can exploit.

Another of Williamson's tables addresses the types of solution likely under different con-ditions (Figure 14.2). As before, if bounded rationality is absent, contracting resembles planning – or is comprehensive. Everything can be specified in advance and the plan simply executed with all parties playing their role. If opportunism is absent, a 'promise' form of contract will function well (general clause). If asset specificity is absent, competitive contracting can function because contracts can be discrete and the market is fully contestable. Opportunism can be punished by withdrawal from contracts. In the example above, the waste-disposal unit can be redeployed and the hospital will have to find another willing supplier. However, everything fails when all three are present – a need for 'governance' of contracts is introduced.

Governance implies a retreat from 'classical contracting' which is equivalent to the comprehensive contracting and planning concepts above – it is assumed possible to account for every aspect of the transaction in the contract. However, there are degrees of governance (Figure 14.3). 'Neoclassical' contracting is characterised by greater flexibility and third-party arbitration of disputes – for example, public purchasers and providers in the UK or Zambian health system can appeal to a government body to settle a dispute. 'Relational contracting' reflects progressively increasing duration and complexity of contract: contracts relate not to a single discrete purchase but to long-term agreements over many

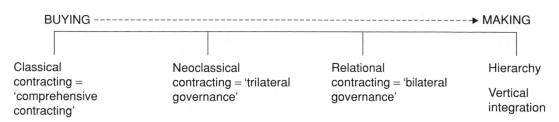

Figure 14.3 Contractual governance, 'making' and 'buying'

different exchanges. The role of *trust* becomes increasingly important. The last point on this continuum is hierarchy or vertical integration – for the public sector the equivalent is reversion to direct provision. The classical, neoclassical, relational classification is used by Williamson but originates from the work of Macneil (1978).

The astute reader will have noticed that the movement from classical to neoclassical to relational contracts resembles the movement from formal explicit to informal contracts discussed above. Williamson's framework implies that more complex contractual situations are best governed by a greater degree of informality or use of implicit contracting.

This is a point of departure for other contributors to contracting debates for whom this appears as more of an assumption than a conclusion. For example, Alchian and Demsetz (1972) and Demsetz (1993) have characterised the firm as a 'nexus of contracts', implying, as does section 14.2 above, that contractual difficulties are not avoided, just altered, by greater use of hierarchy than markets. Alchian and Demsetz write about 'market-like' and 'firm-like' contracts, implying that it is the different nature of the two kinds of contract – either of which may be implicit or explicit – that are differently equipped to deal with the contractual difficulties resulting from opportunism, bounded rationality and asset specificity.

A solution which Williamson largely discounts, but which is given substantial attention elsewhere in the literature, is 'reputation effects'. The argument is that, in a multi-period 'game', participants are constrained from opportunism by the effect of being observed to cheat on future rounds. This suggests that a world of 'promise' or 'general clause' contracting is more feasible than might otherwise seem. Reputation effects depend on how observable cheating is to those who have not participated in the contract, suggesting that 'contract performance transparency' might usefully be considered another component in a framework categorising the viability of alternative forms of contract.

14.5 Health Sector Contracting

14.5.1 Bounded Rationality and Opportunism

The major question addressed in the health contracting literature which immediately responds to an environment of bounded rationality and opportunism is the issue of effective monitoring of contracts. In the 'bliss' of these behavioural assumptions being absent, no monitoring would be necessary.

Health services present notorious monitoring problems in relation to both the quantity and the quality of services delivered. In most cases it is therefore not only *difficult* to attempt 'classical contracting', it is probably *inefficient*, since difficulty implies high costs of achieving complete monitoring. Providers can act opportunistically *ex ante* in the development of monitoring mechanisms (for example, proposing measures which conceal the weaknesses of their provision), and *ex post* in their response to the monitoring mechanisms imposed.

For example, in the US the 'diagnosis-related group' (DRG) as the basis of payment became a feature of contracts between insurance companies and health service providers during the 1980s. Diagnosis-related groups categorised patients according to their expected cost profile, based on the initial diagnosis, and co-diagnoses. Patients with higher expected costs claimed higher fees but the intention was that hospitals would face no incentive to over-provide unnecessary services, as they had under fee-for-service arrangements. However, in the years following this reform, 'DRG creep' became a well-acknowledged phenomenon. It was argued that diagnoses were arrived at bearing in mind the fee schedule and patients were increasingly diagnosed as suffering from more expensive to treat conditions (Simborg 1981; Steinwald and Dummit 1989). This diagnostic behaviour on the part of hospital doctors can be interpreted as an opportunistic response to the incompleteness of the hospital's contracts with insurance companies. In general, imperfect indicators of performance imply scope for providers to respond to the letter rather than the spirit of the measure and to distort statistical returns where those are under the provider's control.

In any given context, since classical contracting is excluded, the question to be addressed is the degree of monitoring difficulty and the type of contract most likely to minim-

ise the costs associated with the transaction. This involves consideration of the type of governance appropriate (trilateral, bilateral or hierarchy), and the types of contracts possible within each type of governance.

In Zambia contracts have been introduced between a central purchaser (the Central Board of Health) and hospitals, and district health management teams who manage the provision of primary- and secondary-level care (see Box 25.2). Contracts stipulate that hospitals will be reimbursed according to a budgetary formula calculated on the basis of bed numbers. Many hospital operating decisions are subject to review by the Ministry of Health. This may be interpreted as the choice of a 'relational contract' mode. The choice of arrangements has been explicitly related to monitoring difficulties by Ministry of Health and Central Board of Health officials. Under more classical contracts, government officials fear the creation of perverse incentives, responses to which they would be unable to monitor. We can interpret these concerns within the frameworks introduced in this chapter, which would also suggest the identification of potential perverse incentives associated with current contractual arrangements and consideration of the ability to monitor those.

14.5.2 Risk and Reimbursement Mechanisms

Reimbursement mechanisms govern incentives and also distribute risk between contracting parties. Examples of reimbursement mechanisms are the DRG and fee-for-service systems and capitation (exemplified in Box 7.2), which pay a provider a fixed price for the coverage of a patient's health care costs over a given time period, whatever they may be.

Adding 'bounded rationality' to this uncertainty, approaches to using reimbursement mechanisms as a means to shift risk and mani-pulate incentives can be developed – but not precisely. In the literature on contracting in the UK the types of contract are categorised as 'block contract' (treat a defined patient population, for a fixed reimbursement); 'cost and volume' (provide a given number of treatments for a reimbursement set accord-ing to the estimated cost of that); and 'cost per case' (provide variable number of treat-ments and receive a payment related to number provided). These broadly correspond to capitation and fee-per-patient reimburse-ment mechanisms (of which diagnosis-related groups are also an example), with number of patients fixed under 'cost and volume' and variable under 'cost per case'.

Capitation shifts risk to the organisation paid on this basis. If a higher number of patients than expected seek to use a service, the additional cost must be absorbed by the provider; so must a higher than expected cost per patient. Fee-per-patient mechanisms shift risk back towards the payer, but not as fully as fee-for-service reimbursement. If the average patient imposes a higher cost than expected, that risk still lies with the provider, but the risk of higher than expected patient numbers now lies with the payer.

The principal consideration that is usually applied to this issue is the incentive to cost control. Since the provider is in a better con-dition to control costs, it is argued that it is appropriate for the risk of excess costs to be felt there. Certainly US experience suggests that failure to address this issue can be cata-strophic. However, Roberts (1993) suggests that the dangers of 'supplier-reduced demand' under capitation have not been adequately considered.

It is also important to understand the im-plications of alternative reimbursement mech-anisms on the distribution of risk between payer and provider. Propper (1995) argues that in the UK, when formal contracts were first introduced, District Health Authorities (DHAs), which purchased care for the popu-lation of the district, were likely to be risk-averse, given the political environment. Under arrangements in which DHAs were more exposed to risk (for example, by increased use of cost-per-case contracts), they might make compensating sub-optimal risk-avoiding decisions from society's perspective. For ex-ample, they might keep a sub-optimally high financial reserve to cope with emergencies. If the same is not true of providers, there are arguments for maintaining block contracts. Returning to Zambia, an explicit reason for working with block contracts is that pur-chasers are wary of accepting risk.

Like the monitoring arguments, these con-siderations may suggest the need to maintain more rather than less 'governance' in health service contracting.

14.5.3 Asset Specificity

Consider again the different types of asset specificity. The level of physical asset speci-ficity can be seen to be related to market structure. Given the wide range of medical equipment that has no non-medical use, phys-ical asset specificity is likely to be prevalent where there is an *ex ante* monopsony in the health sector – for example, in the British NHS. This could lead to reluctance among private sector firms to invest in medical equip-ment, given the risks of appropriation. In the UK the Private Finance Initiative operates by renting equipment to the NHS. Reputation factors may be important in explaining this – or perhaps the UK government plans to renege on these agreements in the future?

The same market structure point would appear to apply to human asset specificity

– since there are clearly a great many health sector-specific human assets but there is mobility between health sector jobs. In any given situation it is worth thinking also about whether there are any other factors causing human asset specificity of the generic type described above. For example, a chief executive of a health authority may have to sacrifice considerable human assets to change job.

'Dedicated assets' seem to give rise to few generic health sector issues, but could be an important consideration in any specific situation – for example, where a hospital invests in facilities under a contract to cater for the employees of a company.

Note

1. 'A spot market contract is a contract for the immediate market exchange of goods or services at current prices' (Milgrom and Roberts 1992).

Chapter 15

Market Structures

....

15.1 Introduction

The role of markets and competition in health care has been brought to prominence in the discussion of health sector reforms all around the world. In many countries there is a large volume of private health care activity. In others, reforms have introduced a greater role for market mechanisms within the public sector, an issue which is further discussed in Chapter 25. Understanding the theory of markets may help government to form appropriate regulatory- or incentive-based policies to ensure the appropriate operation of these markets. When a substantial private market exists in parallel with the public sector then forming public sector policies, which ignore the dynamics of the private market, would seem an unwise strategy.

A simple definition of a market is that it is a set of arrangements by which buyers and sellers exchange goods and services. From Part I we know that the market is the interplay between demand and supply.

In Chapter 6 we compared markets operating under perfect competition and monopoly, and saw that the level of output which a firm selects and the price which it charges for its product depends on the structure of the market. In simple terms, market structure can be thought of as a description of the characteristics of buyers and sellers (for example, size and number). Although pure forms of these structures are uncommon they are useful in showing the range of possible outcomes. This chapter considers the behaviour of firms and markets under intermediate forms of market structure.

15.2 Imperfect Competition

Between the two extremes of perfect competition and pure monopoly there are a range of market forms. These can be analysed by combining the features of the perfect competition and monopoly models. Common problems occur when there is a small number of firms providing a service.

Imperfect competition covers a range of market structures from many firms to a few but, in contrast to perfect competition, relies on each firm facing a downward-sloping demand curve. This results from the relaxation of at least one of two perfect competition assumptions – homogeneous product or perfect information. Departure from perfect elasticity of the demand curve results from the firm differentiating its product from those of other firms – on the basis that some consumers will prefer the differentiated product sufficient to pay some higher price than similar products are sold at. Alternatively, if information is imperfect, some consumers will pay a higher price to one seller rather than incur search costs in finding the lowest-price product on the market. This also means that any one seller will not lose all his sales by pricing above the minimum.

Demand will be more inelastic where there are relatively few sellers who differentiate their products to an extent inducing strong brand loyalty, or where information problems are acute, and search costs therefore high. Imperfect competition is also known as *monopolistic competition* in some texts, and *oligopoly*, a market characterised by a small number of firms, covers the range of cases at relatively demand-inelastic points on the range between perfect competition and monopoly.

The key feature of an oligopoly is that the decision made by one firm depends on the decision made by other firms, i.e. there is a high degree of interdependence between firms. Firms therefore can only decide upon their best strategy in light of what they know about other firms. Many different possible models exist depending on what assumptions the firm is assumed to make about other firms in the market.

An example of this type of model is the 'kinked demand curve' model under which firms assume that, if they raise their prices, other firms will not follow but will seize the opportunity to gain market share. However, price reductions will be imitated as other firms seek to avoid losing market share. This implies that the firm's demand curve is elastic above the currently prevailing price and inelastic below it. The model predicts price stability and that competition will take non-price forms.

Figure 15.1   Incentive to form a cartel

For example, competition may take the form of increases in quality without corresponding increases in price.

A substantial part of the literature looks at *collusion*, where there is a conscious attempt by the different firms in the industry to co-ordinate their pricing and output strategies so that together they can reap monopolistic profits. By colluding (agreeing on price and output levels), firms can jointly generate the profits which would be associated with monopoly and share them among themselves, rather than competing supranormal profit away. Formal collusion in the form of cartels is usually illegal within national economies. However, international export cartels such as OPEC have been successful in supporting higher prices of commodities through international agreements to restrict export quantities. Such examples also demonstrate the difficulties of maintaining the agreements necessary since it is in the interest of each to cheat on the rest of the cartel. Consider Figure 15.1 which presents a two-firm case. The cartel may maximise joint profit by producing where total marginal cost (derived by horizontally summing the marginal cost) intersects the marginal revenue curve derived from the market demand. Output is shared so that MC = MR in each firm and the monopolist's profit (shaded area) is shared between the two firms.

The problem is that both firms have an incentive to increase their share of profit by cutting price and capturing a larger share of total demand. This incentive exists up to the point where each individual firm's marginal cost curves intersect with the market marginal revenue curve. Formal collusion through cartels is very vulnerable to price cutting among members and this has not only at times caused disarray within OPEC, but has undermined the development of similar commodity-based cartels despite attempts.

Such collusion can occur in the health sector. Price agreements are quite common. For example, hospitals jointly agree a price schedule for insurers in Brazil, and it is not uncommon for groups of surgeons to agree fee scales for different operations. It is quite difficult to establish whether or not such agreements set prices at monopoly profit levels, have the intention of restricting competition or have another purpose – but at least in some cases it would seem that they are set at a rate judged to be what the market will bear and aim to prevent competitive strategies which involve undercutting on price.

Game theory attempts to model the behaviour of firms by seeing them as players in a game. The classic game is that of the Prisoners' Dilemma. Two prisoners have been taken in for questioning and they are held in separate cells: there is not enough evidence to prosecute them without at least one prisoner confessing. If neither confesses they are both released. If both confess they each get a prison sentence of ten years. But the worst scenario for each is if his fellow prisoner confesses and he does not – a prison sentence of twenty years. What decision would you make under such circumstances? Your answer is probably dependent on your prior relationship with, and knowledge of, your fellow prisoner. Similarly, firms' decisions about outputs in the market are likely to be affected by the number of times these decisions are to be made and firms' beliefs about each other. These become critical factors determining outcome.

The presence of asymmetric information between producer and consumer may also give rise to forms of imperfect competition. For example, consider a situation where the product is not homogeneous and consumers have preferences over different products. There are likely to be search costs associated with finding their preferred product. Consumers will invest in search activity only up to the point where the expected marginal benefit of search is equal to the marginal cost. Under such conditions, consumers may not search the whole market and hence producers may retain a degree of market power. The smaller the search cost, the better informed the consumer will be and the more closely the model will approximate perfect competition.

The presence of asymmetric information and search costs is pronounced in health markets, as has been discussed in Chapter 7. There are high costs associated with 'shopping around' for the best health care. This has implications for the degree of market power wielded by health service providers.

15.3 Alternative Models of Provider Competition in Health Care

Traditional theories of competition suggest, crudely speaking, that as the concentration of the market declines and competition becomes more intense, prices will fall. Decreasing degrees of market power, reflected in more elastic demand curves facing the individual firm, are expected to lead to profit levels approaching the 'normal' and prices closer to the minimum points of average cost curves. However, in the health sectors of some countries there is a commonly observed association between lower market concentration and higher prices. This has led to attempts by health economists to explain this conflict with the predictions of traditional economic theory.

The models discussed below are not mutually exclusive and it is possible that they occur in parallel with price competition. Thus even in health care markets where lower market concentration is associated with lower prices, one cannot conclude that there is necessarily no simultaneous presence of other forms of competition. The supplier-induced demand model of Chapter 7 is a further example of a possible monopolistic competition explanation of perverse market response.

15.3.1 Quality competition

This is perhaps the most straightforward model. It suggests that providers respond to lower concentration (more competition) not by dropping price, but by increasing quality. Within a profit-maximising framework, this strategy would be rational if it costs the provider less to gain additional customers by increasing quality than by reducing price. In other words if, per unit of expenditure, 'quality elasticity of demand' is higher than price elasticity of demand, it will be more profitable for the provider to increase quality than to reduce price.

This relation between 'quality elasticity' and 'price elasticity' may be particularly likely in the health sector if consumers are not very sensitive to price because of extensive insurance coverage and/or because quality dominates in their utility functions. In addition, the objective functions of actors in the hospital market may differ from those usually assumed. Hospital managers may seek to pursue quality rather than profit-oriented objectives. Physicians may seek to work in hospitals with a good reputation for high-quality care, implying some rather peculiar features of this particular labour supply curve. Chapter 16 gives more attention to these possibilities and it is important to note here only that these also provide an explanation of 'quality competition' models.

Quality competition is often (but not always) associated with higher investment in high-technology equipment and hotel aspects of care. It is less commonly suggested that quality competition leads to improvements in technical aspects of quality (the medical appropriateness of the treatment provided). Technical aspects are those patients are least likely to be able to judge in comparison with the availability of certain items of equipment or the luxury of the building. Investing in easily observable aspects of quality is consistent with profit-maximising explanations, since these aspects play the most important role in the demand function. It may also be consistent with managerial theories of hospital motivation, if what managers are interested to maximise is the observable quality of care in their hospital rather than technical aspects. According to either explanation, hospitals invest in these aspects in order to 'signal' to the patient the quality of the service they provide. As more and more facilities attempt to signal quality, the 'louder' the signal must be in order to be heard against the background noise. Thus problems of excessive high-tech-equipment accumulation occur. Box 15.1 considers evidence of this kind of competitive behaviour for the hospital market of Bangkok, and the Further Reading on p. 140 considers trends in the US.

International Case Study

Box 15.1 Market Structure and Competitive Strategy in Bangkok

By 1993 there were 105 private and eighty public hospitals in Bangkok. Eighty per cent of the private hospitals were 'for profit'. Forty-five per cent of the population was estimated to be covered by some kind of health insurance.

An analysis of the hospital market aimed to differentiate between price competition, supplier-induced-demand (see Chapter 7) and quality competition, by estimating the correlation between measures of competition within a 2 km and 5 km radius of Bangkok, and measures of price, service intensity and indicators of quality.

Correlations between price levels and measures of competition (numbers of hospitals and Hirschman–Hirfendahl indices based on bed numbers for areas within a 2 km and 5 km radius) were insignificant, suggesting that price competition, if present, did not dominate competitive strategy. There was positive correlation between measures of competition, expenditure per bed, and a measure of asset value per bed providing some evidence of quality competition. However, this result had to be interpreted cautiously. The highest levels of competition were found in central Bangkok, areas where there may have been other reasons for high expenditure and asset levels per bed.

The issue of quality competition was further explored by generating 'quality-adjusted prices' (Cowling and Cubbin 1971) which indicate an expected price given quality characteristics. There was no relation between the actual and quality-adjusted price, suggesting that the Bangkok market would bear 'significant and unjustified' price variation. Further, the difference between the two prices correlated positively with the level of competition, assessed by all measures. This implies that, after quality factors were taken into account, prices were higher in hospitals which faced greater competition – possibly explained by the presence of supplier-induced demand.

Privately owned hospitals which were floated on the stock market offered higher quality, charged higher prices and made higher profits. They tended to charge considerably higher prices than were apparently warranted by their quality of care characteristics. There may be a virtuous circle (from the hospital's perspective!) by which hospitals develop their reputation (for example, through quality signals), 'premium price', above the levels justified by their quality standards (Cleverly 1992) and in turn signal quality through the act of 'premium pricing'.

This evidence tends to urge caution in advocating or encouraging a greater role for the private sector, as was done in Thailand, where regulatory capacity is weak. Quality competition described by increasing prices associated with possibly irrelevant quality dimensions used to signal, does not result in better value for money in health services for patients.

Source: S. Bennett, 'The nature of competition among private hospitals in Bangkok', in Bennett *et al.* (1997).

15.3.2 Increasing monopoly model

Pauly and Satterthwaite (1981) argue that health care is a 'reputation good', meaning that (1) sellers' products are differentiated and (2) consumers' search among sellers is conducted by asking friends and relatives for recommendations. The model is thought to be mainly relevant to primary care. Primary care services are frequently used, assumed to imply that reputation is a more important factor than for more rarely used services. Primary care services are also less sophisticated than higher levels of care, and so patients may feel they are in a better position to judge the service provided.

The argument is as follows:

1 If the number of health care providers within a community increases, the available consumer information about each decreases. Therefore consumers find it hard to collect information about a new provider.
2 If the search for information becomes more difficult, consumers become less price sensitive.

Therefore an increase in supply of health care providers makes the consumers' search more difficult and may cause the equilibrium fee to rise.

However, the increasing monopoly model makes a number of questionable assumptions about consumer search behaviour. If consumers seek information by asking a question like 'What do you know about Dr Black?' then indeed as the number of providers increases the people with knowledge about Dr Black are more thinly spread and information is harder to find. On the other hand if consumers seek information by asking questions such as 'Do you know a good physician around here?' it is not clear that search costs will rise with the number of physicians – they may even fall.

There is no substantial evidence supporting the increasing monopoly model but the questions it raises are interesting and relevant. For example, how do different facilities form 'a reputation'? Is it through good reports or avoiding bad ones? We understand little about the processes through which consumer information in health care markets is generated.

Further Reading – Price versus Quality Competition: Changes through Time

Managed care and health maintenance organsations (HMOs) have become a significant force in American health care over the past thirty years. Keeler *et al.* (1999) examine the influence of these changes on the nature of competition in California, focusing on the distinction between non-profit and for-profit providers.

In 1996 a US court refused to halt the merger of two hospitals which when combined accounted for 73 per cent of the market. The argument underlying the ruling was that the merging of non-profit hospitals would lead to different results from the merging of for-profit hospitals, and thus the merger would be unlikely to increase market prices, even though there was an effective monopoly operating in the market. This decision was based on research which suggested that in California for-profit hospitals would raise their prices following a merger and that non-profit hospitals were more likely to reduce their prices (Lynk 1995).

Lynk's results were largely based on the observation that higher costs were found in areas of less concentrated markets. This notion is contrary to the expectation that, with larger numbers of providers, one would obtain greater competition and thus lower prices and costs. The explanation for this has been that these providers are competing on a non-profit basis, maximising objectives such as education, charity care, higher quality, higher wages or dividends for managers or trustees. Thus hospitals were thought to compete by providing (and signalling) higher-quality services, including advanced technology.

In 1982 California began to pursue pro-competition policies, encouraging price competition in the health sector. Hospital costs have risen more slowly. Keeler and colleagues explored potential changes in the market. They found that while measures of competition, market share and the Hirschman–Hirfindahl index (HHI) did not change greatly, the relation between prices and market concentration strengthened over time. Prices were generally higher in less competitive areas, even among non-profit hospitals. This suggests that, given the nature of competition in the market place, a merger among non-profit hospitals may now increase prices. Sources: Lynk (1995); Keeler *et al.* (1999).

15.4 Monopoly, Oligopoly and Contestability

We have seen that monopolists and collusive oligopolists can make positive (supra-normal) profits where other firms do not enter the market. More recently it has been suggested that monopolistic and oligopolistic profits may be eroded by the threat of competition even if it remains a threat and no entry in fact takes place (Baumol *et al.* 1982). This idea is often referred to as *contestability*. Baumol argues that having one firm does not mean there is no competition, and potential competition (the threat of entry) may serve to discipline the established firm.

Perfect contestability requires only one of the conditions for perfect competition: entry is absolutely free and exit is absolutely costless. This implies that the potential entrant will enter if profit can be made and does not consider entry and exit costs. It further implies that:

1 No entrant can make a profit, at the market price.
2 If the incumbent producer(s) price(s) above average cost even for a very short period,

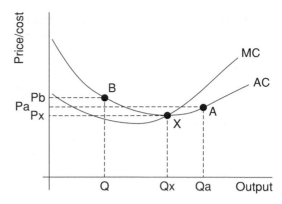

Figure 15.2 Pricing under perfect contestability

it is vulnerable to 'hit and run' entry which may result in losses for the incumbent. The incumbent will not therefore price above average cost.

3 Technical inefficiency offers the same opportunity to a potential entrant. By setting up efficient production, the entrant can undercut the incumbent and force her out of business. Production must therefore be technically efficient.

4 Price must equal marginal cost, since other choices represent profitable opportunities to potential entrants. Consider Figure 15.2, which assumes normal cost curves. We have already seen that price must not be set above average cost to avoid profitable opportunities for entrants. Suppose the incumbent prices below marginal cost (for example, at point A on Figure 15.2). The incumbent is producing a number of units of output (Qa–Qx) which are loss-making. This implies that an entrant could sell a smaller amount at a lower price without making a loss. (The lower price can be set so as to compensate for the reduced loss from moving towards Qx.) Suppose, instead, the incumbent sets a price such as B, above MC. Profitable opportunities exist through increasing production along

Qb–Qx and the entrant could cut the incumbent's price by selling a slightly larger output, and ensuring that additional profit offsets the lower price. Here there is a condition, however – elasticity of demand must be such that the increased production will be purchased. In a two-incumbent case, it is always possible to increase production above the average level of production of each firm by replacing existing production without relying on an increase in total market demand.

At the level of the market, structure is determined by the ratio of Qx to market demand at Px. While excess demand exists, profitable opportunities arise from the replication of the incumbent's activity. In the case of economies of scale, one firm will operate at the point at which demand is exhausted at P = AC. Figure 15.3 describes this case. P*Q* is the price and output decision of an incumbent monopolist. This scenario illustrates the exception to the P = MC rule given above. An entrant is constrained from undercutting P* by being unable to increase demand suffici-

ently to compensate for the price reduction. Normal profits could be maintained while cutting price by moving to a position further along the AC curve (such as A), but the position and elasticity of the demand curve indicates that this is not possible.

Under perfect contestability the welfare implications are identical to those of perfect competition, since no supra-normal profits are made, and outputs are priced at marginal cost, implying efficient consumption and production decisions in own and related markets.

While perfect contestability is likely to be no more prevalent than perfect competition, this theory suggests that markets may be disciplined by potential competition as much as by actual competition. The theory strengthens the arguments of anti-interventionists, suggesting that markets may be getting it more or less right, most of the time. Its less restrictive assumptions suggest that conditions may more frequently approximate contestability, and therefore efficiency.

In a health sector context, the theory of contestability has been used to argue that health sector reform which relies on the operation of competitive pressures (such as the creation of an internal market for example, see Chapter 25) can function even when it is clear that markets are not competitive by conventional definitions.

It is therefore highly relevant to ask to what extent contestability might apply to such markets. How easy is it for firms to enter and exit relevant health services markets? One factor that severely inhibits entry and exit is that of 'sunk' costs. Sunk costs are costs of investment which cannot be transferred to a new industry if that investment fails. (Similar to the concept of asset specificity introduced in the previous chapter.[1]) These kinds of costs are thought to be significant in health services provision at higher levels of technology,

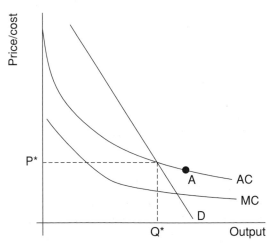

Figure 15.3 Contestability and economies of scale

and include the specialised nature of hospital buildings and of much medical equipment. In general, barriers to entry are likely to be quite important across the health sector.

The contestability theory may not satisfy us that monopoly will not cause problems for health markets as a whole. However, many specific markets within the health sector look more contestable. For example, the market for the provision of family doctor services may be readily entered by those with medical qualifications who otherwise practise in more specialised health markets. If premises, equipment and ancillary services can be rented or bought in easily, that market may be quite contestable over a range of output levels. The pharmaceutical retailing market may be low-cost to enter and exit if pharmacists can be employed on short contracts, premises are easily convertible to other types of shop and stocks move quickly.

15.5 *Measurement of Market Structure*

Most of the market structure models we have described assume that market structure (number of sellers in the market, their degree of product differentiation, the cost structure) determines conduct (such as price, research and development, investment, advertising) and so yields market performance (efficiency, ratio of price to marginal cost, profits). This is commonly known as the structure–conduct–performance paradigm.

It is clear that there are limits to this perspective. Most important, the paradigm offers no explanation of structure but rather starts with structure given. The contestability model departs from this by also providing an explanation of why a market is structured as it is structured, in terms of the relationship between production functions, cost functions

and demand functions – market structure would follow from the least-cost replication of production. In Chapter 14 we saw that transaction cost economics offered a different explanation of market structure – market structure would follow from attempts to minimise transaction costs. There has been further criticism of the structure–conduct–performance paradigm from the perspective that the firm's conduct can be targeted at changing the structure of the industry in pursuit of objectives other than efficiency. For example, advertising strategies may explicitly aim to concentrate market power in the hands of fewer competitors.

However, from any of these perspectives, attempts to operationalise and test the implications of market models require measurement of market structure. The simplest measure is the *concentration ratio* that is given by:

$$Cr_n = \sum_{I=1}^{n} S_I$$

where S_I is the share of the ith firm in the market and n represents the number of firms chosen to include. This measure only considers the n largest firms in the industry.

An alternative measure is the *Hirschman–Herfindahl index* (HHI):

$$HHI = \sum_{I=1}^{N} S_I$$

where N is the total number of firms in the industry and S_I is the share of the ith firm. This ranges from close to 0 (large number of competitors all with small market shares) to 1 (single monopoly supplier). Box 15.2 shows an example of the calculation of the Hirschman–Herfindahl index within the health care market in New Zealand.

Another problem with empirical work which aims to measure market structure is the

International Case Study

Box 15.2 Measuring Market Concentration: Secondary Services in New Zealand

Ashton and Press (1997) consider the market concentration of a number of services in New Zealand before and after the introduction of health sector reforms to promote competition in 1993. Seven secondary services were selected: tonsillectomies and/or adenoidectomies, prostatectomies, knee-joint replacements; hip replacements, cataract removal; angioplasties and coronary artery bypass grafts (CABG).

Several issues arose when they tried to define the market, including how to delineate the market area. They calculated the HHI for a number of scenarios. (H is multiplied by 10,000 to make interpretation easier.) When is a market concentrated? The cut-off is arbitrary, but in practice a value of 1,800 has been used. Thus an HHI above 1,800 is considered to indicate a market which is highly concentrated. This value is used as the cut-off for US anti-trust cases by the US Department of Justice.

One set of results from Ashton and Press is given in the table. Since they were looking at a number of different markets carrying out the same procedures, they categorised the procedures according to what proportion of markets were considered to be relatively unconcentrated.

Market concentration

Procedure	No. of markets	% of markets with HHI < 1,800
Angioplasty	7	71.43
Cataract removal	23	64.71
CABG	5	80.00
Hip replacement	23	45.45
Knee-joint replacement	22	42.86
Prostatectomy	19	27.78
Tonsillectomy	21	65.00

The results suggest that the markets for the selected procedures were all highly concentrated. The CABG and the angioplasty were the least concentrated markets. Interestingly, these two procedures also involved the highest degree of specialisation, and one would expect the highest barriers to entry, and thus relatively more market concentration. One possible explanation is that these services are often not available locally and patients expect to travel to use them, increasing the geographical area that constitutes a market.

Source: Ashton and Press (1997).

question of how to define a market. Definitions can be product or geographically specific. Highly product-specific definitions of markets lead to high concentration ratios (for example, the market for MRI) relative to more industry-specific definitions (for example, diagnostic technologies). This explains part of the rationale for firms to try and differentiate their products through advertising and other marketing strategies. Zwanziger *et al.*

(1994) ask the question 'What is the relevant market for hospitals?' They find that it can vary according to the reimbursement scheme, and that there may be less competition than initially appears to be the case. Propper and Bartlett (1997) take a different view of the UK hospital market, suggesting that, when viewed from the perspective of individual procedures and specialities, there is more competition than might be imagined. For example, for certain kinds of elective surgery, patients travel quite significant distances for care, implying higher levels of competition than might be expected between hospitals considerable distances apart.

15.6 *Markets, Hierarchies and Networks*

As we saw in Chapter 14, a central feature of the analysis of the 'make or buy' decision is the role of transaction costs in the evolution and interaction between institutions both internally and externally within a market. As it becomes more difficult to contract through market organisation, theory suggests that the firm or organisation may decide to integrate with another firm, rather than try to exchange goods by buying and selling. Vertical integration occurs when firms merge with other firms at a different stage of the production process (for example, when a car manufacturer buys the manufacturer of some of its component parts). Horizontal integration occurs when firms merge with others at the same stage of the production process, and either produces greater market concentration (for example, when two brewers merge) or firms with more diversified product ranges (for example, when a manufacturer of chocolate confectionery merges with a firm producing breakfast cereal). Organising transactions

within a firm, in contrast with organisation between firms, has been described as 'hierarchy'. Hierarchical transactions 'are ones for which a single administrative entity spans both sides of the transaction' (Williamson 1985). On this understanding as discussed above, one can view market structure as dependent on transaction costs.

The market and hierarchy duality may miss important intermediate forms of relationships. In Chapter 14 we discussed relational contracting (where the contracting relationship is long term and stable). Recent developments in new institutional economics emphasise the role of norms and networks as mechanisms to reduce transaction costs, consider more dynamic approaches to institutions and look at how over time they evolve to seize efficiency-increasing opportunities. These developments imply that new approaches need to be taken to the understanding of market structure and its implications.

What is a network? In simple terms, it can be thought of as a link or relationship between individuals or organisations. A network can be formally defined in terms of tasks or activities, which involve the actions of one organisation or organisational unit. A task network refers to a set of organisations involved in the activities needed to accomplish a task. The set of organisations may include, for example, government units, non-governmental organisations (NGOs) or the private sector. Thus outcome or performance is related to how well these networks function in terms of both co-ordination and communication. Primary organisations have a central role in performing the task, while secondary organisations are complementary or supportive of the primary organisation (Grindle and Hilderbrand 1995).

Networks can be seen as an alternative (to markets and hierarchies) way of organising activities, able to represent individuals and activities in the context of a broader system of structures or organisations. In addition to price and governance structures, emphasis is now also placed on factors such as trust and reputation.

The design of the network can emerge from collaboration or inter-firm alliance (e.g. the aligning of airlines in competitive networks). This view of networks as an alternative form of organisation is underpinned by both transaction cost minimisation and oligopolistic market competition strategy.

Given these characteristics, it is difficult to distinguish different forms of organisation. Indeed, Bradach and Eccles (1989) suggest that different forms of institutions (markets, networks and hierarchies) are not mutually exclusive.

Formal networks have become a common feature of more market-oriented health care systems such as those of Taiwan (Lin and Wan 1999) and the US (Broyles *et al.* 1998). These new perspectives on market structure give us new frameworks with which to evaluate and understand relations between organisations in the health sector. For example, the introduction of 'internal markets' in health care provision (see Chapter 25 and especially Box 25.2) can be viewed, from a classical perspective, as an attempt to tap the benefits of competition and market forces. However, from a new institutional economics perspective, these reforms can be interpreted as the attempt to move from hierarchical to market modes of transacting in order to economise on transaction costs. However, as new structures emerge, they may not resemble those intended, as organisations manoeuvre to exploit new possibilities in the market. Merger activity is an easily observable response, and has been prevalent among purchasers and hospitals responding to the reforms in the UK, for example. Equally important, if less observable, is the emergence of networks in formal and informal varieties. At the extreme, these may virtually reinstate hierarchical relationships, for example, informally reintegrating purchasers and providers through long-term relational contracts, personal relationships and evolving 'norms' of behaviour which govern the parties of the network.

Note

1. Although specific assets constitute sunk costs, not all sunk costs are specific assets. For example, the legal work involved in establishing a new company is a sunk cost, but not a specific asset.

Chapter 16

Hospital and Health Provider Behaviour and Motivation

....

16.1 Introduction

We have now discussed the model of perfect competition extensively, and have also looked at other market models such as those of contestability and monopoly. Throughout these discussions, we have assumed that firms are profit maximising. As with the other assumptions of the model, it is worth considering the implications of relaxing this assumption. In this chapter we consider the extent to which health care providers may be motivated by factors other than profit maximisation and how this might affect their behaviour.

16.2 Profit Maximisation and Alternative Motivations

The goal of profit maximisation provides the motivation in much of the economic theory of the firm. If firms do not maximise profits, it follows that they may not minimise costs or maximise revenue. There are reasons to question the realism of profit maximisation in health care provision in many parts of the world. In this section we explore alternatives to profit maximisation which can be found in the literature of the economic theory of the firm.

In the next section we will explore the insights this literature generates into the motivation and behaviour of health care providers.

16.2.1 Managerial theories of the firm

In many large firms the owners (shareholders) are not the managers. Owners effectively employ managers to act on their behalf. As with the doctor–patient relationship, principal–agent theory provides a useful framework to analyse the implications of this arrangement. Managers may act as imperfect agents for the owners and may pursue objectives other than profit maximisation. One model suggests that managers maximise revenue subject to a profitability constraint imposed by shareholders and possibly by the danger of takeover by another firm. There are several reasons why managers may maximise revenue:

1 Earnings of top managers tend to be related to sales.
2 Large sales give prestige to managers.
3 High revenue avoids having to make staff redundant.

The situation for a firm with some degree of monopoly power is reflected in Figure 16.1. Under profit maximisation managers would

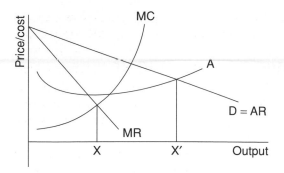

Figure 16.1 The firm under revenue maximisation

choose to produce at point X (where the excess of total revenue over total cost is greatest). If managers are attempting to maximise revenue subject to a 'break-even' profit constraint (profits must not fall below zero), they will choose a rather higher output level at X'. If the profit constraint is binding at some positive level, then the chosen output level will lie between X and X'.

Under perfect competition, managers cannot pursue non-profit-maximising strategies, as they would make losses and would be driven from the market. The degree to which managers are able to pursue objectives other than profit maximisation (i.e. their discretionary power) depends on the nature of the market within which they operate and the strength and nature of competition.

Revenue maximisation (like profit maximisation) may be an over-simplification of the objectives that the manager is likely to have. A more realistic theory is that managers maximise a managerial utility function (subject to constraints) and this contains a number of arguments. For example:

Managerial utility = f(Salary, security,
power, status)

Of these variables, only salary is easy to measure. Many economists dislike this kind

of model, since it is hard to derive clear predictions about behaviour.

Managerial theories have been applied in the health sector. Some studies have assumed revenue maximisation as the manager's objective, in some cases with a quality constraint. Others have compiled a rather more complex set of objectives. For example, Hornbrook and Goldfarb (1983) consider the following list of dimensions which they consider are important to the managers of US hospitals: level of emergency stand-by capacity, total admissions, the diagnostic mix of admissions and the hospital's 'style of practice' with respect to ancillary services and length of stay. It is suggested that different hospitals may attach different weights to these dimensions, depending on their particular utility function, but will try to maximise utility subject to constraints (such as the community's ability to pay for hospital care and community epidemiology). Health care providers with different types of ownership (public, private-for-profit, private non-profit) are likely to put different emphasis on these dimensions.

16.2.2 Behavioural theories of the firm

The managerial theories described above assume that the firm/health care provider has a single utility function. In contrast behavioural theories recognise that firms are made up of diverse sets of actors, who may not share the same goals. The firm (or hospital) therefore is treated not as a single decision-making unit but as one with multiple actors and objectives. There may be conflict between the goals of different individuals and groups within firms. The way in which firms behave depends upon the relative power of different actors and how the institutional arrangements within firms lead to conflict resolution.

The roots of behavioural theory are in the work of Herbert Simon (1957). Simon drew a distinction between substantive and procedural rationality. Economic theory is based on substantive or unbounded rationality, that is, rational agents are said to make decisions which maximise the achievement of their own goals, given existing constraints. Procedural rationality occurs when agents may not necessarily succeed in maximising their own goals but, given the relative importance of the decision, give it appropriate deliberation. Procedural rationality allows for the use of rule-of-thumb measures.

In the context of a hospital behaviour theory this approach has considerable appeal. Managers may have different objective functions from clinicians, different doctors may have different goals. Different types of agents may have control over different elements within the hospital (e.g. doctors may control the use of beds but managers may have control over how many beds can be managed by each doctor). How competing objective functions are reconciled is likely to depend on the internal structure of the organisation.

It was suggested earlier that there may be differences in objectives between provider institutions according to their ownership. Ownership may also affect the internal structure of hospitals and other provider institutions, and this may be another route through which ownership affects the behaviour of different health care providers.

16.3 *Models of Hospital Behaviour*

The development of hospital models can be seen to parallel the development of the theory of the firm (McGuire 1985). Some fall within the tradition of the profit-maximising firm. Others parallel the managerial theory of the firm where the hospital pursues managerial objectives. Still others parallel behavioural theories, where the concern of the model is with internal bargaining between rival interest groups within the hospital, rather than with the specification of an objective function for the purpose of predicting behaviour within the market place.

However, more recent models have applied composite objective functions consisting of both profit and managerial (or perhaps even clinical) objectives (for example, Ellis and McGuire 1986; Dranove 1988; Hodgkin and McGuire 1994). Pure profit maximisation and pure managerialism have given way to mixed-objective functions, and duopoly (or bilateral monopoly) models have been applied to doctor–manager bargaining (Muurinen 1986; Custer *et al.* 1990).

16.3.1 The hospital as a physicians' co-operative

Pauly and Redisch (1973) describe the not-for-profit hospital as a 'physicians' co-operative', implying that the objective function consists of the incomes of physicians who dominate among groups of hospital decision makers. This is the closest a model specifically focusing on hospital behaviour comes to espousing profit maximisation. In this model the full price of care is determined by consumer demand and the amount of care produced and offered to patients depends in turn on the quantity of inputs chosen by the decision makers (e.g. capital, labour and physician inputs).

In a model where the number of physicians is fixed (closed staff model) the hospital maximises net average revenue to physicians:

Net average revenue to physicians
$= (P.Q - rK - wL)/M$

where P is the total price for care, Q, r and w are the input prices of capital and labour and M is the number of physicians on staff. The hospital is viewed as a profit maximiser with all the residual profits given to the physicians as income, but the physicians are the decision makers.

The physicians may either follow the co-operative strategy, operating as a cartel, or follow a non-co-operative strategy. Within the co-operative strategy three possible sets of arrangements are considered: (1) the 'closed staff' model in which the physicians regulate their numbers in order to maximise average net revenue and each takes an equal share; (2) the 'discriminatory hiring' model in which some physicians are partners who share equally in the net revenue and other physicians are hired and paid their marginal product; (3) the 'open staff' model in which any physician wishing to join the hospital can do so and share equally in the net revenue.

Pauly and Redisch analyse optimal staffing from the point of view of the physicians in each of these sets of arrangements. An interesting result from their model is that an increase in demand could lead to higher price levels, lower output and fewer physicians, as the cartel seeks to maximise net revenue per physician (a result also found in models of soviet collective farms). Under the non-co-operative strategy the cartel breaks down (or never forms) if the incentive structure encourages the individual physician to free-ride. Pauly and Redisch (1973) suggest non-co-operation is more likely where there are larger numbers of physicians, and it results in a smaller number of physicians working in the hospital. By employing more non-physician labour and utilising other hospital inputs an individual physician might be able to charge a higher price for his/her own services. But this inflates hospital costs, reducing net revenues.

16.3.2 The quantity/quality non-profit theory

One prominent theory of hospital behaviour is that proposed by Newhouse (1970) to describe non-profit firms of all kinds. Under this theory, the objective of the hospital is to maximise utility. The hospital's preferences are defined over quantity of output (number of cases, etc.) and quality of output.

This objection function implies that a hospital will be prepared to make sacrifices in terms of quantity (for instance, number of patient days) in order to provide higher quality. This can be represented by an indifference curve. For each level of quality, the hospital faces a given demand curve and a given cost function. Increases in quality from low levels would bring increases in demand, as improved quality attracted patients. There would therefore be no trade-off at these low-quality levels. But at higher levels of quality the higher costs of provision would deter those with lower ability to pay, leading to a reduction in quantity of service provided. The result is the unconventionally shaped budget constraint of Figure 16.2. Chosen quantity–quality level is Ql*Qn*.

The model yields a number of predictions, including: least-cost production; a bias

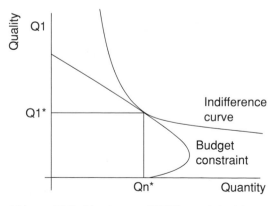

Figure 16.2 Newhouse (1970) model of hospital behaviour

towards high-quality services and away from low-quality services, even where the low-quality services would be in demand; duplication of equipment and capital intensity.

Newhouse's model is an example of a managerial approach, stressing the role of non-financial objectives and the decision-making influence of the manager rather than the clinician. Other examples of this approach include Reder (1965), Feldstein (1968), Lee (1971) and Joseph (1975). Feldstein assumes an objective of maximum output for a given quality; Rice assumes output maximisation; Reder models clinicians as quality maximisers and administrators as having a combined quality/quantity maximising objective related to prestige and salary; in Lee's model, managers are motivated by the prestige acquired for the institution through high-input utilisation; Joseph includes quality, quantity and also the number of patients turned away. What all have in common is that they are based on the specification of a utility function that consists of objectives defined in terms of quantity and/or quality of care provided. High on the list of human motives in these accounts of hospitals is the prestige felt by managers (and perhaps medical staff also) at working in an institution of high reputation.

16.3.3 The Harris model

The Newhouse model maximises the utility function of the managers in the hospital, whereas the Pauly–Redisch model assumes *de facto* control by physicians. The Harris model (Harris 1977) presents the hospital as a scene of continual conflict between two groups.

Harris describes the hospital as composed of two separate firms, rather than as a single firm. One of these firms is made up of medical staff, who comprise a demand division. The hospital administration comprises a second firm, or supply division. Harris views these two firms as quite separate structures: 'Each half of the organisation has its own managers, objectives, pricing strategies and constraints.' He describes the interaction of these two firms as a 'non-co-operative oligopoly-type game'. The level of spare capacity forms a key battleground. He writes:

I have in mind here a disequilibrium model in which everyone behaves as if the hospital is not big enough. The administration, on the one hand, wants the hospital filled. But the doctors want bigger defensive margins. The administration will expand capacity only if doctors can fill up the beds. Since there is internal conflict over the control of these defensive margins, doctors will expand utilisation and increase quality to obtain their share. As a result, the administration will tolerate the creation and perpetuation of these separate empires even though it negates the advantages of risk pooling.

In Harris's discussion the doctors would seem to be the more powerful group. But, despite his emphasis on conflict, his conclusions are in fact similar to those of Newhouse: quantity and quality dominate in the objectives which the conflict results in the hospital pursuing. This discussion predicts conflict over the level of spare capacity and a tendency to expand (given a soft budget constraint).

The model offers an explanation of the expansionist tendencies of US health care in the 1970s and 1980s, which are a key concern of the next section. The model also offers some other perspectives which may be useful for policy making and regulation of the hospital sector. First, given the role of physicians, we can expect that the hospitals' preferences for technologies will be driven by the preferences of the physician demanders. Second, hospital regulation aimed primarily at the trustee–administrator group may have little effect. Regulation to limit hospital costs must establish incentives for and constraints on the physician-agent as well as the administrator.

Harris's model is an example of a behavioural model which is concerned with the potential for conflict in the objective functions pursued by different decision makers within the organisation. Models of internal bargaining in hospitals described in Muurinen (1986) also fall into this category, as do the models of Custer *et al.* (1990), who describe the relationship between hospitals and their medical staffs as variously 'non-co-operative', 'co-operative' or 'dominant–reactive', and consider the implications of prospective and retrospective reimbursement under each characterisation of the relationship.

16.4 The Relevance of these Models to Provider Institutions in other Health Systems

These models all originate in the US and thus describe the consequences of incentive structures common there. Since these provide a snapshot of provider institutions operating in perhaps the most private sector-oriented health system in the world (see Part IV), it is useful to consider the relevance of these models to different types of hospital environment, taking public hospitals in publicly oriented health systems as the opposite case.

While some of the models focus particularly on the not-for-profit hospital (e.g. Newhouse), in general there are difficulties in applying this body of work to public hospitals operating in public health systems. There is clearly a range of differences which might be considered. For example, in a public system the payment mechanism for the hospital does not usually permit payment to vary with activity levels in contrast to arrangements on which the models described above are based, where the majority of care is funded through cost-per-case and fee-for-service contracts. Similarly, in contrast to the US situation, salary reimbursement is the more common means of paying individual health professionals. With respect to the internal hospital budgeting process, in traditional public budgeted systems, financial administration is usually centralised. Individual departments have limited control over their allocation or use of resources.

To some extent the models described above can be adapted. For example, in the absence of a payment–activity relation, the upward-sloping part of Newhouse's budget constraint (Figure 16.2) is eliminated. An objective function represented by an indifference curve reconciling the trade-off between quantity and quality through tangency with a normally shaped budget constraint could be proposed. However, differences between the two operating environments may have implications for the objective function itself. Might such hospitals maximise quality subject to the relevant constraints? The other models suggest some alternative possibilities for the objective function which might predict something different. Under fixed physician salaries, the physician-income or profit-maximisation model of Pauly and Redisch is excluded, but the possibility that doctors' interests are pre-eminent, resulting in maximisation of doctors' objective functions, or factors closely associated with medical promotion criteria, are not ruled out. This might translate to the unwarranted selection (for example, judged by cost-effectiveness criteria) of research-valuable patients, for instance. Alternatively, where they work in both public and private sectors, decisions which benefit physicians' parallel private practices might dominate. Where there is conflict between the objective functions of doctors and managers and both have significant influence on decision making, conflict focusing on resource use within the hospital might ensue, similar to that described by Harris.

However, given the differences in incentive structures, the balance of tension between the two 'firms' is likely to be different. To conclude that the model of Harris applies because some kind of tension is apparent can provide only a starting point to an understanding of hospital behaviour in public systems.

16.5 Models of Hospital Behaviour and Health Policy

Why do we want to better understand the motivations and therefore behaviour of hospitals or other health service providers? Much of the content of health policy is designed to influence the behaviour of health service providers. For example, changes in hospital reimbursement mechanisms have usually been designed in order to change the incentives facing hospitals and therefore their behaviour – perhaps on the assumption that provider institutions are profit or revenue maximising. The introduction of separation between purchasers and providers seems to assume that providers will respond to market forces by trying to improve the quality and efficiency with which they offer services – but why should they, if profit maximisation is not their objective? Even interventions such as in-service training programmes designed to improve the appropriateness of care provided, or attempts to improve management information systems, assume a particular set of motivations. In these cases, perhaps the assumption is that hospital decision makers will strive to make the most technically appropriate decisions if only they are provided with the necessary

technical skills and information – in other words, that they are the perfect agents of their patients, or even of society. On the basis of the insights provided by the hospital models presented in this chapter, all these assumptions appear rather simplistic. In order to manage incentives, it is important to understand motivation.

One example of the application of the kinds of models discussed in this chapter to these kinds of policy concern is a study by Ellis and McGuire (1986), who use this type of model to explain how hospitals responded to the introduction by the Medicare programme in the US in 1983 of prospective reimbursement for hospital services. Their model is set up within a principal–agent framework (see Chapter 18) under which the doctors are considered as agents to two principals, the patient and the hospital. Imperfect agency (in the doctor–patient relationship) results in two adverse outcomes, depending on the payment scheme. Under retrospective hospital reimbursement, there is a danger that doctors will be induced to over-treat in order to boost hospital net revenue. Under prospective payment, the incentive might be to under-treat. The incentives provided by these payment schemes lead to agency costs in the form of inefficiency. They propose a solution in the form of mixed reimbursement comprising both prospective and retrospective payments. They argue that a mixed-reimbursement scheme is more likely to lead to an efficient level of supply, fewer inappropriate admissions, more appropriate competition between hospitals, and less 'DRG creep' (see Chapter 14.5).

It is useful to view the various models we have reviewed above through the lens of principal–agent theory (see also Chapter 18). Agency relationships between the payer and the hospital, and between the hospital and its employees, are both of interest. The objective of hospital reform may be to reconcile the objective functions of principals, agents and the goals of social welfare. The problem is to align incentives so that the tension between the objective functions of doctors and managers produces hospital behaviour approaching that consistent with maximisation of social welfare as closely as possible.

The Newhouse approach can be seen as one in which there is implicitly a fairly (but not perfectly) successful alignment of incentives of the behaviour of the hospital with social objectives. (The hospital aims at balancing quantity and quality, but with overemphasis on quality relative to the efficient solution.) However, under the Harris account of hospitals, where the hospital is essentially split into two firms, the agency problem appears more pronounced, with considerable costs associated with the active conflict between the two groups. Managers find themselves giving way to more powerful doctors, presumably with considerable social welfare costs. The model described by Pauly and Redisch is one in which the hospital, dominated by doctors who pursue their own ends, is likely to be very far from an effective incentive alignment.

Custer *et al.* (1990) argue that the degree of incentive alignment between hospital and doctor determines the efficiency of production. Such an alignment may imply productive efficiency, but this alignment may not necessarily be one that improves social welfare. Internal incentive alignment may be a necessary, but not sufficient, condition for improving social efficiency.

Within public health system structures, there is evidence to suggest that public sector hospitals in the UK, and in other parts of the

world (for instance, Zimbabwe: Hongoro 2001), are, and have been, largely controlled by doctors. Strong and Robinson (1990) described the UK reforms of 1974 as institutionalising a system of medical syndicalism, in which contracts between the health service and its medical staff specified very little, and distributed residual power largely to doctors.

Both Sloan (1980) and McGuire (1985) have suggested that hospital behaviour cannot be explained by a single model. A focus on the agency relationship and property rights implicit in the contractual arrangements that constitute the hospital helps explain what makes hospitals different from one another and how they might change in response to changes in their environment. Transformation in the hospital sector in the US brought with it a new set of hospital models in which prospective payment systems replaced retrospective, cost-based reimbursement (Ellis and McGuire 1986; Dranove 1988; Custer *et al.* 1990; Hodgkin and McGuire 1994).

This highlights a key difference between the 'theory of the hospital' and the 'theory of the firm'. While the alternative models of firm behaviour which were used to introduce the chapter are viewed as permanent descriptions which can predict the firms' response to changing conditions (such as price, or level of competition), models of hospital behaviour themselves change in response to changing conditions. For example, prospective reimbursement might better align the objective functions of hospital managers and physicians, and consequently a behavioural model such as that of Harris might give way to a managerial model. In other words the reform might lead to a single objective function better characterising the hospital.

Chapter 17

The Economics of Regulation

17.1 Introduction

The economic rationale for regulation arises from market failure. As we have seen repeatedly, perfect markets produce efficient outcomes. Therefore, if inefficient outcomes are observed, they must stem from market failure. The aim of regulation is to correct market failure on the understanding that if one market distortion exists, introducing another (regulation) can lead to efficiency improvement – the theory of the second best which was introduced in Chapter 6. Given the extensive failures of health markets as introduced in Chapters 7 and 8, it is unsurprising that health markets are among the most extensively regulated in most economies.

Regulation may also arise to correct inequity, although, as discussed in Chapter 1, it is usually rather difficult to disentangle inequities from inefficiencies in health markets. Most observed inequities (for example, lack of access to care for part of the population) are also inefficiencies (a failure of the health system to address high-priority demands from a social welfare perspective). For this reason we will not separately address efficiency-focused regulation and equity-focused regulation, although it is clear that some of the regulations we describe below address both kinds of problem.

17.2 What is Regulation?

Regulation may be thought to occur when a government/state exerts control over the activities of individuals and firms (Roemer 1993). The exact 'action' is described as the *regulatory intervention* or *regulatory mechanism*. Interventions that are used to affect variables such as price and quantity can be categorised as being either:

1 *Legal restrictions or controls* where participants must conform to legislated requirements. If participants do not abide by these laws, they will face punishment.
2 *Incentives* to which participants change their behaviour and lead to changes in the target variable. These incentives could take both monetary and non-monetary forms, and may be used in the context of both government and non-government roles.
3 *Incentive regulation* is a further extension of the use of incentives. The use of incentive regulation can be thought of as 'rules' which regulate the relationship of

verifiable outcomes such as price (Laffont and Tirole 1993). Here rewards or punishments are related to observed behaviour.

These definitions are broad, and include market interventions such as taxes and subsidies as well as rules that are legislated or set by administrative fiat. In this chapter we will largely concern ourselves with the second kind of regulation (legislated or administratively set rules) – though in principle other kinds of market intervention are also 'rules'. For example, a tax is a rule that a particular activity carries a particular penalty, even if the intention is not punitive.

In addition to these formal rules, more informal codes of conduct, guidelines or recommendations may exist. Formal rules mix formal rule setting and explicit contractual agreements. Informal regulation is a system which uses co-operation between parties (e.g. health professionals, the Ministry of Health and other interested parties) to achieve outcomes (Mackintosh 1997). Interventions in this case may be the development of good practice norms, for example. These informal rules are not binding on the regulated (Moran and Wood 1993). There may also be 'informal controls' which occur through day-to-day social interaction. People behave in accordance with social rewards such as the approval or disapproval of others (Allsop and Mulcahy 1996; Lindbeck 1997).

17.3 Regulation in the Health Sector

The key roles that regulation can play within the health sector (Allsop and Mulcahy 1996) are:

1 control of market entry and exit;
2 control of competitive practices;
3 control of market organisation;

4 control of remuneration;
5 control of standards/quality;
6 ensuring safety.

Each of these may be explained in terms of the correction of one or more market failure. The first three respond to concerns regarding the implications of monopolistic market structure (although some kinds of controls over entry may create problems of monopoly – see section 17.4.1 below). The fourth, control of remuneration, may respond to a number of different market failures. This measure may correct for monopoly power, it may aim to motivate providers through rewarding particular desired features of performance, or it may involve the use of monopsonist power to hold wages and health services costs downwards. The last two, control of standards and quality, and ensuring safety, aim to correct for information asymmetry problems. If consumers cannot observe standards, quality and safety features, there is a case for expert inspection or review.

The extensive size of private sector activity and deliberate policies promoting it, especially in low-income countries, have led to the increasing 'marketisation' of the health sector and a concomitant need for stronger regulation (Bennett *et al.* 1994).

Figure 17.1 explores three dimensions related to regulation: what to regulate, who to regulate and how to regulate. The figure shows three levels at which target variables may be addressed by regulation, together with the nature of the instruments used. The 'what to regulate' is reflected by a range of target variables, described in terms of entry, quality, quantity, price, distribution and competitive practices. The choice of 'who to regulate' must encompass successively complex levels in the provision of services, addressing individual inputs such as unqualified drug sellers and

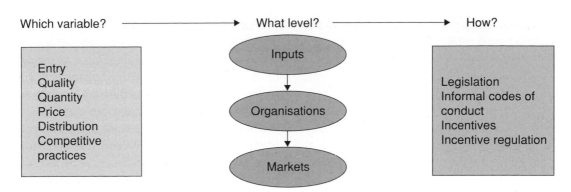

Which variable? ──────────▶ What level? ──────────▶ How?

Entry
Quality
Quantity
Price
Distribution
Competitive
practices

Inputs

Organisations

Markets

Legislation
Informal codes of
conduct
Incentives
Incentive regulation

Figure 17.1 The process of regulating
Source: Kumaranayake *et al.* (2000).

licensed pharmaceutical retailers, organisations such as solo physician practices, hospitals, nursing homes and the market in general. The levels are obviously linked (for example, combinations of inputs create organisations) and a number of organisations coexist in the market. The 'how' to regulate refers to the instruments used to affect these variables, and are described later in this chapter.

The target variables can apply at different levels and are aimed at different actors within the health sector. Entry refers to initial acceptance into the market. There are issues regarding entry at each level:

1 the entry of individual inputs to the organisation: the selection of personnel, drugs, or medical equipment;
2 the entry of organisations to the market: licensing of facilities, clinics and individuals.

Quantity regulation can be used to affect the volume of inputs in health service provision (for example, 'certificate of need' laws restricting the purchase of equipment or facility development); restrictions on the number of organisations (for example, limits on the number of private clinics which will be granted licences within a given area); or the promotion of an increased number of providers in

the market through anti-monopoly legislation. Quality regulation refers to standard setting and quality assurance, and covers such areas as quality control of drugs and approved curricula for the training of health professionals. Price regulation includes the articulation of minimum salary levels of health workers and the setting of fees for the provision of particular services. Regulation of distribution may set quotas so as to locate health professionals in under-served areas. Regulation of competitive practices aims to reduce adverse outcomes from anti-competitive behaviour. In practice, these areas may interact and even conflict for example, regulations aimed at ensuring a minimum quality of services or goods in a market also work to restrict entry into the market.

The third dimension in Figure 17.1 is the 'how' of regulating and refers to the manner in which regulation is undertaken, i.e. the nature of the regulatory instruments. These instruments range from formal legal controls enacted through legislation providing for sanctions if the regulations are not followed to informal codes of practice or policy guidelines. A second way of regulating is through the creation of incentives, both financial (whether a tax or a subsidy) and non-financial, aimed at encouraging participants to change their behaviour. A more formalised approach to incentives is seen in the use of incentive regulation, which can be thought of as rules which use verifiable outcomes such as market prices to affect individual participant's behaviour (e.g. prices can only rise by some proportion of market price). This is often seen in the regulation of utilities (such as energy and telecommunications) in industrialised countries (Abbott and Crew 1995).

17.4 Review of Regulatory Mechanisms

This section reviews the performance of regulatory mechanisms that have been used in the health sector. Most are legislative. Regulatory mechanisms chosen must depend on the structure of the health care (e.g. the way it is organised, and how health care is produced and distributed). Within a health system there are many markets – for instance, the market for supplies, for medical equipment and for services. The appropriateness of any given regulation is specific to the system and market under consideration.

17.4.1 Entry

The licensing of professionals before they are allowed to be employed in the sector is one of the earliest forms of regulation (the professional guilds of the Middle Ages served a similar function). Licensing serves to regulate the labour input into the production of health care services for all professions involved in health care.

The rationale for licensing is that consumers are unable to judge for themselves the quality of the professionals they seek services from. An expert evaluation of competence to practise which can be clearly signalled

provides information with public good characteristics (see Chapter 8), since the information is non-rival. There is therefore a rationale for a collectively organised licensing system. In theory, licensing can provide two types of information about quality: it can certify that the licensed person has obtained a sufficient level of knowledge and it can provide information about the performance of individuals. In reality, the first type of information is a much more common feature of licensing systems. The second type is usually provided only in relation to extreme cases, in the form of provision to de-register those established to under-perform grossly. It is also sometimes provided more routinely – for example, where mandatory refresher courses run by professional organisations are a prerequisite of continued registration.

However, licensing also restricts entry to the market. Organised professional groups may use licensing to promote their own interests by limiting entry and reducing competition (e.g. by raising licensing standards for potential entrants). This will allow them to earn economic rents (monetary return which is greater than what is necessary to persuade them to supply their services), as shown in Figure 17.2. In this case, the licensing causes a restriction

Figure 17.2 Potential impact of licensing requirements on physician income

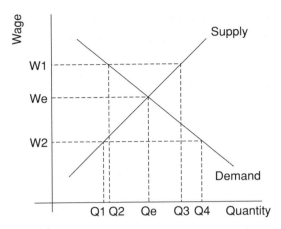

Figure 17.3 Price control in a competitive market

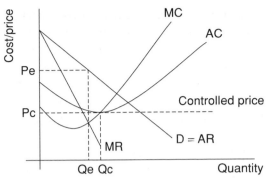

Figure 17.4 Price control in a monopolistic market

17.4.2 Prices

One approach to controlling prices or fees charged is through the negotiation of payment schedules between government and professional associations. This approach is contingent on the relative power of the negotiating parties. Figure 17.3 shows the impact of price control on the market for nurses. This analysis suggests that shortages or surpluses are likely to arise in the relevant labour market in response to price control, depending on the relationship between the controlled price and the equilibrium. If the equilibrium is at wage We and quantity Qe, if the controlled wage is

in supply, and so the likely wage that physicians who are in the market is much higher than if there were no supply restrictions. Leffler (1978) attempts to estimate these rents for American physicians and argues that they are not as high as might be expected. Many countries have requirements to register facilities before they can open. In order to register, facilities such as hospitals, clinics and nursing homes must meet minimum standards established in the registration legislation.

at W1, a surplus of nurses Q3–Q2 results. However, if the controlled wage is at W2, a shortage of nurses Q4–Q1 results.

However, Figure 17.3 relies on an assumption of an underlying competitive market characterised by an upward-sloping supply curve. Suppose instead the input for which price is controlled is supplied through a monopolistic market. Price controls might then be intended to imitate the price that would result from a perfect market. Regulators may aim to set price at the minimum point of the average cost curve, or, as is common for regulated utilities, at the marginal cost of production. Since there is no supply curve, this does not necessarily create any shortage or surplus of the input in question. The intended effect is to force the monopolist to price-take, rather than price-set, and thereby to induce the monopolist to supply in accordance with the marginal cost curve. In Figure 17.4 a price control which reduces the equilibrium price from Pe to Pc results in the monopolist increasing production of the service or input from Qe to Qc. In the UK price regulations mandate marginal cost pricing for NHS trust hospitals – although the absence of cost information makes this a very difficult regulation to enforce.

In insurance-based systems, consumers do not face prices as such, but there is extensive rate regulation which establishes the terms under which public and private insurers pay hospitals and other providers. American physicians are reimbursed under Medicare at the prevailing rates for services in the area. In addition, volume-type standards have been put in place.

17.4.3 Quantity

Quantity restrictions are common. Controls have been put on staff levels, operational budgets, equipment, physician training and even on patient numbers. Motivated by the need to reduce costs and to prevent duplication of services, *certificate of need* (CON) laws have been used to control the construction of new capital facilities, gross investment in new equipment, expansion of special services and the purchase of expensive equipment such as CT and MRI scanners in the US. CON laws require that state agencies approve the entry of new hospitals, expansion/ modernisation of hospitals and provision of services. By 1979 almost all states had enacted some form of CON law.

The rationale for CON laws is that natural market forces lead to excess capacity and cost inflation. One model of competitive behaviour which predicts this is the quality competition model (see Chapter 15). However, an unintended effect of CON laws is that they may reduce competition in the provision of services, leading to increased monopoly power and price increases. Some studies suggest that hospitals favour CON laws on the basis that they protect them from competition (Campbell and Fournier 1993).

Regulation of particular hospital inputs makes those inputs more expensive. For example, a case may need to be prepared to argue for a licence to purchase a particular input incurring transaction costs, or other hospitals may need to be 'bought off' from making a competing bid. The impact is to alter the relative prices of different inputs in the production function. Hospitals will therefore substitute non-regulated inputs for regulated ones, again offsetting cost reduction. To the extent that the regulation intends that less use is made of the regulated input, this is the effect desired. However, understanding the mechanisms through which hospitals will respond to regulation highlights the need for regulations to be carefully 'fine-tuned', since inefficient substitutions may also result. If certificates of need are issued on the basis that existing treatment profiles justify replacement or expansion of equipment, there is a danger that perverse incentives to over-treat using the given technology will be reinforced rather than undermined by the regulation (Abbott and Crew 1995).

17.4.4 Quality

Quality is not unidimensional. For example, good quality requires appropriate facilities and equipment, short waiting times, good clinical outcomes, timely and accurate information and good food.

Accreditation is one mechanism which aims to assess and ensure quality. Originating in the US, accreditation occurs when an independent agency defines and monitors the standards of facilities that voluntarily participate in the scheme (Scrivens *et al.* 1995). Accreditation was originally developed by physicians to support improvements to conditions in hospitals and was seen as an instrument of self-education.

However, accreditation has evolved to serve a control function in the US while still acting as a process of peer review in other countries.

In the US accreditation became linked with hospitals receiving funds from Medicare. During this process, the concept of accreditation based on 'minimal standards' was upgraded to being based on 'achievable optimal standards'. Currently more than 80 per cent of American hospitals are accredited. The Accreditation Committee which assesses the facilities is comprised mainly of health professionals and has a few consumer representatives. Accreditation occurs in a peer review context in Australia, Switzerland, Spain, Italy and Brazil.

Accreditation provides a way for hospitals to 'signal' improved quality based on accepted standards and may thus limit the need for excessive investment in high-technology products in a market characterised by quality competition (see Chapter 15). Accreditation systems could be developed for facilities other than hospitals such as private clinics.

The use of quality registers has also been discussed in terms of quality assurance. In contrast to accreditation, which is quite macro in nature, generating a summary statistic for the entire facility, the quality registers operate at a micro level. Their purpose is to help various specialisms to control quality by comparing their performance with overall specialism averages. Participation is voluntary and the register can be disease or method oriented. Such 'league table' approaches have been criticised in other contexts, however. Devoid of context they may be as misleading as they are helpful. For example, evidence that a specialism group in a large hospital is a particularly heavy user of a technology may not be very helpful if possible case-mix differences are not well understood. Case mix is influenced by the mix of alternative providers and their sub-specialisms and the structure and functioning of referral relationships as well as by the designated role of an institution in the health system.

The approach has characteristics similar to systems of 'performance indicators' systems which have sometimes been exercises in peer review, sometimes linked with financial rewards, and sometimes part of a 'naming and shaming' exercise. There has been interest in and experimentation with such systems in the UK, where a set of performance indicators was compiled in the 1980s, and where a system of rating hospital and health authority performance on a league table basis was published in 2000. These tables have been criticised for failing to take account of context, and for showing a close correlation between socio-economic deprivation and poor health service performance.[1]

Complaints mechanisms provide another opportunity for quality regulation. Many countries have provision for recourse in the face of medical malpractice or negligence. However, there has been limited use of this in most countries, in contrast to the litigious environment of the US. Self-regulating professional bodies are hesitant to impair their professional reputation. In response to this phenomenon, there seems to be a swing towards complaints mechanisms which involve or are controlled by non-professionals, much to the displeasure of the medical professionals (Bartlett 1996). In India the Consumer Protection Act of 1986 attempted to strengthen the rights of consumers and their ability to seek redress through the courts in cases of medical malpractice. Bhat (1996) reviews experience under this legislation but concludes that such measures are not in themselves sufficient to significantly impact poor quality of care in the private sector. For example, 71 per cent of cases filed in the state of Gujarat were decided in favour of the defendant, complainants faced considerable difficulty in getting experts to support their cases, and half the outstanding cases at the time of the review were 'pending'.

All these regulatory mechanisms aim to induce providers to choose higher levels of quality. They either aim to exploit providers' interest in pursuit of profit to do this, or to exploit providers' interest in quality for its own sake, which follows from the identification of motivation in some of the alternative models of hospitals described in Chapter 16. If quality *per se* is the motivation of health service providers, regulation will not be necessary, since providers will anyway maximise quality within the constraints of their market. However, if the quality emphasised in hospital managers' objective functions favours particular dimensions which are observable to outsiders, the attempt to render otherwise unobservable characteristics observable (for example, through accreditation) makes sense.

Operating on the assumption of the profit motive, regulatory mechanisms can focus on the demand side – aiming to increase consumers' willingness to pay for higher-quality providers, for example. Such mechanisms must be successful in shifting the demand curve to the point where it becomes more profitable to provide high-quality care, or they will not succeed in increasing quality care in the market. This is likely to be particularly difficult in low-income economies.

Alternatively, they can focus on the supply side, aiming to make it more expensive to provide poor-quality than good-quality care – by increasing the chances that poor-quality care will result in compensation payments in medical negligence cases, for example. In that case the average costs associated with making compensation payments must more than account for the difference in cost between offering low and high standards of care.

Different approaches are likely to favour particular features of health markets and address different kinds of quality concern. Increasing the viability of litigation is likely to influence only the worst instances of medical malpractice, while an accreditation system addresses only those aspects of quality it is able to measure through its monitoring system.

17.4.5 Pharmaceuticals

Many countries have agencies that approve whether drugs can enter the market, the purposes for which the drug can be used (for which diseases doctors can prescribe the drug), and even the information contained in the drug package when it is sold. Regulations in most industrialised countries require drug manufacturers to establish not only the safety of the new drug but also its efficacy and even its cost-effectiveness. The process of approval is often long and costly.

In contrast to the considerable regulation of drug safety and efficacy, no comparable regulation exists for new non-pharmaceutical treatments (like keyhole surgery), and treatments which were standard practice before the introduction of the regulation are not subjected to the same evaluation. Thus while market entry is controlled in the case of drug treatment, there are no constraints on other new interventions. This distorts the economic incentives regarding these alternative forms of therapy, probably tipping us towards 'too much surgery' and not enough 'pharmaceutical treatment'. This is a relevant comparison for many diseases for which either surgical or non-surgical intervention is indicated.

A second type of regulation tries to restrict monopoly profits thought to be enjoyed by the pharmaceutical industry. Price controls are often suggested as a remedy. We have already considered some simple models of the effect of price regulation in section 17.4.2 above. The pharmaceutical industry argues that price controls, by inhibiting profit potential, stifle investment in research and development. Taking the monopoly model used in section 17.4.2, it is reasonable to suggest that applying a marginal cost pricing rule to the pharmaceutical sector would diminish interest in speculative investment in research and development, since the normal profits which result can be achieved without such investment. Patent-protection law recognises monopoly profit as a reward for successful research and development and as providing necessary incentives. However, this need not be accepted as an argument against all price control. Drug company profitability is the third highest of any economic sector in the US, expenditure on advertising and political lobbying is typically higher than on research and development, and much research and development into new drugs is financed publicly (Bond 1999). This may suggest that the failure to regulate to control pharmaceutical prices owes as much to 'public choice' explanations of regulatory practice, to which we now turn, as to 'public interest' ones.

17.5 From Theory to Practice

Up to this point we have considered regulation through a 'public interest' approach – from the perspective of an enlightened government serving the public interest. Each of the areas of regulation has been addressed from the perspective of its potential to improve on the outcomes of the market.

'Public choice' theory suggests that regulation, as it is practised, is the result of the bargaining, power play and self-interest of the actors who are involved or involve themselves in the regulatory industry. The theory, first developed by Stigler (1971), and further developed by Peltzman (1976) and Becker (1983), suggests that regulation is the result of the interaction of special interest groups who provide financial and political support in return for favourable legislation. The cost of securing regulatory change is high whereas the amount of effort and resources that any group will expend will depend on the probable gains (rents) that group can capture as a result of the legislation.

For the general public, the effect of any given regulatory change is very small whereas for special interest groups it is very high. There will therefore be uneven investment in securing regulatory change by the groups affected. Special interest groups will devote considerable resources while the general public will take little interest. This results in 'regulatory capture'. Those organisations and individuals which a public interest motivation of regulation seeks to regulate take control of the regulatory process. The theory therefore predicts that the impact of regulation is to redistribute wealth away from the general public and towards special interest groups, and that, as the power of special interest groups changes, legislation will change over time.

From this perspective, far from improving on market outcomes, regulation may reduce welfare. This model is an example of a model of government failure that we came across at the end of Chapter 6. The interaction between voters, special interest groups, politicians and bureaucrats leads to public choices which will not improve (and may worsen) efficiency or equity relative to an unregulated market.

From a public-choice perspective, doctors can also be seen as economic participants with skills to sell as well as being part of a special interest group with interests to defend

Box 17.1 Public or Self-interest?

Studies have attempted to test empirically the relevance of these theories to the health sector. Paul (1984) looked at the timing of the decision to license physicians by different states. He found a strong negative relationship between the year of licensure and the *per capita* number of physicians in a state, and interpreted this as rejecting the public interest theory. However, the interpretation of this is difficult. The observed relationship could mean that the physician lobby was strong enough to demand licensure.

Moran and Wood (1993) suggest that US doctors lacked power to influence state governments with respect to licensing (which would be in its self-interest because it would restrict entry) owing to their lack of social standing and authority. In contrast, UK doctors were organised early (1518) and developed a self-regulatory body which limited entry and dominated the supply of services. Aljunid (1995) suggests that in many low- and middle-income countries professional organisations pushed for licensure or registration in order to control entry to the profession.

While there seems to be quite mixed evidence, it seems reasonable to suggest that most governments are likely to formulate government policy for both public and self-interest reasons. This suggests that the impact of regulation will in some cases improve efficiency or equity, but in other cases interventions will yield a cost to the public as a whole and lead to inefficient and inequitable allocation of resources. Each case of regulation is worthy of analysis with respect to its impact on social welfare, and this may be understood in terms of either public interest or public choice theories.

or pursue (Moran and Wood 1993). From this perspective regulation can be viewed as a constraint or control but also as an opportunity to secure income or power. Box 17.1 discusses self- and public-interest perspectives further.

Even from a public-interest perspective, there are a number of reasons why the implementation of regulatory intervention may not lead to the desired gain:

1 *Transaction costs.* The traditional analysis assumes that there are no transaction or other operating costs of implementing, monitoring and enforcing the regulatory intervention. In practice the regulatory process can become both cumbersome and bureaucratic. In the extreme, parallel state machinery can be created with a large staff, lobby groups emerge to pressure regulators on behalf of interested parties and

further groups may emerge to counter the influence of these.

2 *Rent-seeking behaviour.* Theory suggests that once a regulation is implemented (regardless of the cost), the desired outcome is achieved. However, this does not take into account the response of those being regulated. In situations where large rents (profits) are being made, providers will attempt to protect those rents and this rent-seeking behaviour may lead to adverse consequences. For example, increasing cigarette taxes may spur the growth of a black market which may ultimately reduce the price of cigarettes to the end user and reduce the revenue from the tax.

3 *Informational asymmetries.* The regulator will to a large extent be dependent on the regulated organisation to provide information about the firm. The firm is in a position

to delay or mislead the regulator by delaying the transmission of data or by presenting inaccurate information.

It is therefore difficult to predict the impact of regulatory intervention without knowledge of market structure, cost conditions and objectives of firms. 'Dead-weight loss due to high profits, rent seekers, transaction costs, asymmetries of information, economies of scale and moral hazard issues represent barriers to creating an efficient health care delivery system through a regulatory model' (Liss 1995).

Note

1. 'Warning over hospital ranking system', *Guardian*, Wednesday 6 December 2000.

Chapter 18

Incentives and Agency

....

18.1 Introduction

Throughout the book we have referred extensively to incentives – but we have rather taken their meaning and implications for granted. This chapter takes a closer look at what we mean by incentives, and develops the framework of principal–agent theory through which incentives operate. Sections 18.6–9 go on to review the difficulties of managing the mix of incentives that are present in any context, and some examples of policy measures which can be used to intervene in the incentive environment in the health sector.

18.2 What is an Incentive?

For economists, the nature of incentives is the driving rationale behind observed market behaviour. Economic incentives are defined as allowing 'individuals to behave in accordance with expected material rewards or favours that can be traded for such rewards including leisure'. This can be contrasted to social norms where people behave in accordance with social rewards such as approval or disapproval of others (Lindbeck 1997).

Incentives are present in every situation. For example, the market provides a set of incentives to a firm. If the firm is profit maximising, these incentives result in the firm aiming to minimise its production costs. This argument is by now very familiar. In Chapter 16 we suggested that some firms, including hospitals, might pursue objectives other than profit maximisation. In some of the models examined there, the owners of the firm were still assumed to wish to maximise profits. However, the managers, as the imperfect agents of the owners, might pursue other objectives. This suggests that in any departure from an owner-operated business without employees the assumption that the market provides all the relevant incentives is flouted. In most contexts, therefore, incentives can be understood only within a principal–agent framework.

18.3 Further Insights from Agency Theory

We have already encountered the principal–agent idea in the context of doctor–patient relations (Chapter 7). Although the problem there deserves special attention, as it is at the centre of all types of health service provision, in practice principal–agent relations are ubiquitous. Within the health system, for example, there is an agency relationship between the Ministry of Health and a health authority or local government authority with health responsibilities. There is an agency relationship between a hospital manager and hospital employees. Sometimes agency relations operate in both directions between two organisations. For example, national medical associations are the agents of doctors who employ them to advance the interests of the profession, but individual doctors are also agents of the associations, in upholding standards and the good name of the profession. Wherever there is an agency relationship there is an explicit or implicit contract (see Chapter 14) and, within that, a set of incentives through which the principal aims to direct the agent to act on her behalf.

Where these contracts and incentives are implicit, it is interesting to consider their nature and effectiveness. For example, how does the Ministry of Health try to direct local health authorities to deliver on its policy measures? Sometimes there are quite explicit measures – for example, financial penalties for failing to deliver against target performance measures. However, the systems are often subtle and may be unobservable to outsiders. They are sometimes hidden in the trading of political favours, or well-understood criteria for promotion (or dismissal, or for relegation to a dead-end post) which may not be written down.

The combination of *agency* and *information problems* (information asymmetry combined with uncertainty or risk) produces interesting economic problems. Where information is perfect, principals easily specify the actions required from agents to secure payment. As in the doctor–patient relationship, problems arise when one party is privy to information and the other is not. (We will concern ourselves with problems where information is 'impacted' in the agent, or 'asymmetric' on the agent's side.)

The standard set-up for principal–agent problems contains the following components (Strong and Waterson 1987):

1 The principal delegates to the agent responsibility for selecting and implementing an action.
2 The agent is compensated by the principal.
3 The principal is the 'residual claimant' to the outcome of the agent's actions.
4 The principal's problem is to negotiate a contract which specifies the agent's remuneration, knowing interests are not in complete harmony.
5 Both agents and principals select from the alternatives on the basis of their utility functions.

18.4 Moral Hazard

Strong and Waterson (1987) give the following numerical example of moral hazard which enables us to understand the nature of moral hazard and the problems it causes:

> Moral hazard arises where there is shared information up to the point of selection of an action. The principal does not observe the action – only the uncertain 'pay-off'.

There are three possible 'states of the world' (s1, s2 and s3) that have an equal probability of occurrence. The pay-off from actions a1 and a2 depend on the states of the world according to Table 18.1. (Note that there are no circumstances in which the pay-off reveals the action with certainty.) The utility functions of the two parties are assumed to be:

Table 18.1 Example of situation giving rise to moral hazard

	s1	s2	s3
a1	£60,000	£60,000	£30,000
a2	£30,000	£60,000	£30,000

$$U_P = f - z$$
$$U_A = z^{0.5} - a^2$$

where f = pay-off, z = agent's pay and a = effort associated with action. Action $a1$ costs the agent more than $a2$ in effort: $a1$ requires six units of effort; $a2$ requires four units. The agent has a 'reservation utility' of 114 – this is the minimum for which she will work for this principal.

If the action could be observed, the reservation utility could be achieved with a flat rate payment of £22,500 and the principal simply directing the agent to take action $a1$ in return for the payment. Set the agent's utility function equal to 114 in the case of action $a1$ ($a = 6$):

$$U_A = Z^{0.5} - a^2 = 114$$
$$Z^{0.5} - 36 = 114$$
$$Z^{0.5} = 150$$
$$z = 22,500$$

Under these circumstances, the principal's utility level is 27,500 and the agent's 114. (The agent does not have the option of pursuing $a2$ since his action is observed, but if he did, the principal's utility would decline to 17,500, and the agent's increase to 134 – this illustrates the agent's incentive and the cost to the principal of failing to design an outcome-dependent contract.) Figure 18.1 shows how the agent's utility responds to income without any effort, and under effort levels $a1$ and $a2$. The result above simply sets the $a1$ function equal to 114.

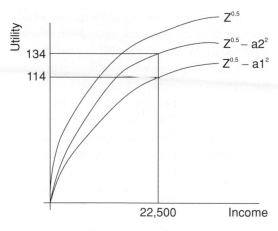

Figure 18.1 The agent's utility function

Given action unobservability, the principal's problem is to define an outcome-dependent contract that provides the agent with the incentive to pursue action $a1$. The problem is to derive the basic and bonus salaries that will make the agent indifferent between actions $a1$ and $a2$, and ensure that the reservation utility is achieved under action $a1$. (Either assume that, when otherwise indifferent, the agent will prefer to please the principal, or assume that once the problem is solved the principal has to add 1 to the bonus payment.) The problem can be solved at a basic salary of 12,100, and a bonus payment of 16,800 payable if the 60,000 result is achieved.

Solve the following simultaneous equations:

$$0.67Z_{60}^{0.5} + 0.33Z_{30}^{0.5} - 36 =$$
$$0.33Z_{60}^{0.5} + 0.67Z_{30}^{0.5} - 16 = 114$$

$$Z_{60}^{0.5} = x \text{ and } Z_{30}^{0.5} = y$$

$$0.67x + 0.33y = 150 \text{ and } 0.33x + 0.67y = 130$$

$$2x + y = 450 \qquad x + 2y = 390$$
$$2x + 4y = 780 \qquad 3y = 330 \qquad y = 110$$
$$2x + y = 450 \qquad 2x = 340 \qquad x = 170$$

$$Z_{60}^{0.5} = 170, \quad Z_{60} = 28,900$$
$$Z_{30}^{0.5} = 110, \quad Z_{30} = 12,100$$

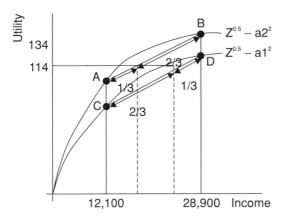

Figure 18.2 The agent's utility function and action unobservability

In terms of Figure 18.2, the principal must define a contract so that the agent prefers the pay-off chances 0.67A + 0.33B to 0.33C + 0.67D and still achieves utility level 114. The solution has the characteristics of the figure.

However, the principal's utility has now fallen to 26,700 (the agent's remains at 114) – Pareto sub-optimal compared with the situation in which the action is observable.

$$U_P = 0.67(60,000 - 28,900) +$$
$$0.33(30,000 - 12,100)$$
$$= 26,700$$

Under a1,

$$U_A = 0.67(28,900)^{0.5} + 0.33(12,100)^{0.5} \quad 36$$
$$= 114$$

This just confirms the previous calculation.

The reason for the welfare loss is that, in order to achieve the desired result, the risk-neutral principal has had to shift risk to the risk-averse agent. Risk neutrality and risk aversion are inherent in the assumed utility functions. (Risk aversion is inherent in the diminishing shape of the agent's utility function.) The more general point – independent of which utility functions have been chosen for which party to the transaction – is that, to solve the moral hazard problem, a specific distribution of risk is implied. This is unlikely

to coincide with the optimal distribution of risk according to the role of risk in the two utility functions.

You may already have come across moral hazard in the context of insurance markets. (If not, see Chapter 22.) Here, rather counter-intuitively, the agent is the enrolee, and the principal is the insurance company. The agent has to avoid risks on behalf of the insurance company. The insurance company cannot observe risk avoidance. The principal may try to induce risk avoidance by paying differentially according to the outcome. A good example is the 'no claims bonus' typical of car insurance. Such schemes imply less than perfect insurance. As in the example, the agent may be more risk-averse than the principal because the insurance company has large numbers of clients and is therefore most interested in the average outcome, whereas the agent is interested in only one outcome. Perfect insurance and the observation of risk avoidance would therefore likely be Pareto optimal. Information asymmetry therefore induces a Pareto sub-optimal result.

18.5 Adverse Selection

In situations of adverse selection, only the agent has the information relevant to the selection of an action. The principal can observe the action and the outcome only.

We can set up a similar problem to the previous one, to see how this works. Suppose again that:

$$U_P = f - z$$

and (slightly simplified):

$$U_A = Z^{0.5} - a$$

Now there are two possible states of the world (s1 and s2) – with equal probability of

Table 18.2 Example of situation giving rise to adverse selection

Probability of pay-off	s1		s2	
	a1	a2	a1	a2
£60,000		0.67	0.33	0.33	0.67
£30,000		0.33	0.67	0.67	0.33

occurrence; and two possible actions that can be taken (a1 and a2). Suppose the pay-offs look like Table 18.2. In order to maximise the pay-off, in situation s1, take action a1; and in situation s2, take action a2. However, the principal cannot observe s, and action a1 is preferred by the agent. For example, action a1 is 'do nothing' and action a2 involves effort (effort levels a1 = 0; a2 = 10). Again note that observing neither pay-off nor action enables the principal to identify s.

Assume again that the reservation utility of the agent is 114. In the event of s1 occurring there is no conflict between the utility functions of the agent and the principal – under a fixed- or incentive-based reimbursement. In the event of s2, a bonus system is required to induce effort from the agent. Therefore, if her interests are to be promoted, the principal will use a bonus system, even in the absence of knowing whether s1 or s2 has occurred.

If s2 occurs, is observable to both agent and principal, and the agent is paid at a fixed rate, the salary required to achieve the reservation utility level is £15,376. At this point the agent's utility level is 114, and the principal's 34,624.

$$U_A = Z^{0.5} - a2 = 114, \quad a2 = 10$$
$$Z^{0.5} = 124; \quad Z = 15,376$$

$$U_P = 0.67(60,000 - 15,376) + 0.33(30,000 - 15,376) = 34,624$$

As before, the problem is to derive the basic and bonus salaries that will make the agent indifferent between actions a1 and a2, and ensure that the reservation utility is achieved under action a1. A basic salary of £10,816 and bonus in the event of achievement of the £60,000 outcome of £7,140 is just sufficient to induce the agent to make the effort required. The agent's utility level remains at 114, the principal's falls slightly to 34,423. Again, this is because of the costs of transferring risk to the risk-averse party.

Solve the following simultaneous equations:

$$0.67Z_{60}^{0.5} + 0.33Z_{30}^{0.5} - 10 = 0.33Z_{60}^{0.5} + 0.67Z_{30}^{0.5} = 114$$

$$Z_{60}^{0.5} = x, \quad \text{and} \quad Z_{30}^{0.5} = y$$

$$0.67x + 0.33y - 10 = 0.33x + 0.67y = 114$$
$$2x + y - 30 = x + 2y = 342$$
$$2x + y = 372 \quad x + 2y = 342$$

$$4x + 2y = 744 \quad x + 2y = 342$$
$$3x = 402 \quad x = 134$$

$$x + 2y = 342 \quad 2y = 208 \quad y = 104$$

$$Z_{60}^{0.5} = 134, \quad Z_{60} = 17,956$$
$$Z_{30}^{0.5} = 104, \quad Z_{30} = 10,816$$

$$[1]U_P = 0.67(60,000 - 17,956) + 0.33(30,000 - 10,816) = 34,423$$

You may have come across adverse selection in the context of insurance markets. (If not, see Chapter 22.) The insurance example parallels the example above less perfectly than in the case of moral hazard. (The characteristics of the insurance case can be found in a different class of adverse selection model than the standard one presented above.) The hidden information is the underlying health risk of the agent (enrolee) – low (s1) or high (s2). We assume that enrolees know more about their existing health status than the insurance company. A standard set of insurance benefits is offered at a standard price – which parallels fixed salary in the above problem. At this point, the parallel with the stylised example breaks down, since the situation is not such that the principal seeks to induce a particular type of action from the agent.

18.6 *Applying the Ideas*

'Incentive compatibility' means 'getting the incentives right' and, in the terms of the above examples, implies solving the problem so as to maximise welfare. This has been a main thrust in the design of a range of interventions including contracts and regulation within the health sector.

Incentive compatibility was first used as a concept to identify the range of actions for which participants in the market would not find it advantageous to break the rules or behave opportunistically. The concept of incentive compatibility can be thought of as the process of designing mechanisms to restructure the incentives or rewards facing individuals in order to achieve a desirable outcome.

As suggested above, agents, information asymmetry, risk and uncertainty are pervasive in the health sector as elsewhere. They imply that the information deficit has costs, in Paretian terms, and leaves principals with options of seeking missing information (which may be costly), tolerating agent 'opportunism' (defined, as before, as any strategy involving guile intended to further self-interest – here meaning the agent's maximising her own utility function by concealing information) or seeking, through contract specifications, to induce appropriate action on the part of the agent. Here, we have focused on comparisons of the last two options. In real contexts 'pay-offs' are more likely to be uncertain than risky

as described here (i.e. the probability distributions are not known), thereby making attempts to use strategies to induce agent behaviour in line with principal utility functions an approximate science.

It is worth exploring the concept of incentive compatibility because its application to economics has been widespread and 'getting the incentives right' has been a main thrust in the design of a range of interventions including contracts and regulation within the health sector.

In this chapter we consider in detail two areas where the issues of incentives and incentive compatibility have become prominent within the health sector: regulation and contracts. Within these sections we explore the role of incentives and the design of mechanisms.

18.7 *Incentive Management*

Whether or not explicit and deliberate, all organisational structures embody sets of incentives (encouraging people to work with or against the organisation). In Chapter 17 we recognised that institutional, informational and capacity constraints limited the implementation and impact of legislated mechanisms. Given these informational, transaction, administrative and political constraints, interest has turned to examining whether incentive management (defined as deliberate attempts to manipulate incentives to achieve desired objectives) may better accomplish the objectives of regulation. In Chapter 17 we recognised 'incentive regulation' a form of regulation but said little about it. Here we consider this type of regulation in more detail.

Incentive management may take two forms. First, the government can subsidise or tax regulated firms. Subsidies can take several

Figure 18.3 Effect of subsidy on a competitive market

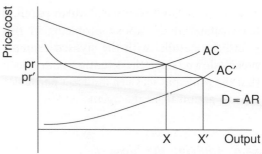

Figure 18.4 Effect of a flat-rate subsidy on a revenue-maximising firm

forms: direct subsidies (which may be paid as a lump sum or as a 'price subsidy' which is effectively a subsidy per unit of output sold), government loans at low interest, or government guarantees for borrowing on the private markets (Laffont and Tirole 1993).

Figure 18.3 shows the effect of a government price subsidy on a competitive market (with upward-sloping supply curve). The price subsidy implies that a fixed amount (ab) is paid for each unit of production sold. This is equivalent to each firm receiving a higher price for each unit of the good – which is equivalent to a shift of the demand curve outwards, from each firm's perspective. Firms respond so that the market reaches a new equilibrium (at a) where production is higher. Firms receive price p1 for each unit sold, whereas consumers pay only p2. The effect of the subsidy is therefore to lower the price paid by the consumer (but not by the full extent of the subsidy paid – compare pe–p2 and ab), and to increase output. The extent to which these two effects occur depends on the relative elasticities of supply and demand curves. The effect of a unit tax is the opposite – it can be viewed as the opposite shift in the demand curve and will reduce output and increase price (but not by the full extent of the tax).

However, many subsidies in the health sector are not of a price subsidy nature, but rather flat-rate subsidies to specific institutions. A flat-rate subsidy would not affect the decision making of a profit-maximising firm – it would be received as a windfall payment and profit-maximising decisions would be made regardless. It follows that flat-rate subsidies can work only in the context of non-profit-maximising behaviour on behalf of the firms subsidised. For example, if the firm is a revenue maximiser subject to a 'break-even' constraint (like the firm of Figure 16.1), the flat-rate subsidy has the effect of reducing average cost (for example, to AC′), and reduces price and increases output as might be expected (Figure 18.4).

Financing health service provision through a public provider and a budget mechanism is analytically similar to a flat-rate subsidy – although the assumed objective function of the provider is apparently neither profit maximising nor revenue maximising. Rather, the provider's interest in delivering appropriate services to the population covered as efficiently as possible seems to be assumed. It is worth considering whether such altruistic motivation seems reasonable in any given context, and which other mechanisms are used for the principal (the provider of finance) to achieve the behaviour intended by the agent (the providing institution).

Combining user fees with a flat-rate public subsidy – perhaps the most common set of arrangements for public provision in low-income countries – provides an odd-looking mix of incentives to provider institutions. Countries with this set of arrangements need to consider carefully their assumptions about the objective functions of provider institutions, and the contractual arrangements (implicit or explicit) which govern providers' use of subsidy.

The second form which incentive management can take is that the government can make transfers to participants through its purchasing function. This is no different from subsidy in analytic terms but is associated with a greater explicitness of contractual arrangements. For example, in the UK contractual arrangements between health authorities and hospitals have been classified as 'block', 'cost and volume' and 'cost per case'. Block contracts are equivalent to fixed-rate subsidies whereas 'cost per case' contracts are equivalent to price subsidies. 'Cost and volume' contracts agree a specific price–quantity point in the terms of Figures 18.3 and 18.4. In the UK case, additional user fees are ruled out by regulation, however.

Incentive management is practised actively in low-income countries too. For example, in Malaysia and Thailand there are allowances paid to encourage physicians to forgo private practice, a form of subsidy to the services provided by those physicians. Why might this be a good way to solve the problem of 'dual practice' whereby salaried public sector doctors spend a substantial share of their time in the private sector? Figure 18.5 looks at the situation from the perspective of a doctor who chooses how to spend an eight-hour working day (the time budget). The analysis assumes

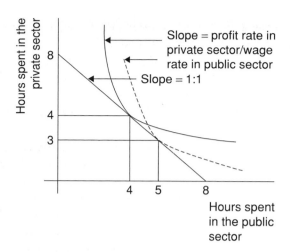

Figure 18.5 Model of a physician's 'dual practice' decision

that there is a flat-rate wage in the public sector, and a diminishing marginal wage in the private sector. (The doctor can choose to work the most profitable opening hours in her private clinic.) This produces a curved 'iso-income' line (with slope equal to the relative wage rate across the two sectors) that holds the doctor's income constant. At the point of tangency between the iso-income line and the budget line the doctor will choose to divide her working time.

If the time offered to the public sector is thought to leave the public sector short-staffed, the government might increase wages to alter the physician's decision. This would alter the iso-income line – for example, to the dashed one in Figure 18.5 – and increase the number of hours offered. However, this would be quite costly, and to secure all eight working hours, the government would have to pay at the rate of the most profitable hour of operation of the physician's private clinic. A non-private practice allowance can instead attract the full working day of the doctor by at least matching the total income she would have earned from private sector

Table 18.3 Possible schedule of earnings in public and private sectors (shillings)

Hours	Profit in private sector	Wage in public sector
1	10,000	6,000
2	9,000	6,000
3	8,000	6,000
4	7,000	6,000
5	6,000	6,000
6	5,000	6,000
7	4,000	6,000
8	3,000	6,000

work in the part of the day allocated to that. Suppose that the schedule of earnings possible in both sectors is as in Table 18.3. In order to attract all eight hours of the doctor's working day to the public sector, the government would have to pay a wage of 10,000 shillings per hour, or a total of 80,000 shillings per day. However, the same could also be achieved by paying a non-private practice allowance of 10,000 shillings per day and maintaining the hourly wage at 6,000 shillings – a total wage of 58,000 shillings per day, equal to the income the doctor would have earned by dividing her time as in Figure 18.5.

In practice, non-practice allowances may be more expensive since doctors who operate dual practice often continue to earn as if they were working a full day in the public sector despite spending a significant proportion of that time in the private sector. That would imply that the full extent of private sector earnings would have to be compensated, but would still be cheaper than trying to induce full-time public sector work through the wage rate. Alternatively, measures to monitor public sector work and pay only for hours worked might be considered.

18.8 Incentive Regulation

Incentive regulation can be thought of as 'rules' which regulate verifiable outcomes such as price (Laffont and Tirole 1993). Rather than attempting to micro-manage an individual participant's behaviour, incentive regulation can adopt market-based criteria. For example, in the regulation of telecommunications in the UK, a price-cap incentive scheme has been put in place, replacing the rate-type regulation. Price-cap regulation attempts to address the same problems as rate regulation but breaks the link between revenue and costs. The firm or market price is based on last year's price, corrected for inflation and then decreased by some percentage x. This x factor means that the real price falls over the period of the price cap. There is some incentive to lower quality and so the regulator must monitor this. There is also an incentive problem. Since this year's regulated prices are based on last year's achieved efficiencies, there is certainly no incentive to achieve efficiency gains higher than the x per cent required. Such achievement will only drive further efficiency demands the following year. Depending on the penalties for failing to meet the x per cent efficiency gain, firms may try to game the system by using failure to meet targets this year as a means to negotiate a less stringent target the following year. Much depends on the regulator's ability to monitor the firm's costs and effort in seeking efficiency improvement.

Other incentive regulation schemes are based on the government and regulated firm sharing costs or profits. For instance, firms may be allowed to charge higher prices, but some proportion of their profit is taxed. Alternatively, if x is constant, firms are allowed to keep cost improvements that are greater than x per cent (Propper 1995). The advantage of such schemes is that if the variables are well specified and easily observable, the monitoring and implementing cost of such regulation is relatively low.

In comparison with other approaches to regulation, mechanisms based on incentives seem to be associated with much lower transaction costs. However, monitoring is still important. Both incentive management and incentive regulation can be implemented through contractual obligations, rather than legislated requirements, and an example of incentive regulation in the health sector is considered in the Further Reading that follows.

Further Reading – Incentive Regulation in the Health Sector

In a social experiment on incentive regulation of nursing homes, Norton (1992) looked at whether monetary incentives can improve the access and health of Medicaid residents in nursing homes while saving money. Nursing homes were given three kinds of financial incentives:

1 *Tied to admission*. Daily reimbursement rate to depend on case mix in order to increase the admission of sick patients.
2 *Tied to case outcomes*. A lump sum bonus was awarded when a resident improved her health.
3 *Tied to discharges*. A lump sum bonus was awarded when a resident was promptly discharged to home or to an intermediate care facility to encourage nursing homes to fill their beds with people who could most benefit from their care.

Norton found that the incentive regulation had beneficial effects on access, quality and cost of care. The admission incentives induced the nursing home to take in people with severe disabilities. Nevertheless the need to have independent confirmation of discharges was emphasised. Incentive mechanisms seem to have much lower transaction costs. However, the Norton experiment suggests that monitoring is still important, particularly to see whether the incentive is having the desired effect on behaviour. Source: Norton (1992).

18.9 Contract Design: the Incentive Compatibility Constraint

Different contract types are seen in the health sector, both between and within organisations. In order to restructure incentives there are two important constraints: first, within the design of a contract each person would be willing to participate – the *participation* constraint. Second, the contract needs to structure incentives in order to meet the desired objectives: the *incentive compatibility* constraint. In section 18.5 we encountered the participation constraint in the form of the 'reservation utility' of the agent, and the incentive compatibility constraint required the contract to be structured so that the agent took the action that furthered the principal's objectives.

In contrast to the arithmetically solvable problems of section 18.5, real contract design raises a number of difficulties for which there is no solution but which require the development of carefully judged strategies. As we saw in section 18.5, the problem of designing incentives arises because there are unobserved hidden actions or asymmetrically observed factors relevant to the choice of action. There are many examples of both kinds of problem in the health sector. For example, there are difficulties for payer organisations in verifying exactly what treatments have been administered to each patient (hidden action), and there are difficulties in verifying the symptoms of disease and the appropriateness of diagnoses recorded (asymmetrically observable relevant factors).

In any payment system, rewards must be linked with some aspect of performance that is observable. Under incentive management and regulation, the objective is that the aspect chosen should also be that which is intended to be encouraged. In the examples of section 18.5 the pay-offs were observable (financial returns) and the solution was therefore calculable. However, in situations like many found in the health sector, the observable aspects of performance may bear very little relation to unobservable actions or underlying objectives. The equivalent of pay-off in the health sector might be health outcome, but contract reimbursement is almost never linked with health outcome – an exception can be found among traditional practitioners in some African countries (see Box 18.1). One reason why health outcome is not usually used as a basis for payment is that in many situations it is not primarily dependent on health service inputs. An outcome-dependent contract would not provide incentives for health workers to make heroic efforts to revive patients with a poor chance of recovery. Yet we may want to ensure our contracts contain such incentives. Health outcome is also not easily observable by third-party payers – and may be opportunistically concealed even in the case of a direct transaction (see Box 18.1 for more discussion of this).

The design of incentive management or regulation depends on how participants respond to incentives and the clarity of the formula or rule linking rewards with actions. If there exists some vagueness about the formula or 'rule' that is used, individuals will also respond to these incentives in ways that are not desirable. For example, if lecturers' salaries are geared to the number of new courses designed or innovations in teaching,

individuals can try and respond by influencing or 'corrupting' the related outcome measures (Kreps 1997). For example, teachers might re-label existing courses or teaching techniques, so that they are counted as 'new'.

Hughes (1993) discusses different types of financial payments used to increase the preventive activities of family doctors in the UK. The contract by which private family doctors are paid by the National Health Service was substantially revised in 1990. New initiatives included the introduction of 'target payments' for immunisation and cervical cytology paid only if specific coverage levels were achieved which replaced per-service payments, and 'sessional payments' of a lump sum for the provision of health-promotion clinics. Hughes suggests that target payments may fail to induce appropriate behaviour, since they do not reward the targeting of the service to the patients most likely to benefit or effort to increase coverage levels if targets are not believed attainable. Sessional payments might reward the reorganisation of health-promotion activity from a routine component of doctor–patient interactions to special clinic activity – not self-evidently a positive change.

Further design issues arise when tasks or outcomes are multi-faceted (Holmstrom and Milgrom 1990). Individuals can more easily alter behaviour that is perverse to the original intention of the incentive where outcomes are multi-characteristic or multi-task-dependent. When the organisation performs several tasks or outputs, which vary in the degree to which they can be observed, tasks or characteristics that are observable would have a 'higher-powered' incentive effect relative to other outcomes.

If rewards are related to observable tasks or characteristics, there is an incentive for regulated firms and individuals to neglect other tasks or characteristics. The contractor has

---

International Case Study

Box 18.1 *Traditional Healers and Incentives in Rural Cameroon*

Traditional healers in Cameroon are paid according to a 'contingent payment scheme' under which payment increases according to the success of the treatment. Leonard (2000) argues that this payment scheme will induce effort on the part of the traditional healers in cases where the condition of the patient implies that the success of treatment is dependent on the healer's effort. It also implies that where patient effort is an important determinant of outcome, healers will be very interested in mechanisms to induce patient effort in order to secure higher payment.

In contrast, employers of those working in clinics and hospitals within the public and mission systems use a 'penalty-based scheme' to manage incentives. Records are kept of activities, and if these indicate inappropriate practice, sanctions can be applied. Sanctions are more serious in the mission system, where dismissal and demotion are options, than in the public system, where relocation is the most serious credible sanction. Since this reward system is not directly related to outcome, patient effort is predicted to be of little interest to workers in these two systems.

Medical skills also differ among the three systems, with untrained personnel available in the traditional system, and semi- and fully trained personnel in the public and mission systems. (Note that Leonard's comparative analysis of the three systems does not rely on the existence of *different* skills in the traditional sector.)

Leonard argues that 'These combinations of skill and incentives lead people rationally to choose different types of practitioners depending on the disease from which they suffer.' He develops a scale which quantifies three dimensions – medical effort, patient effort and medical skill – with respect to common conditions experienced by the population of rural Cameroon. It was predicted that traditional healers would be most likely chosen where the combination of patient and medical effort was high; mission hospitals (and to a lesser extent clinics) where medical effort and medical skill were most important; and public hospitals or clinics where medical skill was important but effort less so.

On this basis, a utilisation decision was predicted for each of 537 episodes of care, and compared with the actual patient utilisation decision. The model generated correct predictions for 50 per cent of cases over the five provider types (whereas a model with no predictive power would be expected to predict correctly in about 20 per cent of cases).

These results suggest that not only does the characterisation of incentives capture the key features of the incentives operating in the different provider institutions, but that incentive characteristics are well understood – at least implicitly – by those making decisions regarding where to seek care.

Source: Leonard (2000).

---

the incentive to increase production or manage production in such a way as to skew observed characteristics to meet the target. In Uganda there has been a change from reimbursing hospitals on the basis of bed numbers to bed occupancy (Ssengooba *et al.* 2000). While both bases of reimbursement can present problems, the switch to bed occupancy is likely to result in longer lengths of stay – unless these are monitored and credible penalties are attached to gaming the system in this way. It is tempting to judge evidence of an existing association between an indicator such as bed occupancy and desired activity characteristics as a basis on which to manage incentives, but the act of using the indicator as a basis for reimbursement may well undermine the relationship.

Propper (1995) suggests that this can also occur within the UK NHS structure where hospitals are assessed on the basis of an efficiency index that is heavily weighted in favour of in-patient activity. Then there is an incentive to over-emphasise in-patient activity in the hospital's service mix, and to over-record in-patient activity – and evidence that both have been occurring.

The designers of contracts have to weigh the advantages and disadvantages of relying on incentives related to tasks and characteristics which are observed with more certainty, but with less impact on performance, and those tasks and characteristics which are observed with less certainty but are more likely to impact behaviour.

A further design issue arises in the use of relative or group targets – and where outputs involved rely on teamwork. There has been extensive work in the area of labour economics which looks at comparative pay schemes such as 'tournaments' (e.g. the most 'successful' will achieve the prize). The underlying principle is that the firm ranks competing agents in terms of relative performance and allocates remuneration according to the ranking. For example, Nalbantian and Schotter (1997) present evidence from an experiment involving different group incentive programmes between workers and firms. Their findings suggest (1) history matters: how a group of individuals perform under one incentive scheme depends on its previous experience under a different one and (2) relative performance schemes

outperform target-based schemes. However, again this result is mitigated by the context of larger groups performing multiple tasks. Holmstrom (1989) argues that larger firms perform more tasks, therefore have weaker incentives and suffer a relative disadvantage in performance because of the multi-faceted nature of the judgements required.

What is the possibility of adjustment in the design of contracts? In the private sector owners or managers can devote substantial effort and resources to maintaining and perfecting rewards systems and adjusting the schemes as they receive information about dysfunctional or opportunistic behaviour. To what degree can adjustments occur when there is an interaction between the state and individuals in the private or public sectors? Courty and Marschke (1997) examine a reward scheme within a bureaucracy. They find that this process is much slower in government owing to the absence of well-defined goals (like profit) and because bureaucracies are controlled by multiple principals with potentially conflicting interests and differing understanding of the impact of incentives. The conflict between bureaucratic discretion and objective measurement imposes moral hazard costs and reduces any efficiency gains from implementing market-based measures. This is particularly the case when output is difficult to measure – installation of specific goals may focus effort the wrong way (Heckman *et al.* 1997).

We saw in section 18.2 that reorganisation of incentives could not avoid simultaneously redistributing risk. The various forms of incentive management and regulation discussed here therefore have differing implications for risk distribution that have efficiency implications. For example, if a payer organisation faces significant risk associated with the reimbursement mechanism, it may respond by conserving inefficient levels of reserve to ensure that crisis is avoided under all possible scenarios. If a provider organisation faces high levels of risk it may also devise inefficient measures to protect itself. For example, under capitation, providers must offer services as required for a fixed payment that does not respond to the level of demand.

Providers may use alternative mechanisms to deter demand or 'cost shift' – such as referring patients to higher-level providers, failing to recommend appropriate treatment or using waiting lists or queues to cope with excess demand. Further consideration is given to the efficiency of such rationing mechanisms in Chapter 21.

Part IV

The Economics of Health Systems

Chapter 19

Health Systems

A Framework for Analysis

....

19.1 Introduction

Markets are arrangements through which people exchange goods and services, giving up those things they value less, and gaining those they value more. When people work, they exchange leisure time and effort for food, housing, clothing and other goods they value. By converting their leisure time and effort assets into money they can exchange for other things of value. In this way we can see money as a device that allows easier use of the market to exchange things we have for things we would value more. As the first three parts of this book have described, in simple markets, such as those for fruit and vegetables, the buyers and sellers are easily identifiable, and are generally well informed. The market can work well with little in the way of rules and regulation. But understanding markets becomes more difficult as the products become more complex and when actors start to include people acting as agents for the consumer or seller.

Well-functioning markets are a common part of most of our lives, and most access to goods and services uses at least elements of market processes. Within health systems markets exist widely, but tend to be complex

and regulated. As we have seen, analysis has to take into account agency, regulation, oligopolistic or monopolistic arrangement of suppliers, monopsonistic organisation of purchasing by agents on behalf of the ultimate consumers, compulsion of payment through taxation or social insurance arrangements. At times we can hardly recognise what we see as a 'market' at all. Yet through viewing a health system as a series of complex markets, and by focusing on elements of exchange, incentives, rationing mechanisms and underlying demand and supply curves, cost and production functions, important insights can be gained into the strengths and weaknesses and likely effects of alternative forms of organisation.

This part of the book aims to introduce the reader to this approach to viewing health systems. There are two major sets of issues that will be addressed. The first is the implications of alternative ways of organising financing for funding levels and rationing. How much in total will be spent, what services will be provided, and who will get them? The second concerns the institutional structures of alternative health systems and focuses particularly on arguments about the incentives to efficiency implicit in them.

19.2 Alternative Health Systems, Funding Levels and Rationing

There are several approaches to the question 'What is the right level of funding?' A common starting point in the political debate about health care funding is to assert that all health care needs should be met. Defining what we mean by 'need' is more complicated (Culyer 1976). One starting point (Matthew 1971) defines need not in terms of the size of the health problem an individual faces, but rather in terms of the feasibility of intervening to remove or reduce the problem. A need is therefore defined as the capacity to benefit from a service. Taking this approach, someone with serious and incurable disease may have great need of care and palliative services, but has no need for curative health care (see Box 19.1). But, even on this more

---

Box 19.1   Normand and McPake disagree on Need

C.N. I really feel quite strongly about the 'capacity to benefit' definition. Too many people talk about 'needs' when they really mean problems – unless there's something that can be done about it, a problem isn't a need.

B.M. Yes, but I think that 'capacity to benefit' trivialises important distinctions. My three-year-old never 'wants' an ice cream, she always 'needs' one. According to your definition, she's right.

C.N. Yes, she needs an ice cream, but we can't meet all needs.

B.M. I prefer a framework that accepts that different claims on uses of resources – whether we call them wants or needs – have an order of importance. Our non-technical language has different words for my grandfather's need for heart surgery and my daughter's desire for an ice cream for good reason.

C.N. Obviously, we can acknowledge an order of importance without trying to draw arbitrary distinctions that inevitably leave grey areas. Is aesthetic plastic surgery a 'need', a 'want' or a 'desire'? A cost–benefit framework enables that ordering, without requiring arbitrary distinctions.

B.M. I accept that drawing a hard line between needs and wants is difficult, and that really we have a continuum of more important and less important claims on resources. There are grey areas between needs and wants, but towards the ends of the continuum the terminology is clear, and that is often all that is needed. A 'need' is a more important claim on resources, a 'want' or 'desire' is a less important one.

C.N. I see no reason for economists to join in the use of imprecise language. At these ends, we have high and low benefit–cost ratios – that tells us what we need to know and keeps the importance of *our ability to tackle the problem* centre stage. My definitions are much clearer and more precise than yours. The cost–benefit framework takes account of the extent to which serious problems can be alleviated. If we consider all opportunities to achieve benefits as 'needs' then we can leave the cost–benefit framework to decide which ones should be met.

B.M. I think we should separate the issue of what is a 'need' from how efficiently we can tackle it. The definition of a need – that it is a more important claim on resources – *is* messier than capacity to benefit. I think that's a necessary evil.

C.N. Your proposal leaves those problems for which we can do nothing, like curing untreatable conditions that threaten survival, within the range – possibly at the high end.

Continued

I thought we both agreed that these were not needs. We waste our time even allowing them into the debate.

B.M. I agree that problems with no effective intervention are not needs for intervention, and that 'capacity to benefit' is a necessary condition of 'need'. I'm not convinced that it is sufficient, though I think it is the most viable definition for the purpose of our textbook. What I'd like to highlight in the book, though, is that using benefit–cost ratios as our sole guide to importance won't bring out the greater seriousness of the problem addressed by heart surgery than by ice cream. The ice cream is cheap and very satisfying to my daughter – if we accept her as a sovereign consumer, the benefit–cost ratio is high. The heart surgery is expensive, and may have quite a low benefit–cost ratio. We may well agree that it has a low priority for resource allocation, given that benefit–cost ratio, but to rank it as a less important 'need' than my daughter's ice cream ignores the acuteness of the resource allocation issues we are talking about. No wonder economists are viewed from the outside as callous pennypinchers! Apparently we think ice cream is more important than heart surgery.

restrictive definition of need, economists seldom accept that all needs should be met. Rather they argue that needs should be met if the benefits of doing so exceed the costs (in other words, exceed the forgone benefits if resources are used for this purpose). This approach was considered in more detail in Part II.

As we have seen, individuals' own valuation (willingness to pay) for goods and services can be charted by a demand curve. Those who value the benefits most are willing to pay the most – these demands can be found on the left-hand end of the demand curve. Those who place a relatively low value on the benefits to themselves are willing to pay less – these demands can be found at the right-hand, lower end of the demand curve.

If we accept consumer sovereignty – that is, that consumers are the best judges of their own interests – and also accept the current distribution of income and wealth, the appropriate level of provision (and by implication funding) can be defined at Q* in Figure 19.1. Q* is easily achieved by setting price at marginal cost. The simplest way to ensure that resources are allocated to those who value

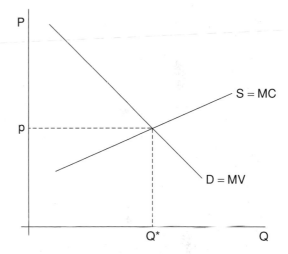

Figure 19.1 Health services rationed through the price mechanism

their own demands most is also via the price mechanism. The 'invisible hand' will direct resources to high-value demands, away from low-value demands, and, at the margin, allocate the last unit of a resource to a demand with a value equal to the price.

Q* could also be achieved in a public system by setting funding levels such that Q* can be provided. However, a public system also has to develop a rationing mechanism that allocates resources to high-value and away from low-value demands. If the values derived from demand curves were satisfactory to society and policy makers, the idea would be ludicrous. Why take the trouble to estimate Q* and aim to develop a rationing mechanism which would exactly mimic the price mechanism when prices already perform the function perfectly and without effort? We have already encountered a response to this question in our analysis of market failure in Chapter 8, and the fact that no society leaves the delivery of health services to be determined by an unregulated price mechanism suggests that no society and no policy makers consider that values derived from demand curves are at all satisfactory.

There are three important sources of divergence between private and social demand. First, values derived from demand curves are determined not only by willingness but also by ability to pay. Richer people's demands are weighted more heavily than the demands of poorer people. If society or policy makers believe that demands should be weighted equally in health sector resource allocation, values derived from demand evidence alone cannot be relied upon. Second, lack of information influences the way individuals order and value their own demands. They may place high value on interventions with limited effectiveness because they have been misled by product claims, or may believe that only an injection will cure an illness best treated by a

Box 19.2   A Social Demand Curve?

We have seen that demand curves measure the marginal valuations of the individuals making up a market for the goods or services being traded. They slope downwards for each individual because we expect 'diminishing marginal utility' to be associated with any goods under consideration. Summing the demand curves of all individuals then also gives a downward-sloping curve (see Chapter 2).

The concept of a social demand curve is a graphical representation of the same idea for social marginal valuations. We also expect diminishing social marginal value. Consider the case of a measles vaccination. We've argued that individuals' values of immunisation are

Figure B3 Demand and social value of immunisation

Continued

likely to be quite low and the private market demand curve might be drawn as curve D in the diagram. The higher values (to the left of the graph) are likely to be associated with the better educated, who understand the value of immunisation, and the rich, who can easily pay for it. A social demand curve gives a value to the immunisation of each individual, equal to society's total value for that immunisation. This includes (1) with full understanding of the likely benefits of immunisation for the individual concerned (correcting for imperfect information); (2) the effect of immunisation on others whose risks are affected (taking account of externalities); and (3) removing wealth-related weights associated with individuals' preferences. Some people would argue for a more radical weighting favouring the poorest – see Box 9.6. On the basis that all adjustments for social value from private values are likely to increase value, we can argue that the social demand curve (SD in the graph) for this service lies to the right of the private demand curve. The social demand curve will still slope downwards. Highest values will be placed on immunising individuals at highest risk of contracting and passing on the disease – those who live in the most cramped conditions, for example – and the marginal value of immunising the next individual will fall to zero at the point that 'herd immunity' is reached. The ordering of priorities within the social demand curve will therefore be quite different from those within the private demand curve. Efficiency requires the equation of social demand with social marginal cost (which may also differ from social private cost in various ways). This concept of efficiency includes the concept of equity in whatever form it has been encompassed in social demand.

tablet. They may not value simple preventive measures through ignorance of risk of disease, or of relative risks of rare side effects.[1] This limits the extent to which the demand curve can be interpreted as the individual's true valuation of health interventions available. Third, there are important externalities in the health sector: individuals' valuations of their own benefits will not usually take account of the benefits, for example, of reduced risk of disease transmission, received by others.

We can hypothesise a social demand curve which would perform the same function as the private demand curve in valuing and ordering demands for the use of resources from a social perspective (see Box 19.2). The balance of consideration could lead to any relative positioning of the private and social demand curves, and different sub-health markets are likely to balance the three sources of divergence differently. For example, private de-

mand for immunisation is likely to lie to the left of the social demand curve owing to substantial externalities. In addition, lack of information may lead the average patient to under-value immunisation. Furthermore, the highest relative values of it are in the poorest populations who suffer most from communicable disease but whose low ability to pay means that they express only a low level of demand in the market. In a market, the demands expressed reflect the relative valuation of goods and services by different individuals, but these are effectively weighted by their ability to pay (wealth). Together these factors mean that the social demand for immunisation is likely to lie above the private demand. On the reverse logic, the opposite may be true of the services of CT scanners.

A better definition of optimum provision and funding is therefore where the marginal social value of the application of a unit of resources equates with its marginal social cost.

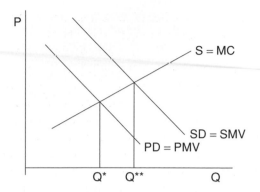

Figure 19.2 Impact of social demand curve on optimal provision level

Since marginal social cost is defined in terms of opportunities forgone, as explained in Chapter 10, comparing marginal social cost and marginal social value is equivalent to asking the question 'Does society have a higher value for the unit of resource used this way, or used another way?' Figure 19.2 shows that where the social demand curve lies to the right of the private demand curve, a new Q* higher than that suggested by the use of private valuations (Q1) applies; a higher level of funding must now be defined as optimum, and levels below that defined as 'under-funding'.

Alternative ways of financing and allocating health services have implications for the total level of finance, the types of health services that will and will not be financed, and the distribution of those services among individuals (or groups of individuals in the case of services with wider application). The following chapters consider the likely implications of each type of system for each.

19.3 Alternative Health Systems, Institutional Structures and Incentives

Alternative ways of organising the health system have implications for the ownership of health-providing and financing institutions, the internal structures of each, the flows of resources within and between institutions and hence the incentives that actors within the system face to pursue the objectives of both 'allocative' and 'internal' efficiency (see Chapter 6 for explanation of these efficiency terms).

A simple framework suggests that incentives to pursue efficiency strengthen as institutions become more private – for example, some literature refers to 'high-powered incentives' operating in markets and 'low-powered incentives' operating within hierarchical organisations such as large companies and public bureaucracies. The argument is that the owner-operator of a 'one-man' business fully internalises the results of her efforts while under other arrangements, at best the results of efforts are shared with others. The responsiveness of individual reimbursement to individual performance varies from 100 per cent in the single owner-manager case to 0 per cent under a fixed salary that does not respond even to the payer's perception of even organisational performance.

Our perspective – that all sorts of institutional structures and mix of arrangements for financing, producing and distributing health services can be viewed as types of markets – emphasises that it is always possible to identify implicit demanders, suppliers, prices and incentive structures, and concords with the perspective that any organisation is a 'nexus of contracts' (see Chapter 14). This suggests that a sharp distinction between a 'market' and a hierarchical organisation as is made above cannot be justified. Instead, following Alchian and Demsetz (1972), we might think of more 'firm-like', and more 'market-like' nexuses of contracts and explore the argument that stronger incentives may be found in more market-like contract structures.

This argument emphasises the financial component of incentives. Those who find rewards in work well done, knowing that they have alleviated suffering, or in social respect, may be more highly motivated by knowing that their services, produced in a public organisation, are distributed on the basis of need, than by being paid more money for their good performance. Nevertheless, there are probably limits to the salary levels consistent with this outlook, as deteriorated salary levels, motivation and performance of health workers in some public systems seem to attest.

Methods of matching rewards to performance vary in degree of directness and strength, and are not necessarily stronger in private organisations than in public ones though they are usually more direct. A well-tuned-to-performance promotion system with a steeply graduated pay structure, that exists in some public sector organisations, aims to reward performance financially and may do so as effectively as a profit-sharing system in a private organisation. Where teamwork is practised, inevitably it is difficult to match pay to performance. This applies as much to private sector as to public sector organisations. Fixed salaries and poor career structures and promotion incentives can be found in both public and private organisations.

However, some of the belief in the strength of private sector incentives is based on faith in the perfect competition model (see Chapter 6). The underlying idea that profit seeking implies concern with cost minimising (internal efficiency) and seeking to meet the demands that consumers express (allocative efficiency) may have some validity, despite the problems with the model as a normative guide discussed in Chapter 6. More market exposure means stronger pressures to perform efficiently than where there is less market exposure. These kinds of pressures may be helpful in a range of contexts – but they can also prove perverse. This is particularly the case in more complex situations in which several market imperfections apply – the divergence between private and social demand discussed at length above may become a source of perverse allocative efficiency incentives, viewed through this lens. Where different incentive structures coexist – such as where doctors work in both public and private sectors – similar perverse incentives may arise, for example for doctors to encourage patients to be treated in the doctor's private practice.

In Chapter 6 we concluded that these questions were impossible to evaluate in the abstract, once a range of market imperfections are admitted. Similarly, institutional arrangements need to be examined in their specifics rather than in general. For example, there are several different possible motivations of individuals (such as altruism or desire for money). There are different objectives that may be followed by organisations (such as profit or growth). Each organisation faces a choice of mechanism to encourage staff to pursue its objectives (such as performance-related pay, or bonuses). In order to understand the likely incentives and behaviour in that organisation it is important to know what are the objectives of staff and the organisation, and what choices are made of mechanisms to motivate staff.

Within each of the following chapters it is necessary to discuss different broad types of health system, ignoring some important differences within the systems. We aim to discuss some of the most common configurations of relevant factors which arise in different types of health system and the likely incentive issues.

Social demand curves are concepts rather than measurable entities – we cannot observe social values, although we may expect them to be closely related to concepts such as 'benefit', QALYs and DALYs, which have been discussed in Part II. In fact, cost–benefit analysis, and certain types of cost-effectiveness analysis, can be seen as aiming to achieve the equivalent of the equation of social demand with social marginal cost.

Abstracting further, we can compare different types of intervention by constructing curves of 'marginal social value minus marginal social cost', as has been done in Figure 21.1. This enables the widely varying costs of different types of intervention to be taken into account in contrasting social and private optima. Instead of creating an optimum where marginal social value equals marginal cost, the optimum is found where marginal social value minus marginal social cost equals zero – an exactly equivalent position. Roughly speaking, 'QALY league tables' locate points on this curve (though see the discussion of the relationship between QALYs and utility

– or welfare – in Chapter 11, especially section 11.4).

Note

1. It is important here to distinguish between mis-valuation, which can be attributed to lack of information, and judgement of mis-valuation, where the underlying difference is of opinion. A medical professional may judge an intervention as advisable on the basis of its capacity to prolong life while a patient may judge its detrimental effects on quality of life too high a price to pay. In the case of underlying difference of opinion, economics emphasises the sovereignty of the consumer as best judge of their own interests, while paternalist approaches might emphasise the superiority of professional values. In practice it is almost always impossible to distinguish between alternative causes of differing judgement, and the dilemmas for medical professionals can be acute. Here we only need concern ourselves with the theoretical implications of lack of information, for the interpretation of demand evidence.

Chapter 20

Health Systems around the World
An Introduction to Variation and Performance

....

20.1 *Introduction*

A health system is made up of users, payers, providers and regulators and can be defined by the relations between them. Governments can play a number of different roles as financers, regulators and/or providers of services. At one extreme, provision and financing can be completely public. Tax revenues pay for building and equipping facilities for service provision, for employment of the people who work within them, and the supply of all drugs and other non-durable inputs. Patients receive services free at the time they use them. Some countries have even outlawed all forms of private practice. There is no example of the other extreme, a country whose whole health care system is completely private. In all countries there is at least some government subsidy (or tax) on components of the health system, regulation of some service transaction (such as minimum standards for the qualification 'medical doctor' or for hospitals) or public ownership or employment of the resources used to produce health services. However, there are some fully private 'sub-systems' in many countries, for example unregulated pharmaceuticals markets.

Health systems are typically characterised by 'insurance'. This is broadly defined to mean that users pay regularly towards health system expenses in order to avoid bills that would make an unacceptable hole in the household budget at the time of use, and in order to share risk between larger population groups so that no one family faces completely unaffordable catastrophic costs. Broadly defined, public systems can be considered a form of insurance, with the relevant share of tax effectively equivalent to a health insurance premium. More commonly, the term 'health insurance' is restricted to arrangements where separate premiums and a separate 'earmarked' fund for health services is created. Even within this narrower definition of insurance a wide variety of arrangements is found. 'Social insurance' implies compulsory membership and usually a public or quasi-public insurance agent. Private insurance is offered by private insurance companies and is usually voluntary (South Korea's private but compulsory insurance is an exception) but is, nonetheless, usually subject to substantial regulation.

There are very few cases of 'pure' health systems that are neatly captured by these archetype descriptions. Wide and increasing variation is possible within each archetype. While many countries' health systems are dominated by one or other archetype (while usually having small sub-components equivalent to another), it is equally common for countries to have a number of important subsectors corresponding to different archetypes. Some country examples will serve to make this case, and to set the framework for the discussion of tendencies and performance that will absorb the rest of the chapter.

At the extreme public end of the spectrum of archetypes, the health system of the former German Democratic Republic was centrally and publicly financed and provided, with almost all services free of charge to patients. All health staff were salaried and the private sector was extremely small (OECD 1992). The system has now been integrated with that of the Federal German Republic. The arrangements were typical of the former Communist countries of Central and Eastern Europe that are now all undergoing substantial reform. However, in practice, divergence from the pure public model is reported in many of these countries to the extent that while intended to be free, substantial 'under-the-counter' payments seem to have been made by patients in order to secure services, a form of default privatisation. Nevertheless, this 'Semashko' system, at least in its intended form, occupies the extreme, most publicly dominated end of the archetypal range.

The UK health system is dominated by the largely publicly provided and financed National Health Service (NHS) but includes some user charges (for example, for dental and optical services, and for prescriptions) and also contains a small private insurance sector outside the NHS. Most of the resources used within the NHS are owned or employed publicly, but primary-care doctors, known as general practitioners (GPs), are contracted private individuals or firms. Further complications have been introduced by two rounds of reforms in the 1990s that have separated purchasing and providing functions (while maintaining the public character of both), and have increased the role of private investment funding in the system (see Chapter 25). Examples of other countries whose systems are dominated by public provision and finance but with more private components than the former Communist countries include Denmark (where non-hospital services are provided under public contract by private practitioners and certain co-payments exist), Sweden (where private practice is common only in occupational health and dentistry), Ireland (where richer people have more limited access to public services and voluntary but public insurance covers 30 per cent of the population) and New Zealand (where primary providers are private practitioners and a range of co-payments apply) (OECD 1992, 1994).

A number of poorer countries have modelled their health systems on either the British or the Semashko model. Taking Uganda as an example, the health system was designed to be dominated by public finance and provision. A range of publicly owned health facilities from small aid posts in most remote regions, intended to provide services for minor illnesses, through health centres, district and regional hospitals and two teaching hospitals in the two largest cities, are all publicly equipped, directly employ all health personnel, and are publicly supplied with drugs and other non-durable items. Recent reform of the system includes major decentralisation, in line with general administrative decentralisation in the country. However, problems of inadequate resources and poor management of resources in the public sector have ensured that the public system has for some time not been as dominant in health service provision as was originally intended. Within the public system, substantial 'default privatisation' is reported, as in the former Communist countries discussed above. In addition, pure private practice fills the gaps the public sector has left, and covers a high, if difficult to document, proportion of primary-care provision. This includes some of the purest private-sector arrangements to be found, with unregulated providers selling unsubsidised or taxed services directly to health service users. At the hospital level private not-for-profit providers (mainly mission-run facilities) play a substantial role. Examples of countries in which similar descriptions apply include India, Pakistan, Bangladesh, Kenya, Tanzania and Ghana, although the extent of 'default privatisation' within the public system varies considerably (Berman *et al.* 1995a, b; Bennett *et al.* 1997).

'Social insurance' dominates the health systems of most of the remaining industrialised countries. The 'Bismarck' model of social insurance, developed in Germany, has often been considered the standard model of social insurance. In the former Federal Republic of Germany 75 per cent of the population were insured compulsorily, about 13 per cent voluntarily with the same (quasi-public) statutory sickness funds while 10 per cent of the population were insured privately. (This situation has changed with the integration of the former GDR into the system.) There are both public and private providers (51 per cent of hospital beds are public; ambulatory care physicians and pharmacies are largely private). Both types mainly operate on contract to the statutory sickness funds (although investment costs are usually directly funded by state governments), and there are only minor co-payments paid by patients at the time of use. Examples of countries in which similar

system models operate include Belgium (however, co-payments are much more substantial and a higher proportion of health service costs are met through tax-based finance), France (with 99 per cent insurance with statutory sickness funds but a 'reimbursement' model for many health sector transactions whereby health service users pay and are later reimbursed), the Netherlands (where recent reforms aim to stimulate competition in both the insurance and provision markets), and Austria (OECD 1992, 1994).

The majority of Latin American countries (defined henceforth as Mexico and the countries of Central and South America, excluding the Caribbean island nations) contain three important sub-systems: public, social insurance and private (both insurance and out-of-pocket financed). Taking Peru as an example, about 30 per cent of health sector expenditure goes to public sector providers, 35 per cent to separate social insurance providers and about 35 per cent to private providers. (About 20 per cent of this last 35 per cent flows through private insurance funds and 80 per cent through out-of-pocket payments.) Theoretically the public sector covers over 70 per cent of the population, the social security sector over 20 per cent and the private sector about 2 per cent. However, this overstates the differences in coverage levels. In practice, as in other poor countries, the public sector achieves less than intended and public documents admit that about one-third of the population have no access to services while the private sector serves a much larger population who seek alternatives to both public- and social-insurance-provided services – about 20 per cent of the population. Although distributions vary between these three major sectors, this 'segmented' health system applies to all Latin American countries except Brazil, Chile, Argentina and Costa Rica

(Ministry of Health, Peru 1997a, b; IADB 1996). Colombia, most notably, is in the process of trying to reform from a 'segmented' to an integrated model (see Chapter 25).

Private, voluntary insurance plays an important role in a limited number of countries and always coexists with some form of coverage or compulsory arrangements for those it excludes, or would otherwise exclude. The US is the most prominent country that substantially relies on this set of arrangements, with employers expected to provide coverage to their employees and dependants (61 per cent of the population are insured in this way), or individuals to insure themselves (13 per cent of the population). Public finance directly covers only the elderly, disabled and poor – 23 per cent of the population. Arrangements for military veterans cover 4 per cent of the population. Fourteen per cent of the population are officially 'uninsured', although this group is indirectly able to access some services.[1] The majority of providers are private, although there are some public health institutions that are established in areas the private sector fails to serve, such as inner cities. Until recently private insurance covered nearly 99 per cent of the population in Switzerland, although a share of the population was already covered compulsorily before this became universal in 1996. Significant subsidy also antedates the recent reforms. This extent of private, voluntary insurance is unequalled anywhere else in the world but some other countries also reach relatively high levels, including South Africa (where private insurance covers about 20 per cent of the population and accounts for about 50 per cent of expenditure) and Brazil, an otherwise 'integrated' exception to the 'segmented' Latin American model, but where 25 per cent of the population have private insurance (OECD 1994; van den Heever 1997; Chollet and Lewis 1997).

These suggested categorisations are only points on the range of system options from the fully public to the fully private. Many health systems have different mixtures of the elements from the systems described above. Some have not been stable in their characteristics, even before the far-reaching and wide-ranging reforms of the 1990s. These have substantially changed the systems of many of the 'model' countries described above. Bearing in mind that systems have become even more complex and even less capable of categorisation in the decade, the following discussion considers evidence relating to system performance up to the early 1990s. Chapter 25 will separately consider recent reform models.

20.2 *Health Sector Expenditure Patterns*

Table 20.1 shows expenditure performance for a selection of OECD countries presented in three categories. The non-OECD countries mentioned have substantially lower GDP *per capita* and less reliable data collection systems, making comparison difficult. The table suggests that those health systems categorised as more public in character exhibit lower expenditure *per capita*, lower expenditure as a percentage of GDP, and lower health expenditure inflation between 1972 and 1992. Some exceptions to these generalisations can be highlighted. Sweden and Ireland spend comparably in their share of GDP to the social insurance group. The UK and New Zealand grew in terms of GDP share at a comparable rate to the social insurance group in the 1982 to 1992 period. Although there is a correlation between health system types and GDP levels, Denmark's GDP is higher than that of the Netherlands, yet both countries' health expenditures have conformed to that expected of their health system groups rather than

Table 20.1 Health expenditure, 1972–92

Country	1992 per capita expenditure (US$000)	As % GDP			% change in health expenditure share	
		1972	1982	1992	1972–82	1982–92
Public systems						
United Kingdom	1,157	4.7	5.9	7.1	26	20
Denmark	1,175	6.3	6.8	6.5	8	–3
Sweden	1,319	7.5	9.6	7.9	28	–18
Ireland	880	6.7	8.4	7.1	25	–15
New Zealand	1,109	5.3	6.9	7.7	30	12
Social insurance systems						
Germany	1,775	6.5	8.6	8.7	32	1
Belgium	1,438	4.3	7.4	8.2	65	11
France	1,748	6.2	8.0	9.4	29	17
Netherlands	1,462	6.7	8.4	8.6	25	2
Austria	1,593	5.4	8.0	8.8	48	10
Private insurance systems						
Switzerland	2,074	5.5	7.5	9.3[a]	36	–[a]
United States	3,248	7.6	10.3	14.0	36	36

Source: OECD (1994).
Note:
[a] Swiss accounts were revised in 1985 and the two data series cannot be linked.

that of their GDP group. The US lies at the extreme in almost all measurements and Switzerland, which over the period of meas urement was characterised by a private-insurance-based system, is in either second or third place in relation to all these measures.

The table also shows that in almost all OECD countries health expenditure growth as a percentage of GDP was higher in the 1970s than 1980s, with some countries in the public group reversing the health expenditure increases of the 1970s (Denmark, Sweden and Ireland) and some in the social insurance group reducing further growth to 1 per cent or 2 per cent (Germany and the Netherlands). The US was the only country in the 1980s that failed to bring health expenditure growth under control.

This is far from conclusive evidence of a causative effect from health system type to health expenditure and expenditure inflation. The simple categorisation of countries misses important differences in the health care systems and obscures important similarities that exist across groups. Important possible confounding factors have not been controlled. However, a correlation between public finance and expenditure control is widely believed, and the evidence is strongly suggestive. As we shall see in the following chapters, there are good theoretical grounds for expecting a causal relationship.

However, normative judgement does not easily follow. These data themselves do not identify which health systems are more efficient. Higher-spending health systems could be technically less efficient – spending more for an equivalent level of achievement – or allocatively inefficient – spending more for a higher level of achievement which would not be judged by society worth the sacrifice of expenditure in other sectors. Alternatively, lower-spending health systems could be allocatively inefficient. They may fail to spend where the increased level of achievement associated with more spending would be judged worth the sacrifice of expenditure in other sectors – a judgement of 'under-funding' in the language of everyday debate. Nevertheless, 'cost control' has become a major preoccupation in many social insurance systems and even more so in the US, while

Table 20.2 Health status performance

Country	Life expectancy 1991	Infant mortality (per 000 live births)	
		1970	1991
Poland	71	33	15
Bulgaria	72	27	17
Georgia	73	–	16
Azerbaijan	71	–	33
Czechoslovakia	72	22	11
UK	75	19	7
Denmark	75	14	8
Sweden	78	11	6
Ireland	75	20	8
New Zealand	76	17	9
Uganda	46	109	118
India	60	137	90
Pakistan	59	142	97
Kenya	59	102	67
Ghana	55	111	83
Germany	76	23	7
Belgium	76	21	8
France	77	18	7
Netherlands	77	13	7
Austria	76	26	8
Peru	64	108	53
Ecuador	66	100	47
Colombia	69	77	23
Mexico	70	72	36
Uruguay	73	46	21
Switzerland	78	15	7
US	76	20	9
South Africa	63	79	54

Source: World Bank (1993).

'under-funding' has been the major preoccupation in many of the public health services.

20.3 Health Status Performance

Table 20.2 shows life expectancy and infant mortality rates for countries in each of the categories. The data show far more association with the income level of countries than with health system categorisation. Health status is well understood to be affected by a wide range of social and economic variables and it would be surprising on the basis of this type of analysis if health systems could be shown to be critically determinant of health status outcomes.

Nevertheless, something other than income differences must explain the differing health status performance of the Central and Eastern European and the Latin American groups. The average GNP *per capita* levels of the selected countries were very similar (US$1,882 for the former and US$1,840 for the latter in 1991; World Bank 1993), yet the former group exhibit superior health status performance in all respects. However, it is impossible to conclude that the main explanatory factor is the health system. A number of factors are similar within the two groups relative to the differences between them, including historical and cultural factors, political systems and geographic locations – and these are so strongly enmeshed with the development of different health systems that it is very difficult to separate them.

A more promising approach has been applied to Latin American and Caribbean data by the Inter-American Development Bank (IADB 1996). Figure 20.1 shows health expenditure as a percentage of GDP plotted against the 'health gap' defined as the difference between observed life expectancy and

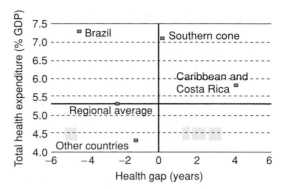

Figure 20.1 Expenditures and health gaps in four sub-regions of Latin America and the Caribbean. Note: the health gap compares observed life expectancy with the expectation based on *per capita* income
Source: Inter-American Development Bank (1996).

that which would be predicted by *per capita* GDP for four groups of countries defined according to their health system type. The four sub-system types are defined slightly differently from the system advanced above as (1) integrated public systems: the Caribbean countries and Costa Rica (similar to the UK-headed group in our categorisation); (2) private provision through contracts financed with public resources: Brazil (not equivalent to any of the groups discussed above but similar to post-reform models of several – see Chapter 25); (3) social insurance systems using contracts with private providers: the 'southern cone' countries of Argentina and Chile (similar to the Germany-headed group) and (4) the segmented system group, described above and containing all the other countries.

The figure shows that the worst performance in terms of outcome is observed in Brazil, despite the highest level of expenditure *per capita*. The segmented system performs slightly better than the regional average in terms of health outcome and spends considerably less than the regional average in proportionate GDP terms. However, the

Deviation from predicted life expectancy (years)

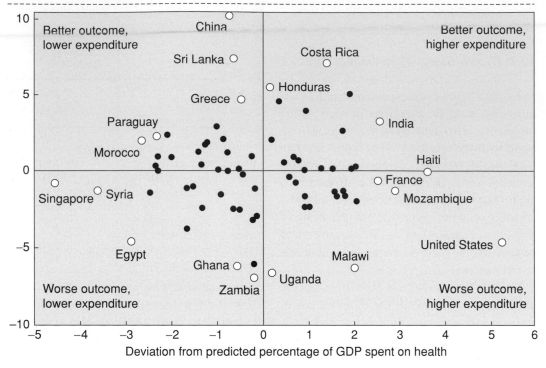

Figure 20.2 Life expectancy and health expenditure in selected countries: deviations from estimates based on GDP and schooling
Source: World Bank (1993).

overall regional performance is poor in this respect, and this group of countries still exhibits a negative 'health gap'. The social insurance countries spend substantially above the regional average and achieve a health gap only just above zero. The best health outcomes are associated with the integrated public systems, despite health expenditure levels only slightly above the regional average.

Can this analysis be considered conclusive proof of the superiority of integrated public systems? Unfortunately for those seeking a clear-cut answer, within this group of countries too there is still a strong association between health system type and income group, and although the 'health gap' and the expression of health expenditure in proportionate

GDP terms attempt to control for this, a higher level of actual health expenditure is still implied in the richer countries (comparing for example the public integrated with the segmented systems). Further, the association between health system type, cultural and historical factors and political systems remains and we cannot be sure which is most important in determining health status outcomes.

A similar analysis suggests that income differences cannot explain the relatively poor performance of the US in terms of health status. Figure 20.2 shows that the US is the most extreme outlier in exhibiting high expenditure and poor life expectancy when compared with levels predicted from *per capita* GDP and schooling. Looking at the other outlying countries in this graph, it is difficult to suggest any further relation between health system and health status outcome. While Uganda and Ghana achieve worse outcomes than expected, India in the same group achieves more. On this evidence, the group including Paraguay and Honduras appears to achieve better outcomes than expected, conflicting with conclusions of the previous analysis (although that did not take account of the expected effect of levels of schooling on health status). Again, the evidence of US performance is only circumstantial evidence of an association of more privatised health systems and poor performance – from both efficiency and health outcome perspectives.

20.4 Health System Satisfaction

A few international surveys of health system satisfaction have been undertaken. One conducted among OECD countries was reported by Blendon *et al.* (1990) and produced the data shown in Figure 20.3. The data suggest that social insurance systems produce the most satisfaction, public health service systems less, and the private health system of the US the least.

A later survey (Blendon *et al.* 1995) considered the underlying causes of these differences in more depth, covering only the US, Canada and West Germany. In the six years between measurements taken in 1988 and 1994 it appeared that satisfaction had grown substantially in the US (to 18 per cent) while falling substantially in Canada and West Germany (to 29 per cent and 30 per cent respectively).

Critics of the original survey had argued that Americans were more cynical and distrustful of all public institutions and the results therefore were not specifically relevant to the health care system – in other words that the factors responsible for the oddly outlying US health system were themselves independently responsible for poor satisfaction ratings. It was also suggested that Americans might have higher expectations of their health system than other populations. Further

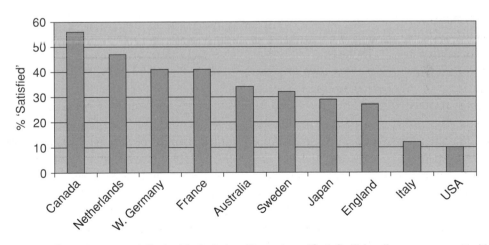

Figure 20.3 Percentage satisfied with their health system. 'Satisfied' implies agreement with the proposition 'On the whole, the health care system works pretty well, and only minor changes are necessary to make it work better'
Source: Blendon *et al.* (1995).

exploration of these factors indicated that Americans expressed slightly less satisfaction with public institutions in general than Canadians and West Germans – suggesting that even if other populations are more satisfied with more public-oriented health systems, Americans might not be. In some, but not all, respects Americans also had higher expectations of their health system. However, the differences in these measures were not comparable with the difference in health system satisfaction. Americans did, however, report a comparable excess of dissatisfaction with the fairness of their system, having faced a problem in paying a doctor or a hospital bill.

A single explanation of growing confidence in the US was not suggested and obvious candidates do not present themselves to the current authors. Falling confidence in Canada and West Germany is likely to be explained by substantially increased cost-control measures in both countries. This suggests that the association between system type, expenditure levels and population satisfaction evidenced by comparing public and social insurance systems may not be an artefact. While the effects of lower health expenditure on health status measures may be too difficult to separate from the effects of the multitude of other determinants, satisfaction measures may be a more sensitive reflection of the impact of expenditure on the health system.[2]

Notes

1. Percentages sum to more than 100 per cent because of duplicate coverage.
2. Controversial data on health system performance were compiled in the *World Health Report, 2000* (WHO 2000). We have chosen not to conduct similar analyses using those data for two reasons. First, the data are controversial owing to the basis of their estimation. Many of the data included in these tables are imputed on the basis of regression analysis which predicts rather than measures the performance of health systems. This creates a circular effect in trying to analyse the impact of other factors (system characteristics) while controlling for those factors which have been used to predict the indicators in the first place. Other data were estimated using information provided by a small sample of respondents in selected countries. We do not believe that such estimates give reliable results even for those selected countries, or that they can be used to predict performance in others. Second, the 'archetypal' character of most health systems in our list had dissolved by the time of the compilation of these data. These categories can no longer usefully distinguish between system types, and new categorisations are appropriate.

Chapter 21

Reliance on the State

Public Health Service Systems

....

21.1 Introduction

As we have seen in Chapter 20, public health service systems have better controlled cost inflation than other types of system, but it is often argued that they are 'under-funded', leading to more rationing of essential care and poor-quality services. Evidence of any direct effects of rationing and service quality on health outcomes is hard to assemble. There are many factors determining health status, and they are not precisely understood. Furthermore, health status improvement is not the only valued outcome of a health system – others that may be considered important include freedom from anxiety, and comfort during illness. Palliative care may be valued for its own sake. Achievements of this sort should be added to health status improvement to reflect population satisfaction. Satisfaction levels might prove to be highly sensitive to levels of health system adequacy.

In the archetypal public health service system, simplified and stylised for the purpose of this chapter, funding is provided through general taxation and the system is characterised by public ownership, providers of care are given fixed annual budgets, and health workers are direct employees. Health services are free to users at the point of use.

21.2 'Under-funding' and Rationing of Services?

Where the source of all funding for the health sector is public, policy makers should aim to ensure that the funding provided equals their estimate of the optimal level of provision (Q^{**} on Figure 19.2).

Getting the funding level right is a necessary condition for ensuring that resources are rationed to the highest-priority uses. In place of the price mechanism, public systems must use alternative measures to decide who gets how much of what. There are four means to ration in a pure public system: setting the pattern of supply; gatekeeping; waiting lists; and queues. A fifth means – applying user charges – has been ruled out in our characterisation of an archetypal public system. Issues relating to user charges will be considered in Chapter 25.

No matter how well funded, all public systems must set the pattern of supply, and in so doing enable some demands on the health system and disallow others. The pattern of supply determines access costs and the level at which other rationing mechanisms have to be applied. A new hospital can always be built and will always reduce access costs for someone. In the situation of most public systems, where resources fall short of the ability to meet a wide range of legitimate demands facing them, setting the pattern of supply involves making more critical choices. Limiting the growth of premature baby units implies higher gatekeeping thresholds (see below) and increases the probability that a baby capable of survival will be denied treatment. Despite this, the level of funding may be appropriate, given the opportunity cost of resources for this purpose. Costs per QALY reach high levels in this area (Rogowski 1998). In the public systems of poor countries, routine and unquestionably high-priority health services, such as caesarean section capacity in the case of complicated births, are out of reach of millions of women at the time of need. Even this does not necessarily imply poor rationing through poor planning of the pattern of supply. All uses of resources have extremely high opportunity costs in poor countries, and even in an ideally allocatively efficient context it is difficult to see where resources could be found to staff and equip operating theatres in remote and sparsely populated regions.

It is easy – and common – to assume that such problems indicate the failure of public decision making, both in ensuring optimal funding levels and in setting patterns of supply appropriately. Decisions on setting the pattern of public supply should, at least in principle, attempt to order demands for health resources according to marginal social value. By using the results of economic evaluations where they are available, and by attempting to apply social values more generally where they are not, public systems have the oppor-

tunity to improve on the pattern of supply which would result from a price-rationed system. In practice, there is wide variation in the extent to which supply planning achieves its potential (for example, see Box 21.1).

Most public systems attempt to use 'gatekeeping' (or a referral system) in an attempt to ration services to those with the highest-priority demands. In the UK it is intended that the whole population should be registered on the list of a general practitioner, who should act, in all cases other than emergencies, as the first point of contact with the health system. Whenever a case falls outside the general practitioner's areas of competence, or requires specialist facilities, the general practitioner should refer the patient to an appropriate provider. In theory, this process should ensure that specialist and referral services are rationed towards those patients whose demands have been sanctioned as appropriate, or as 'needs that should be met' (see Box 19.1). In practice, the mechanism works imperfectly, general practitioners have widely varying rates of referral (Wilkin *et al.* 1989) and large numbers of patients directly attend Accident and Emergency departments for minor complaints that could be dealt with by the GP. In some cases this is because it is more convenient and in others because they have not been able to register with a GP (Lowy *et al.* 1994). Direct use of hospital outpatient departments is a common problem in developing countries (for example, in Zimbabwe: Hongoro and Musonza 1995), where mechanisms to enforce referral systems are not or cannot be applied. However, if the price mechanism were used to ration between levels of care, reliance would be placed on the patient's own assessment of need for specialist services weighted against their higher price, and assessment of the risk of paying twice by paying a generalist for advice as to

Box 21.1   Setting the Pattern of Supply in Public Systems: Geographical Resource Allocation

The pattern of supply is determined in public systems directly by public decision making. This usually has more centralised and decentralised components. Building a hospital will seldom be an option for a local health authority, but decisions to increase levels of equipment, or to develop a new service, may be.

From a central perspective, one major question is how to distribute resources among local health authorities. Typically, public health systems have developed rather inequitable and allocatively inefficient financial distribution among local areas. In many countries, this resulted from funding criteria being facility rather than population based. Inequitable facility distribution from a population perspective was commonly the result of historical factors: the facilities and their distribution existed prior to the development of the public system.

South Africa's health sector resource distribution reflects the peculiar historical factors of that country. Zwarenstein and Price (1990) document the disparities in the availability of hospitals and hospital beds to urban and rural populations and by 'race'. For example, bed ratios varied from 130 people per bed for the urban white population to 460 people per bed for the rural, black/Asian/Coloured population outside the 'homelands'. McIntyre *et al.* (1991) propose a formula which would allow these inequities to be addressed. The formula would determine the resource allocation to each region or 'homeland' on the basis of an estimate of need for curative and preventive services and population size and structure. Comparing the results of the formula with the existing allocation of resources suggests that one region, Western Cape, receives 183 per cent of the estimated appropriate allocation while another, KwaNdebele, receives only 10 per cent. Including an allocation for teaching, the estimates change to 141 per cent and 12 per cent respectively.

Some countries already apply a formula such as that proposed by McIntyre *et al.* (1991). In England such a formula was first introduced in 1977. It adjusted population numbers for standardised mortality ratios weighted by their importance in bed use and patterns of use of facilities. At the introduction of the formula, the most over-provided region received about 15 per cent in excess of its fair share of resources; the most under-provided region about 11 per cent less. After ten years the formula had achieved a narrowing of that range from +7 per cent to −4 per cent (Mays 1995). Such formulas have the advantage over traditional resource allocation mechanisms of transparency, and almost certainly move health systems in a more equitable direction in resource allocation, but cannot be perfectly objective. Since 'need' cannot be directly measured, debate remains as to the variables which best proxy for need and how they should be combined – for example, mortality or indicators of social deprivation (Sheldon *et al.* 1993; Mays 1995).

whether specialist services are necessary and then paying for those services recommended. In practice, countries which do not use gatekeeping systems encounter problems of inappropriate use of specialists for generalist advice and sometimes an absolute lack of a source of generalist advice for patients as to the appropriate type of specialist to consult (Rosenblatt *et al.* 1998; Franks and Fiscella 1998).

The third rationing mechanism in public systems is waiting lists. Waiting lists are administered queues by which patients referred to departments where an out-patient appointment, day case appointment or hospital bed is not available are listed and allocated the resource as it becomes available in order of registration on the list. In principle, the waiting list mechanism does not prioritise higher-value demands. There is no reason to suppose that the highest value should be placed on the demand of the potential patient who has waited longest. In practice, however, waiting lists do adopt prioritising mechanisms – emergencies are prioritised and sometimes a numerical scaling of priority is proposed (Culyer and Cullis 1975; Gudex *et al.* 1990). The underlying assumption is that all cases receiving the same weight on the list have the same priority and that waiting is a fair means of rationing among cases of equal social value. Again, it is easy and common to assume that evidence of long waiting lists is in itself evidence of inadequate resource allocation to the health sector, and poor rationing within it, whereas it is at least plausible that the opportunity costs of increasing provision of services with long waiting lists are higher than the social value placed on shortening the lists (see Further Reading on pp. 204–5).

From the point of view of the economist there may be a further worry about using waiting lists, especially in cases of chronic diseases. The 'output' of cataract surgery is really years of improved vision, and of hip surgery, years of pain-free mobility. By making elderly people wait for treatment we may be reducing the overall benefits associated with a given operation or treatment.

The final rationing mechanism in public systems to be considered is that of queues in which patients physically wait to receive services. Queues ration on the basis of the patient's willingness to allocate time in order to receive a service. There is no reason to believe that there will be a strong relation between this willingness and the social value of the service. Although controversial, it is sometimes argued that higher social value should be placed on the receipt of services by breadwinners and mothers on whom the rest of the family rely – such people are likely to place a high value on time and be least able to spend long hours queuing. The system of 'triage' by which a nurse or doctor quickly assesses the emergency status of patients attending Accident and Emergency departments attempts to impose prioritisation on the basis of social value. In general, queuing is an inefficient and inappropriate rationing mechanism – its use is often a means of maximising the efficiency with which health professionals' time is used (which may or may not be justifiable) rather than as a means to ration services.

In extreme emergencies, waiting cannot be used as a rationing mechanism – patients will die before they reach the top of a waiting list or the front of a queue, supply constraints are absolute, and gatekeeping assumes critical importance. The case of premature baby units has been mentioned above. Organ transplant is another example of critical and time-limited demand but absolute supply constraints that in this case are independent of the funding level of the system. In such cases there is likely to be explicit consideration of gatekeeping thresholds – days of gestation which warrant admission to a premature baby unit, the age and health condition of a candidate for organ transplant. These explicitly ration on the basis of social value and unsurprisingly are controversial.

Further Reading – The Dynamics of Waiting Lists

Street and Duckett (1996) divide typical approaches to waiting lists into demand- and supply-side approaches. A large literature supports the view that supply-side approaches are misguided. If expected waiting time is understood to be acting as the price of the service concerned, it follows that supply-side approaches, by reducing that price, will increase demand, and a number of UK studies of waiting lists in practice support that view. It would follow that mechanisms to restrict low-value demands prior to their registration on waiting lists would have more potential to reduce lists. These include prioritisation mechanisms, about which there is a growing body of evidence – Meiland *et al.* (1996) in the Netherlands and Langham *et al.* (1997) in the UK provide two recent examples.

Demand has largely been viewed as originating from general practitioners and patients, but a number of authors have focused on the role of hospital specialists in the system. According to one argument, conditions for which long waiting lists develop are of low scientific interest – a factor discussed in this chapter as capable of distorting incentive structures in public systems. According to another, consultants use waiting lists as a signal of their reputation with patients and general practitioners, creating the incentive to maintain them unnecessarily. Whatever the underlying explanation, consultants who control the rationing of hospital resources may face perverse incentives, and these can be further entrenched if hospitals are rewarded for long waiting lists by receiving additional resources – as is implied by supply-side approaches.

Street and Duckett explain how politically motivated approaches to solve the problem in the UK have been misguided from the perspective of the social demand value framework we are using in this book. For example, setting targets for the number of patients waiting over a given period reallocated resources between patients on the list towards those who would have waited longest – precisely those deemed low priority according to previous weighting decisions. They argue (after Iverson 1993) that the solution is to introduce enforceable contracts between funders and providers; and to ensure that funding is linked with work load. Arrangements in Victoria, Australia, which follow these guidelines are shown to have reduced lists dramatically. Sources: Iverson (1993); Meiland *et al.* (1996); Street and Duckett (1996); Langham *et al.* (1997).

21.3 Provider Behaviour in a Public System

Public health service systems have traditionally owned the physical resources necessary to provide services and directly employed the health professionals working in them. Under public ownership, provider institutions have traditionally been reimbursed by budget, which may be global, or may be made up of separate expenditure 'votes' for different types of expenditures (such as salaries and drugs) between which limited virement (reallocation of expenditures between votes) is permitted. This situation is criticised as providing little incentive for the provider institutions to improve either efficiency or quality of care.

A number of perverse incentives are commonly attributed to these institutions. Those institutions which succeed in reducing their costs may be penalised by reductions in their budget the following year – hence the infamous end-of-year spending sprees which ensure that an institution does not appear to have excess resources. Efficiency improvements that imply a higher rate of patient 'throughput', such as switching from in-patient to day surgery, may increase expenditure over a given period of time, causing a budget short-fall. Measurable improvements in quality such as improvements in survival rates will not automatically attract new resources and, if costly, are unlikely to be pursued.

Crude attempts to measure and reward performance within a budget-governed system are capable of inappropriate manipulation. Mullen (1985), for example, argued that the use of 'performance indicators' in the UK was likely to produce behaviour aimed at improving the indicator rather than improving performance. A crude example would be unnecessarily increasing length of stay to meet a bed occupancy performance indicator.

When health professionals are directly employed, the most common form of reim-bursement is by salary. Salaries are criticised for providing little incentive to performance, as they are fixed and paid regardless of per-formance. In Central and Eastern European countries a salary system certainly seemed to be associated with poor performance and motivation on the part of health profession-als. However, this may be an excessively harsh view of the potential of a salary system. Arguably the problem in those countries arose from the demotivating impact of inadequate

salaries combined with failure to relate pro-motion and career prospects to fair judgement of performance. In practice, whatever people think is measured and used in the promotion process will be encouraged within that salary system. For example, if research and publica-tion ensure the fastest route to promotion, it is likely that junior doctors will prioritise them at the expense of patient care. To the extent that salary reimbursement systems fail to pro-mote good performance, the cause is probably the difficulty of measuring good performance and perverse institutional incentives to recog-nise other types of merit (or demerit).

21.4 Conclusion

Figure 21.1 characterises the relative positions of different types of health services on curves of marginal private and social value that are standardised for marginal cost (as explained in Box 19.2). While the characterisation may be accused of verging on caricature, the under-lying point – that health service priorities are likely to be completely reordered from a social rather than private perspective – is difficult to contest. It follows that the price

Figure 21.1 Ordering priorities on the basis of marginal social value compared with marginal private value

mechanism is a poor allocator of resources in the health sector. This is recognised in virtually all health systems around the world. Most countries use elements of service planning, gatekeeping, waiting lists and queues in place of prices for rationing, at least in some parts of the sector. They also intervene in the market to support delivery of priority services – to the poor – and of preventive and public health services that are not prioritised by price rationing.

The principal problems of public systems are the lack of mechanisms to push funding to appropriate levels; weakness in the application of rationing mechanisms; and lack of incentives to promote performance improvement within traditional reimbursement mechanisms both of provider institutions and health professionals, especially where public sector capacity is weak. In the worst cases the results may even be inferior to what would

arise from price mechanisms. The populations of rural areas in poor countries would be better off if their taxes were not collected and used to provide services for the elite in teaching hospitals in capital cities. Nevertheless, evidence from lower-, middle- and upper-income countries – that better solutions to geographical and service pattern resource allocation questions can be found using the available rationing mechanisms – suggests that where policy makers genuinely support the distribution of health sector resources on the basis of social values, pure public systems are more likely to deliver than reliance on the price mechanism.

Yet, real debates are not about choosing between purely public and purely private systems, but about configuring systems with the most useful components of each. We will continue to build the foundations of this debate throughout the rest of Part IV.

Chapter 22

Voluntary Insurance-based Systems

22.1 Voluntary Insurance

Insurance companies will sell insurance only if the premiums are sufficient to pay for claims and the costs of administration and they normally aim also to make a profit. The policies offered will therefore be (on average) actuarially unfair; that is to say, on average policy holders get back less than they pay in. People will voluntarily choose to purchase such insurance only if they are *risk-averse*, in other words, they are willing to pay more than the *actuarially fair premium* (the probability of an event multiplied by its cost). The extent to which individuals are risk-averse determines the viability of insurance markets.

Risk aversion can partially be explained in terms of diminishing marginal utility of wealth. If individuals are *risk-neutral* with respect to utility (that is to say, they are willing to sacrifice only the amount of utility equal to the probability of an event multiplied by its utility cost), they will still be 'risk-averse' with respect to income, since the actuarial premium would have a lower utility value than the utility cost of the event multiplied by its probability.

Figure 22.1 demonstrates this point. The graph shows the relationship between wealth

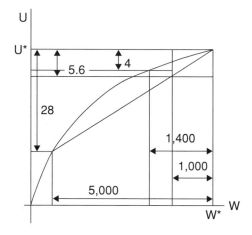

Figure 22.1 Decision to purchase insurance

levels and utility measured in imaginary 'utils' for a skier. The skier considers the purchase of insurance against a risk of accident on the slopes. An accident would cost her £5,000 and there is a 20 per cent chance of an accident occurring. The actuarial premium is £1,000. The utility loss associated with paying the premium is shown on the graph to be four utils, while the utility cost associated with the risk is twenty-eight utils. If the skier is risk-neutral with respect to utility, she will be willing to sacrifice up to 5.6 utils (28 × 20 per cent) for insurance, an amount which can be identified graphically on a straight line between the starting point and the point associated with the risky outcome. She will therefore be willing to pay up to about £1,400 according to the graph. It follows that the more utility of wealth diminishes (the more the utility of wealth curve bends) the more an individual will be willing to pay for insurance, for any given level of risk aversion with respect to utility.

It is expected that risk aversion with respect to utility varies from individual to individual and is a component ('an argument') of his or her preference function (see Chapter 2). The extent of risk aversion with respect to wealth determines the viability of insurance markets. This varies according to individuals' diminishing marginal utility of wealth and level of risk aversion with respect to utility. In the example above, insurance will be exchanged only if transaction costs and profits can be contained within the £400 'slack'.

A major problem associated with private insurance is *adverse selection*. Individuals' risks vary and their own knowledge of some aspects of their particular risks is better than that of the insurance agency. If the insurance agency sets a single premium that is capable of covering the actuarial risks of the whole population, those who perceive their risks as higher will purchase insurance. Depending on profits and transaction costs, some individuals who perceive their risks as lower than average will purchase insurance, but those who perceive their risks as substantially lower, or who are less risk-averse, will opt out. The average risk will increase. This will cause the actuarial premium (based on the insurance company's claims experience) to increase and further individuals will now perceive the premium offered to be a bad deal (see Figure 22.2).

The equilibrium depends on the distribution of risk in the population and levels of

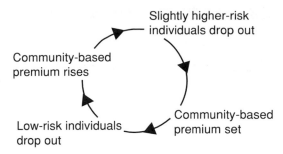

Figure 22.2   Adverse selection problem

risk aversion. If risks are identical the problem does not arise; the problem worsens as the risk distribution broadens. If risk aversion is very high, even the lowest-risk individuals may be willing to pay a premium which covers average risk, transaction costs and profits. In most cases insurance agencies attempt to deal with the problem by offering individualised premiums requiring the gathering of more information about individual risks. While many markets succeed in functioning on this basis, the process increases transaction costs, and some risks become 'uninsurable', assessed at too high a probability to be offered at a premium much different from the cost of the risk itself. In the case of health insurance, the old and chronically ill may find themselves in this position (see Box 22.1).

A second problem affecting all types of insurance parallels the rationing problem considered in the previous chapter. Since full insurance implies that price will not be paid by the consumer of services at the point of use, price will not serve the function of a rationing mechanism. The extent to which the insured, when not faced with the price at the point of use, increase their use of services is known as *moral hazard*. (See Chapter 18 for a fuller discussion of moral hazard.)

If we assume (as discussed in Chapter 19) that the values derived from demand curves and prices represent social values of benefit

Box 22.1   The Uninsured in the US and Adverse Selection

Rowland *et al.* (1994) report on the profile of the uninsured based on census bureau information for 1992. Some 37.1 million people (approximately 15 per cent of the US population) were
uninsured on average on any given day in 1992, 18 million (7 per cent) were uninsured for the
entire year and 51.3 million (20 per cent) were uninsured for some period of the year. The
diagram describes some characteristics of this population.

The average cost of insurance cover for a family was $5,232. Where employers bought group
insurance they covered approximately 70 per cent of its cost. Individual policies which could be
purchased privately by the unemployed, self-employed and those who were not offered insurance by their employer were more expensive and more restrictive with respect to deductibles
and co-payments and the exclusion of existing conditions. Fifty-nine per cent of the uninsured
gave inability to afford insurance as their reason for non-insurance; 22 per cent cited loss of
a job; 3 per cent cited ill health or prior illness and 7 per cent were uninsured by choice.

What can be concluded about the level of adverse selection? Those who choose not to
purchase insurance (7 per cent) can be assumed to consider it poor value and their own risk
of ill health low. It is difficult to assess what further proportion of those who cite loss of a job or
lack of affordability as their reason also consider the option of private insurance purchase poor
value rather than absolutely unaffordable. The 13 per cent who earned more than the equivalent of $46,280 annually for a family of three (more than 400 per cent of the official poverty line)
are unlikely to be absolutely unable to afford insurance, especially in a context in which their
expected health care costs are at least as high as the premium. This 13 per cent may constitute a minimum estimate of the proportion of the uninsured who consider insurance bad value.

Those who are excluded on the basis of ill health or prior illness (3 per cent) are also
uninsured because of the individualisation of risk assessment that follows from the adverse
selection problem.

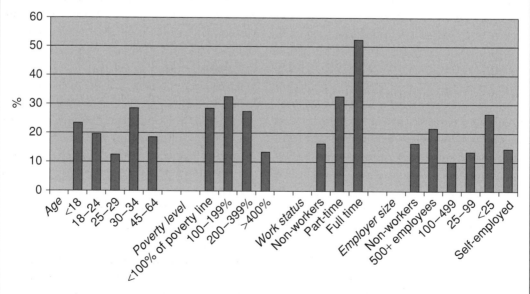

Figure B4   Characteristics of the uninsured population

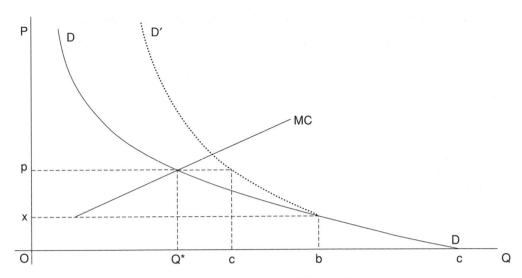

Figure 22.3 Moral hazard under full insurance, deductibles and co-payments

and cost, the optimal point of consumption and provision of services can be defined as the point at which demand equals price (Q* on Figure 22.3). Under full insurance, demands will be expressed up to point a, where the demand curve intersects the horizontal axis. 'Excess demand' can be defined as Q*a. Insurance agencies are also faced with the need to devise rationing mechanisms. In Figure 22.3 we have replaced our usual simple assumption of a straight-line demand curve with a more realistic curved one, to emphasise that a large proportion of excess demand ab/aO can be rationed by using prices that are a relatively small proportion of the marginal cost-based price (xO/PO).

Common rationing mechanisms used by insurance agencies are price based: deductibles that require the insured to pay the first fixed amount of any bill, and co-payment that requires the insured to pay a fixed proportion of the bill. A deductible of x reduces demand from a to b, and also has an important effect on proportionate transaction costs, since they are likely to be relatively high for small bills.

Co-payments swivel the effective demand curve upward from the point of intersection with the deductible, or from the horizontal axis if there is no deductible (D'D). At price p, demand will be further reduced to c. It is worth noting that only the removal of insurance altogether is capable of rationing demand back to the 'optimal' Q*. Thus these price-based rationing mechanisms are capable of reducing but not eliminating moral hazard.

Returning to the conceptual framework of Chapter 19, we are concerned with the extent to which voluntary-insurance-based health markets provide the optimal amount of health services, and ration in such a way as to allocate health sector resources to uses with the highest social value. Dropping what we have argued to be the highly unrealistic assumption that value derived from demand curves can be deemed even to approximate social value, we find little in voluntary insurance markets that promotes social objectives. In the price rationing of insurance itself, 'uninsurable' demands are eliminated by adverse selection, without any likely relation between insurable demands and the social value of demands. Indeed, we can identify a number of demands likely to prove uninsurable or uninsured for which there is reason to believe that private demand value understates social value – diseases of the poor, especially where communicable, and palliative care of chronic but incurable diseases such as cancer and AIDS. In the rationing of services to the insured, price-based rationing mechanisms reinforce the ordering of private valuation in determining which services will be offered and received and which not. In the absence of other intervention, ineffective but popular treatments will be promoted while effective but unpopular treatments will not.

Insurance agencies use a further rationing mechanism that is not price based, that is, disease and service exclusion lists. These usually exclude high-cost diseases and interventions, and uses of health services that can be considered optional rather than risks, such as cosmetic surgery. Some of these exclusions may imply social-value-based rationing – cosmetic surgery is unlikely to be a high social priority, while others may imply the reverse. In any case, at least to some extent, such exclusion lists are likely to 'shift' costs within the health system rather than change the pattern of provision of the whole system, an issue which will be considered at more length in Chapter 24, where health systems delivered through multiple, parallel sub-systems are considered.

22.2 Institutional Structures and Incentives

In the framework of analysis presented in Chapter 19 the simple theory was discussed,

that incentives to efficiency strengthen as institutions become more private – owing to the profit motive, the threat of being driven out of business and the closer relation between the individual's rewards and the individual's effort. To what extent can such a theory be sustained with reference to health systems characterised by voluntary health insurance?

In the archetypal system we are considering in this chapter, provider institutions are privately owned, though they may be for-profit or not-for-profit. In the case of hospitals they are large institutions with multiple decision makers and workers; the distance from the one-man business in which reward equates with the business's performance is therefore great.

In Chapter 16 we discussed the various models of motivation and behaviour of private hospitals, looking at managerial and behavioural theories, and in Chapter 18 we discussed incentives.

These models have differing implications for the nature of incentives in hospitals. For example, if the 'physicians' co-operative' model applies, and fee-for-service reimbursement pertains, incentives to effort will make themselves felt. Physicians will likely be interested in doing more work – but incentives to economise on costs incurred by the hospital, patients or third-party payer will be absent (see below). If Newhouse's quantity and quality model applies, there are incentives to technical efficiency (in the sense of aiming to eliminate X-inefficiency for any given quality of care – see Chapter 16), but the quantity and quality objective may conflict with allocative efficiency (if lower quantity and quality are allocatively efficient). In Harris's model the 'trustee administrators' are likely to have some concern with technical if not allocative efficiency but the physician group may succeed in frustrating it.

The above suggests that even technical efficiency incentives are likely to be weak in this setting, and it is not surprising that evidence of greater technical efficiency in the private health sector is equally weak. For example, Valdmanis (1990) found that public hospitals in Michigan (USA) were technically more efficient than non-profit private hospitals. Studies in other countries comparing private and public hospitals generally fail to find the efficiency effect predicted by the simple theory (for example, in Thailand: Pannarunothai and Mills 1997; in South Africa: Naylor 1988).

If technical incentives are weak, allocative efficiency incentives are likely to be absent altogether. The combination of the lack of allocative efficiency incentives arising from the motivation and behaviour attributed to private hospitals and 'third-party' payment (separation between the insurer and the provider of services: the 'contract' model) is likely to be the more important source of the cost-control problems in private systems discussed in Chapter 20. At least until recently, reimbursement of providers has usually been in the form of a fee for service for both hospitals and doctors, which may encourage both types of provider to maximise the number of services offered to each patient. Furthermore, since the number of patients referred to a hospital or doctor is less under their control than the volume of services provided to each patient, it is argued that fee-for-service reimbursement mechanisms produce high service intensity per patient, possibly associated with a highly technological approach to patient care. It is certainly unlikely that fee-for-service reimbursement will encourage careful consideration of the necessity of marginally helpful diagnostic tests or dubiously effective procedures (see Box 7.2).

The combination of third-party payment and fee-for-service reimbursement has often been classified as inherently inflationary. Under such conditions 'moral hazard' occurs on both the demand and the supply side of the market, since both providers and patients pass their costs on to a third party and do not have to take them into account in deciding the services to provide and use. Under private insurance, patients usually have a free choice of providers. (Again recent reforms and new models such as Preferred Provider Organisations may restrict this.) Where neither providers nor patients bear costs, the most likely form of competition between providers is 'quality competition'. Providers compete using 'quality signals' (which often take advantage of the consumer's relative ignorance) such as high levels of amenity (for example, private rooms, telephone, fax and television facilities) and availability of specialist facilities on the basis that consumers may associate these characteristics with high-quality clinical care (see Chapter 15 and Boxes 15.1–2). However, it is likely that a further element in this mix is required for inevitable inflation – lack of constraints on the demand side. The health insurance inflation of the 1970s and 1980s in the US was grounded in this mix of factors, and South Africa has undergone a similar experience (see Box 22.2). In the US it is probable that the introduction of a range of reforms focused on cost control and the rapid development of various forms of insurance organisation known collectively as 'managed care' have resulted from a perceived need to introduce demand constraints. The experience of recession and widespread concern about international competitiveness seem, albeit belatedly, to have imposed limits

International Case Study

Box 22.2 South Africa's Private Insurance Market

South Africa is one of a small group of countries which have a significant private insurance market. Highly regulated 'medical-aid schemes' and actuarially based health insurance cover 17.2 per cent and 4.4 per cent of the population respectively, and consume 43 per cent and 4 per cent of resources respectively.

Medical-aid schemes are non-profit trusts that were prohibited from applying underwriting principles in setting premiums. More recently they have been administered by contractors working on a for-profit basis and paid as a percentage of income. Their behaviour has become indistinguishable from that of for-profit agencies and they have succeeded in changing the law to allow a degree of risk rating in determination of premiums. The situation has evolved to a classic 'third-party payer' model and inflation in the medical-aid scheme market, which averaged 7–11 per cent for hospitals, and 2–10 per cent overall in the years 1983 to 1989, peaked at 27 per cent for hospitals and 17 per cent overall in 1990, the year following the introduction of risk rating.

As costs in the medical-aid scheme market have spiralled, competition from purely for-profit and actuarially based health insurance, which is not entitled to tax exemption, has become more viable and more attractive to those with the lowest risks in the market. It is also purchased by the relatively rich, but their lower risks are apparent from their consumption of a less than proportionate share of resources. Adverse selection out of the more community-rated medical schemes further threatens the latter's viability, but measures proposed by a public commission charged with investigating the problem have focused on enabling medical-aid schemes to reduce their exposure to the highest risks (or 'cost shifting') rather than addressing cost control. For example, further development of risk rating is proposed, which would shift costs to those individuals who could afford higher-assessed premiums and to the public system for those who could not.

Source: van den Heever (1997).

on the extent to which US industry is able and willing to absorb further health insurance inflation.

22.3 Conclusion

In the 'archetypal' voluntary insurance system there is little to promote rationing on the basis of need, and much to promote both technical and allocative inefficiency, and an inflationary spiral. The finding in Chapter 20 that systems coming closest to the archetype described have the most serious cost-control problems and little to show for their higher spending levels in the form of better health status indicators would seem to be explained. This is clearest in the case of the US, but Switzerland too appears to be achieving very little marginal health status for its high level of expenditure.

Chapter 23

Social Insurance Systems

....

23.1 Introduction

The development of formal systems of health care finance in the nineteenth and twentieth centuries centred mainly on employment and the workplace. Whereas the system in the US developed on a quasi-actuarial basis, in Central Europe the model that emerged involved deliberate solidarity, with contributions based on income. As a legal framework for these schemes was put in place, and the income-based health insurance contributions became compulsory, in principle, the characteristics of 'social insurance' health systems became very similar to systems of 'tax-based finance'. Conversely, tax-based financing can be considered to be government-operated insurance.

One way to distinguish social insurance from tax-based finance is whether the revenues gathered are earmarked for health care (i.e. a fund is established that can be used only for a set purpose). Earmarked insurance funds can be contrasted with systems funded through general taxation in which health must compete with all other applications of government expenditure. Health service revenues are usually earmarked jointly under social insurance with pensions and unemployment

benefits. However, the term 'insurance' is sometimes used where an earmarked tax is not implied. For example, Canada's 'national health insurance' uses a premium basis of collection of revenues only in two provinces (OECD 1994), and the UK's 'national insurance' is treated as a general tax and does not create an earmarked fund.

It has become common to consider both tax-based funding and social insurance as 'public insurance' models which can use either 'integrated' or 'contract' forms (OECD 1992). 'Integrated' forms imply ownership and direct management of provider institutions by the insurer (in the case of tax-based funding, the government), while 'contract' models imply separation of the two and the purchase of services from provider institutions by insurers. This type of model is equivalent to the 'third-party payer' model in voluntary health insurance discussed above. Until recently tax-based financing used 'integrated' models and social insurance 'contract' models. This section will consider the 'archetype' social insurance model as one in which an earmarked fund is created and ownership of provider institutions is separate from the provision of insurance, just as in Chapter 2 'archetype' tax-based finance was considered to imply direct ownership and management of provider institutions by government. Chapter 25 will consider the implications of mixing these characteristics, as is becoming increasingly common.

A second difference (which is usual rather than required) between social insurance and tax-based finance is that social insurance contributions are usually collected by a quasi-autonomous body or bodies which is regulated rather than directly controlled by government. There may be other differences that arise from political interpretation of the distinctive features of the two arrangements. For example, there may be more focus on 'entitlement' under a social insurance system. There may also be greater willingness to pay higher social insurance premiums because uses of the funds are specific and enjoy wide consensus. In contrast, when paying higher tax, the distribution of any increase between alternative uses is not known, and some possible uses such as defence and industrial subsidy enjoy much less consensus.

A third usual rather than required difference is that patients tend to have greater choice of providers under social insurance than under tax-based financing.

This chapter considers only health systems in which social insurance can broadly be considered 'universal', covering 100 per cent or very close to 100 per cent of the population. Chapter 25 considers the quite common situation (characterising most of the Americas and a number of South East Asian countries, for example) in which some social insurance coexists with public and private sub-sectors covering different sections of the population. The implications of competition and movement of population groups between subsystems create significant complications and issues, sufficient to suggest that these systems can only be analysed separately.

23.2 Determination of the Level of Provision and Rationing

The principles a government should apply in setting social insurance premiums should be the same as those used to determine how much tax revenue to allocate to the health system. However, as we have seen in Chapter 20, social insurance systems have tended to allocate a larger proportion of GNP to health services, and to have experienced faster expenditure growth over recent years than tax-funded systems.

There are a number of reasons why we might expect greater pressures on health system expenditures under social insurance than under tax-based financing, which might explain this phenomenon. We have already suggested that there may be greater political acceptability of premium increases than of tax increases. Combined with a more intermediate role of a quasi-autonomous insurance agency which may see itself as representing 'consumers' as much as planning health services for the population as a whole, a greater influence of private demand pressures than under tax-based financing models would be expected. Additionally, as discussed above, a 'contract', or third-party payer, model may contain more pressures for higher costs than an integrated one, both to provide more care per patient and to allow the prices of health sector resources to increase.

It is difficult to conclude from a theoretical perspective whether or not this higher level of resource allocation to the health sector as a whole is more or less allocatively efficient than the lower level associated with tax-based funding. Price increases imply a different distribution of resources between factors of production in the economy, which has no efficiency implications. However, price increases also encourage more resources to be applied to health sector ends and this does have efficiency implications that are context-specific. For example, where doctors are highly paid relative to other professions, more young people may be expected to train as doctors, and an over-supply of doctors could develop. Doctors may carry out activities undertaken by nurses in other countries, suggesting sub-optimal skill mix in the sector. Comparison of the ratio of doctors to nurses in different countries suggests that their roles are very different in different settings.

As we have seen in Chapter 21, it is possible to argue that tax-based funding is unlikely to meet the level of funding which would be achieved under a private-demand-driven system. In contrast, private demand is likely to over-allocate resources to health, since those demands towards which it is biased (high technology, curative care) are likely to consume higher levels of resources than those which it is biased against (preventive and public health measures) both per intervention and in terms of the total resources required by feasible levels of provision.

We can compare the performance of social insurance in terms of its ability to allocate resources according to the priorities of the social demand curve introduced in Chapter 19. Under social insurance, at least in principle, access to services is the same for rich and poor, in contrast to the case where prices are used to ration access to care. However, it is important to look carefully at how characteristics of the system can impose barriers (see Box 23.1). Additionally, social insurance avoids the problem of 'adverse selection' discussed above in relation to private insurance. By enforcing membership of an insurance scheme the drop-out of lower risks which is central to the adverse selection problem is avoided, and as a result, population groups for whom private demand is insufficient but

social demand may be high will receive services. This is an important rationale for social insurance. Its 'social' nature is determined by the *solidarity* created by the inability to drop out. However, to the extent that the population's demands as a whole play a greater role in determining the allocation of resources, we would still expect the problem of information shortages to result in bias towards high-technology curative services and against preventive services. Services known to generate externalities are also likely to be well provided under this system, since the link between receipt of treatment by an individual and payment has been removed. In practice there is a high degree of overlap between externality and prevention, and if prevention is poorly understood these services are likely to be under-provided relative to a tax-based system.

Rationing mechanisms available to social insurance systems include the full range of those available to tax-based finance systems and private insurance systems. Analysis of the likely implications of social insurance for the nature of rationing depends on the balance struck between price-based rationing mechanisms (co-payments and deductibles) and planning mechanisms based on assessment of social demand. This varies widely between social insurance systems. For example, in Germany planning mechanisms are dominant in the setting of a 'benefit package' that all sickness funds (social insurance institutions) are required by government to provide (although this may change with the current reforms; Normand and Busse 2001). This package is amended on the basis of 'benefit', 'medical necessity' and 'efficiency', consistent with a social value framework. Further planning mechanisms include the development of hospital services according to hospital plans, and controls over contribution levels and budgets. Market mechanisms are present

International Case Study

Box 23.1 Access to Health Services under Universal Health Insurance in Korea

Yang (1991) describes the Korean national health insurance system. It is unusual in that it is 'social' in the sense that membership is compulsory but private with respect to the ownership of the insurance societies which offer cover. These societies cover 90 per cent of the population, with the remaining 10 per cent entitled to health services through public assistance programmes.

However, access to health services is constrained by two major factors. First, effective co-payment rates are extremely high – up to 65 per cent for hospital out-patient services (see the first table). Second, the geographical distribution of health resources is extremely uneven (see the second table).

The result is substantial remaining inequity. Both factors have important implications for access to any services, and for a resulting 'two tier' system of high-quality services for the rich and low-quality for the poor. Worse, if compulsory premiums are paid by those who cannot afford to use health services owing to co-payments or lack of geographical access, the result may even be a cross-subsidy from the poor to the rich. The premiums of low-income families subsidise the services received only by those who have the financial resources to pay high co-payments or the geographical luck.

Effective co-insurance rates for out-patient services in Korea

Location	1985	1986	1987
General hospital	50	60.1	62
Hospital	50	62.1	65
Clinic	30	40.3	41.2

Source: Yang (1991).

Distribution of health resources: hospital beds and physicians in Korea

Measure	Seoul	Three major cities	All other cities	Rural areas	Total
Population (000) (%)	9,639 (23.8)	6,932 (17.1)	9,872 (24.4)	14,006 (34.6)	40,448
No. of physicians (%)	8,817 (40.8)	4,431 (20.5)	6,891 (30.9)	1,697 (7.8)	21,626
Physicians per 100,000 population	91.47	63.92	67.67	12.12	53.47
No. of hospital beds (%)	27,721 (30.5)	17,026 (19.0)	–	–	89,463
Beds per 100,000 population	282.9	245.6	–	–	221.2

Source: Yang (1991).

Continued

> The very high co-payments are probably found in only a few countries in addition to Korea. However, geographical access issues are relevant to all theoretically universal systems. In an ideal health system, distribution of hospital and specialist resources would favour more population-dense areas and average distances to all types of health provider would decrease with increased density. These arrangements minimise the average geographical access costs of the population as a whole but inequity of access is then inevitable. In real health systems, health professionals' preference for the amenities of urban areas (especially in poorer countries), historical patterns of health service provision and the location of prestige health facilities in larger cities exacerbates these even in a universal financing system.

but controlled and muted in the setting of physician reimbursement. A point system determined by a joint committee of sickness funds and physicians is used to pay doctors and there are relatively small co-payments for pharmaceuticals – until recently only approximately 5 per cent of sickness fund pharmaceutical expenditure (Busse 1999). In contrast, in France, price-based rationing plays a much greater role. Patients pay 13.3 per cent of health service expenses out of pocket, patients pay at the time of use and are reimbursed later, and financial factors are a commonly stated reason for not seeking care. Increasing co-payments has been the principal response to cost-control concerns alongside decisions to exclude some services from social insurance coverage altogether. Only recently have policy makers started to pay more attention to planning mechanisms beyond constraining the number of doctors and hospital beds, for example in trying to encourage a 'gatekeeper' system to emerge (Lancry and Sandier 1999). In general, social insurance systems tend to make greater use of co-payments than do tax-funded systems, thereby relatively emphasising private rather than social demand.

23.3 *Institutional Incentives*

Contract models in social insurance have typically varied widely and ranged from the salary- and budget-based reimbursement of public systems to the fee-for-service mechanisms of private voluntary insurance systems. For example, under the French system, global budgets and salaries apply to public hospitals whereas individual doctors are reimbursed on a fee-for-service basis, and opt in or out of a pre-negotiated fee structure (OECD 1994). In German hospitals, capital expenditure was directly funded according to the state government's hospital plan while operating expenditure was traditionally reimbursed on a *per diem* basis, with a diagnosis-related group system being introduced in 1993 (Kamke 1998).

Social insurance systems normally have a combination of highly regulated financing, and provision by publicly owned hospitals, or providers working to highly regulated contracts. Along with other characteristics of social insurance systems, the incentives are between those in budget/salary systems and the incentives to over-provide services of a fee-for-service system. These arrangements in the hospital sector prompt questions about the underlying 'objective function' of hospitals, since they cannot be assumed to maximise profit. Only by understanding what hospitals are aiming to achieve can we assess how the incentives they face may impact on their performance. Revenues are a key component of the objective function of most conceivable types of hospital, since revenues determine the resources hospitals can mobilise, the ability to meet managerial objectives, the extent to which services can be offered and their quality. Revenue-related objectives are therefore likely to appeal to profit-motivated, managerial, professional satisfaction-oriented and public service-motivated hospitals alike. However, attitudes to costs are likely to vary, with profit-motivated hospitals being more likely to seek to minimise costs and others less interested in the control of at least some cost components.

Stepan and Sommersgutter-Reichmann (1999) consider the situation of Austrian hospitals. In Austria hospitals are funded partly by the public sector, via the federal government, and partly through the national insurance companies. Reimbursement rates through this system are such that the margin between cost and revenue is negative or zero in the case of out-patients, and slightly positive in the case of in-patients. However, patients with supplementary insurance can be charged higher prices for in-patient care to include payments to both physicians and the hospital for superior hotel services. Stepan and Sommersgutter-Reichmann comment that the incentives in this situation would appear to promote emphasis on in-patient care at the cost of out-patient care, especially since supplementary insurance does not cover out-patients. This is compounded by the number of beds devoted to supplementary care being limited to 25 per cent of the hospital's total beds – another reason for hospitals to seek to increase their bed numbers.

These unintended incentives generated by organisational and financing structures are likely to contribute to the allocation of health sector resources to services with the highest collective private demand, especially where optional additional insurance offers the most significant additional revenue-generating activities as described above in Austria.

Countries with social insurance health systems do tend to allocate higher levels of resources to high-technology, curative and somatic care relative to preventive and palliative care, compared with tax-funded systems (see Chapter 20).

23.4 Conclusion

The archetypal health systems we have considered so far can be located on a 'continuum' producing outcomes dominated by private demand considerations at one extreme, and by social demand considerations at the other. Providing institutions in these archetypal systems can be characterised as over-providing services and over-emphasising expensive high-technology intervention in the service mix at one extreme and as lacking incentives to internal efficiency and public responsiveness at the other. The continuum ranges from private insurance (private demand, over-supply) through social insurance to tax-based systems (social demand, efficiency incentive-deficient).

By 'archetyping' health systems a number of distinctions may have been overdrawn, and pure versions of the health system types described may be difficult to find, especially as the types of reforms discussed in Chapter 25 are increasingly being adopted.

However, by developing simplified models, we have been able to demonstrate the use of the economic principles developed in the preceding chapters to the building of models that help to explain health system performance. The rest of Part IV will further develop the models to debate highly complex health systems resulting from the coexistence of parallel systems and the implications of combining health system characteristics in less conventional ways – the thrust of health sector reforms around the world.

Chapter 24

Parallel Systems

....

24.1 Introduction

In Chapter 23 a comparison was made of the main archetypes of systems of health sector finance and provision. It was pointed out in this comparison that in reality the health system in almost all countries is more complicated than models imply, and in many cases a wide range of systems coexist.

The 'segmented' health system of the majority of Latin American countries has been described in brief in Chapter 20. In these countries the system is composed of a series of sub-components: tax-financed services, social insurance, private insurance, and out-of-pocket private health care markets for rich and poor. Population groups with no access to any of these coexist. Box 24.1 presents more detail on the range of patterns of provision within this group of countries. Chapter 20 also discussed the parallel coexistence of a range of 'sub-systems' within the overall system of a number of other poorer countries. This tends to occur where the public system has failed to play the role envisaged for it. In these countries, the configuration of 'sub-systems' is different from that of the 'segmented' Latin American countries, in particular containing a much less important, if any, social insurance

component. Finally, the US, while discussed substantially in Chapter 23 as a private health system, is also in reality a parallel health system which includes a much more extensive private voluntary insurance sector than any other country, but also includes important components of public finance and public provision, as explained in Chapter 20.

To some extent, each sub-system presents the characteristic issues of its equivalent archetype system as discussed in Chapters 20–2. Nevertheless, interaction between sub-sectors produces further issues, problems and opportunities that are characteristic only of parallel health systems. We start this chapter, however, with a discussion of the general characteristics of the 'out-of-pocket' sub-system that nowhere approaches universality and has therefore not been discussed as a system in its own right.

24.2 The Out-of-pocket Sub-system

There are many manifestations of 'out-of-pocket' health system components. A market for drugs for which prescriptions are not required operates in almost all countries, often, but not always, in a highly regulated

Box 24.1 The 'Segmented' Health Systems of Latin America

The table indicates the extent to which resources are shared and coverage levels achieved between different segments of a number of 'segmented' Latin American health systems. Data all relate as closely as possible to the year 1990, but some unavailability leads to discrepancies, some quite large, between the total of health expenditure expressed as a percentage of GDP and its component parts.

In almost all the countries in the group, private expenditure is a very high proportion of the total – 63 per cent in the median country reported in the table below. This is comparable to the figure of 59 per cent of the US, and much higher than industrialised countries generally (24 per cent) and the Latin American and Caribbean region as a whole (43 per cent) (IADB 1996).

If social security expenditure is shared between those officially covered and public expenditure between the rest, the measured degree of inequity also varies considerably between countries like Uruguay, Panama, Venezuela and Nicaragua which report spending a lower per capita amount on the covered than on the uncovered populations and between countries like Colombia, Ecuador and Bolivia which report spending more than twice as much per capita on the covered.

However, 'official' coverage levels can be shown in some cases to depart quite substantially from 'real' coverage levels, as shown in the table overleaf, suggesting that some of the first group of countries may in reality perform less equitably than is officially stated. These data indicate the considerable divergence between official coverage statistics and utilisation of services, but still do not take account of the percentage of the population who are unable to access services at all, which is less important in urban than rural areas.

Health resource and access distribution between sub-health sectors: selected Latin American countries

Country	Total health expenditure per capita ($)	Total health expenditure (% GDP)	Expenditure (% GDP)			Official coverage	
			Public	Private	Social security	Social security	Any health services
Uruguay	219	5.7	1.2	2.7	1.8	67	96
Panama	173	8.7	2.5	3.2	3.4	60	79
Mexico	155	3.8	0.3	2.4	1.0	60	77
Venezuela	102	8.5	2.0	4.8	0.6	36	76
Colombia	65	5.7	0.6	2.9	1.0	11	75
Guatemala	37	5.6	1.2	1.6	0.5	17	50
Ecuador	39	6.3	1.6	3.7	0.9	13	61
Nicaragua	31	5.0	6.6	1.3	0.9	32	69
Paraguay	49	3.2	0.4	2.8	–	–	54
El Salvador	58	5.0	0.7	3.7	0.5	9	59
Bolivia	34	4.5	0.3	3.1	0.8	20	34
Peru	59	3.1	0.5	2.0	0.6	33	44

Sources: IABD (1996) and Suárez *et al.* (1994).

Continued

Coverage and utilisation by health sub-sector, Ecuador urban areas, 1988 (%)

	Official coverage	Utilisation of services[a]
Social security[b]	15.5	7.6
Armed forces	1.1	2.2
Private insurance	1.5	n.a.
Uninsured:	81.9	90.2
Ministry of health		25.0
Private providers		65.2
Total	100	100

Notes:
[a] Per cent of total consultations.
[b] Affiliates of the Ecuadorian institute of social security, including the population covered by peasants' insurance.
Source: Suárez *et al.* (1994).

environment. 'Out-of-pocket' financed consultation with primary care doctors, formally registered, exists in almost all countries (other than those few which formally ban private practice) from the Harley Street practitioners in London to the medical practitioners of the slums of Karachi.

The model that most closely resembles a simple 'free' market is where out-of-pocket fees are charged for services provided by for-profit operators especially in the informal sector in poor countries, where supply factors are not subject to restriction by regulation. Prices, and quantities bought and sold, are determined by the interaction of demand and supply. Rationing is strictly on the basis of willingness and ability to pay, and problems of 'moral hazard' do not apply. The implication is that private demand-based values are not challenged in any way: services are not offered to those with inadequate ability to pay and users are not protected from 'catastrophic' illness costs (see Further Reading on p. 226). Most evident, however, are the implications of information asymmetry in a context in which the financial incentives associated with maximising sales of whatever treatments are

available seem often to outweigh the incentives to ethical practice (see Box 24.2). The restricted access of the poor to this sub-sector is consequently a mixed blessing. These markets do not exhibit the type of cost escalation associated with a stronger role for the private sector in the health systems of other countries, simply because they are absolutely demand constrained. The poverty of the populations makes demand price-elastic, even for services considered essential by those making utilisation choices. (For many poor populations in poor countries, elasticities of demand for health care greater than one have been measured – see, for example, Gertler *et al.* 1987.)

These free markets also provide evidence of externality problems. Unrestricted use of drugs is allowing resistant organisms to develop. Resistance to antibiotics and chloroquine is commonly reported in such settings. There is too little use of other services whose effectiveness is increased at critical coverage levels and 'public goods' such as vector control of malaria and schistosomiasis are of course not provided at all by this type of market. In the first two cases, it is difficult to

International Case Study

Box 24.2 The Private Sector in Bombay

Yesudian (1994) collected anecdotal evidence regarding unregulated private health providers in Bombay, India. Among the problems described were the following.

A committee charged to review the situation in private nursing homes found:

1 Less than one-third had qualified nurses.
2 Hardly any disinfected the operating theatre after each use – some did so less than once every three days, others less than once a week.
3 Infectious waste material was dumped in municipal bins.
4 Wards and beds were 'dirty' and poorly lit.

Dangerous medical practice, including:

1 Poor sterilisation of instruments in private hospitals.
2 Negligence in post-operative care, resulting in death in two leading private hospitals, leading to court cases.
3 Careless intravenous fluid administration and monitoring.
4 Improper and wrong administration of drugs.
5 Neglect of patients in lower-grade beds.

Fraudulent financial practice, including:

1 Issuing of false medical certificates and bills.
2 Collusion among general practitioner, consultant, nursing home owner and investigation centre to share fees in return for referrals.

Of course, these anecdotes cannot be assumed to provide a full and balanced picture of the private sector of Bombay, and our selection from them has been pointed. What the anecdotes do at least suggest is that there are elements of private sector activity which come quite close to an unregulated free market in health services. They also suggest that ethical behaviour cannot always be relied upon to resolve the potential contradictions between profit maximising and public health in the presence of significant information asymmetries.

Source: Yesudian (1994).

separate the problems of information asymmetry and externality.

Consider the position of the demand curve in this market in relation to the social marginal value curve. For at least some products, dominant externalities are negative, and lack of information causes people to demand poor-quality and inappropriate drugs that they would not demand in the presence of full information. For these products, the social marginal value curve lies to the left of the demand curve – the optimal production level is exceeded. For other products the reverse might be the case: the valuations which the relatively poor consumers can place on appropriate and effective drugs may be low relative to those implied by a weighting system more equitable than disposable income. Can regulation of the market address any of these problems?

More regulated out-of-pocket markets may be capable of controlling some, but not all, of the problems of this market. Common forms

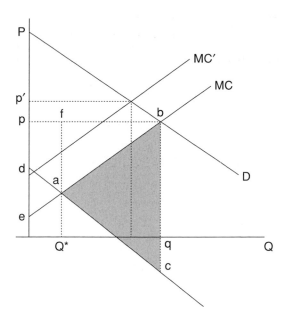

Figure 24.1 Regulating an over-valued pharmaceutical product

of regulation of over-the-counter pharmaceuticals include the licensing of products, qualification standards for pharmacists and restrictions on the activities of unqualified personnel in pharmacy shops.

Figure 24.1 considers the implications of the regulations for an extreme example of an over-valued product – a drug with few effective applications, and potentially harmful effects if inappropriately prescribed, past its use-by date or poorly stored prior to sale. Assume that the free market operates with a high level of demand due to widespread belief in the drug as a cure-all, and there is a supply curve equal to the marginal cost curve because firms are 'price takers' (see Chapter 6). Price is determined at p, and quantity bought and sold at q.

Along the left of the MSV curve are the few effective applications of the drug, and underneath the quantity axis are the negative social values for the many harmful applications. The shaded area abc shows the welfare loss associated with the free market solution in

comparison with the perfect solution (where quantity Q* of the drug is provided in cases where application is most effective). One regulatory option is to refuse a licence to the drug. Assuming this is fully implemented quantity 0 is bought and sold. In comparison with the perfect solution, area (ade) is the welfare loss. In the absence of alternative interventions, the analyst might conclude that since area ade is smaller than abc, the regulation is appropriate – in other words the costs associated with the unavailability of the drug for effective cases are smaller than the costs associated with the unregulated availability of the drug.

Increasing the qualification levels of those who prescribe and dispense (which is the result of the effective implementation of higher qualification standards and control of activities of the unqualified in pharmacy shops) is intended to push the market solution towards the optimum point a. The policy assumes that a qualified pharmacist will not prescribe and dispense dangerous drugs, or inappropriate drugs. Point a might be achieved – but there are two problems. First, like public policy makers, in most cases pharmacists will not have the necessary data to pinpoint a. However, if they ask the right question when they dispense – 'Is this patient likely to benefit to an extent which makes the price worth paying for him?' – they may get as close as possible, given the available information. Second, pharmacy training must be assumed to instil ethical behaviour as well as knowledge in the pharmacist, since the pharmacist must be willing to forgo profits of abf in order to behave ethically. Alternatively, sanctions against unethical behaviour must be effective.

Imposing qualification standards will also increase the cost (and therefore supply) curve (for example to MC′), which will also have the effect of reducing the quantity bought and sold (to q′) – but this alone will not select appropriate uses of the drug over inappropriate and harmful ones. If we assume that price remains the rationing mechanism (i.e. that pharmacists are not ethically motivated to ration according to MSVs), price rises to p′, and the effect is to restrict use of the drug to a smaller number of those willing and able to pay a higher price – who are not necessarily those for whom use of the drug is appropriate.

Further Reading – How do the Poor find the Cash for 'Out-of-pocket' Health Expenditures?

Russell (1996) surveys evidence on the sources of cash for out-of-pocket health expenditure among poor households. It seems possible to identify an order of resort, or a range of options which households are increasingly reluctant to adopt. While any of these options may prove 'catastrophic' in the sense of undermining the long-term health and well-being of the household, they probably represent increasing likelihood of 'catastrophe'.

First, households use available cash. Most studies report a sizeable proportion of households able to do this – for example, 44 per cent of households in a study in Sierra Leone and 41 per cent in a study in Kenya. However, available cash may have high opportunity costs in poor households. In Haiti, costs of consulting medical and traditional practitioners substituted for food expenditures to the extent that children's nutritional status was undermined; savings intended for school fees appear to be a frequent explanation of the existence of spare cash in the household.

Second, households resort to 'extended entitlements' (after Sen 1981), or claims on support networks. These can also prove costly, since there are limits to the individual household's claims on such networks, and future claims are therefore more restricted. Ultimately the whole network can be undermined

by large numbers of such claims, which may result from changes in needs for, or the costs of, health services at the community level – such as epidemics, or changes in financing mechanisms at a local health facility. Loans will usually be repaid when cash becomes available, with the attendant risks suggested by the previous paragraph.

Third, households resort to sales of stores of value that may include clothes saved for special occasions, farm produce or land. All these reduce household wealth and, at the extreme, the ability of the household to support itself. Studies in Kenya and Thailand found that 24 per cent and 60 per cent of land sales respectively were prompted by the need to raise resources caused by expenses associated with illness. Source: Sen (1979).

24.3 Rationing of the Public System, Social Insurance and Private Insurance in a Parallel Systems Context

When public sub-systems are compared with their social insurance sub-system counterparts and those in turn are compared with their private sub-system counterparts, they generally exhibit lower *per capita* expenditure. This pattern matches the results of comparisons of universal systems, but some of the suggested causes of higher and lower expenditure are even greater in this context. If there appears to be reluctance among voters in a democracy to increase tax-based funding in line with health sector cost and technology growth in a universal system, it is likely to be even greater when a significant proportion of voters are not direct beneficiaries of expenditure in the public health sector. Extensive public subsidy of the social insurance sector will not create a more universal interest in public health expenditure if the expenditure votes are separate and com-

International Case Study

Box 24.3   Caesarean Births in Ecuador and the Rest of the World

The data in the table were reported in the Ecuadorian newspaper *El Comercio*. The data show a strong gradient in the tendency to carry out the more interventionist procedures, with very high rates in private clinics, average rates in the social security institute hospital and low rates in the public facilities. This gradient is reflected in global data from the rest of the world, with high rates in the privatised health system of the US and lower rates in social security and public health systems.

Births delivered by caesarean section, 1996 (%)

Ecuador	
Private clinics	65
Andrade Marin hospital (social security)	35–40
Patronato municipal (public)	30
Isidro Ayoro maternity (public)	22
Rest of the world	
World average	20
US	25
Ireland	11
Cuba	10
Japan	7–10

Source: *El Comercio*, 9 February 1998.

petitive rather than jointly determined. The users of the three sub-systems are differentiated by increasing wealth and social status. As the sub-system becomes more privatised this effect is reinforced, since poor and low social status populations are likely to secure a less effective voice in even the most democratic societies.

Arguments about the overall extent of 'under'- or 'over'-funding closely parallel those of their universal system counterparts. From a societal perspective, funding within the public system may be more appropriately spent than that in the private one. The 'public good' measures implemented in the country are usually in the public sector, and sometimes in the social insurance sector. A system aiming to prioritise primary health care and offer lim-

ited access to higher levels of care through referral usually operates. The coexistence of other sub-sectors serving the needs of urban, middle- and upper-income groups may even allow the public sub-sector to concentrate more effectively on an appropriate mix of care for poor rural populations than is possible in more universal systems, especially where private and social insurance systems are well developed and extensively provide referral hospital level services.

At the same time, private demand considerations evidently dominate in the private insurance sector where high levels of technology are present and specialist consultations dominate ambulatory services. Latin American countries are renowned for their high rate of caesarean births, which probably reflects

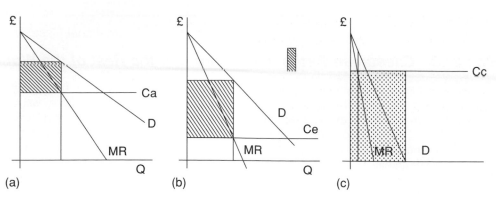

Figure 24.2 Cost-shifting incentives in private insurance: (a) comprehensive, (b) for elective surgery, (c) for chronic illness care

both private demand dominance and level of specialist involvement. Within countries, there is a strong association between location of birth and type of delivery (see Box 24.3). As was discussed in Chapter 23, rationing to control moral hazard largely depends on co-payments, but the implications of failure to provide particular types of services – undervalued ones because of externality and information asymmetry, and services to the poor – may be unimportant if the sector is defined as serving the rich and providing them with curative services. However, the use of disease exclusion as a rationing mechanism which aims to control adverse selection rather than moral hazard is effectively a 'cost-shifting' strategy in a parallel system context. The high level of ability to pay of the rich and relatively healthy can be exploited to offer luxurious services to patients and substantial profit to insurers with a high concentration of elective surgery cases that have predictable prognoses and limited costs. The extent of risk sharing is limited, and the most expensive cases are returned to the public or social security sub-sectors. These sub-sectors effectively cover nearly the whole population for the most catastrophically expensive risks whatever proportion of the population is considered to be covered by the private

sector. Adverse selection, cost shifting and cream skimming are closely related in this context. The incentives to cost shifting can be shown graphically in Figure 24.2.

The figure shows the potential profitability of different types of insurance to a monopolist private insurer, and the potential surplus to be shared in an oligopolistic insurance industry (see Chapter 15). Assume, for simplicity, that comprehensive insurance is the combination of insurance for elective surgery and insurance for chronic illness care only. The demand for elective surgery and treatment of chronic illness is assumed to be somewhat lower than for comprehensive insurance, but demand for elective surgery insurance is the higher of the two. Cost is assumed to be lower for elective surgery, and higher for chronic illness care. The hatched areas show potential profitability. Since it is more profitable to the insurer to offer insurance for elective surgery only, she will not offer comprehensive insurance. Assuming there is some demand for chronic care insurance above its cost, an insurer may offer this separately, but it will represent a relatively minor activity. The public or social security sector is left with the responsibility of offering chronic care to all who are deemed to need it at a cost potentially as large as the larger shaded area in the third figure. (The size of this area depends on the volume of care the public or social security sectors decide to offer.)

Where a social insurance sub-sector exists, it usually exhibits intermediate characteristics with respect to the trade-off between private and social demand factors (for example, in its caesarean birth rates – see Box 24.3), although in some countries it is effectively integrated with the public sub-sector. In contrast to the typical social insurance model considered in Chapter 22, the social insurance model in most segmented Latin American systems is integrated with no competition between social insurance agencies. (This latter characteristic is changing in some countries which have been undergoing reform in the 1990s – see Chapter 25.) The characteristics of this social insurance model leave it more likely to lie further towards the public end of the spectrum than the model of Chapter 22. There are fewer incentives on the part of providers who are not competing with each other to provide services responsive to consumer demand or to maximise performance from a social value perspective. There are also weaker incentives for insurance agencies which are statutorily entitled to their revenues, whatever the views of their enrolees, to steer providers towards private demand responsiveness. In some countries this leads to little distinction between public and social security sub-sectors. Both are considered poor quality, resource inadequate and with poorly motivated staff who are often more interested in a parallel private sector.

24.4 The Interaction of the four Sub-systems: Equity

The most evident deficiency of these parallel sub-systems is the extreme levels of inequity

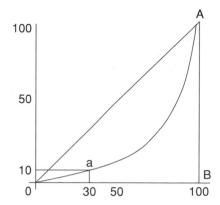

Figure 24.3a The Lorenz curve

implicit in the data presented in Box 24.1. Levels of funding *per capita* have a steep and positive gradient as the population served becomes richer and healthier. While those who can afford private insurance and whose conditions do not exclude them receive services comparable to the most luxurious and well resourced available anywhere in the world, at the other extreme, large population segments are denied access to services at times of need. The characteristics of the different groups vary.

Lorenz curves are a useful technique for measuring inequity in the distribution of any resource. The standard form of the Lorenz curve depicts percentage of population against percentage of income, ordering the population from the lowest- to highest-income earners moving from left to right (see Figure 24.3a). For example, point a on Figure 24.3a shows that the poorest 30 per cent of the population earn only 10 per cent of total income. A 45° line represents perfect equality in income distribution. The greater the curvature of the Lorenz curve, the more unequal the distribution. The information on the Lorenz curve can be summarised by the Gini coefficient, which expresses the area between the Lorenz curve and the 45° line as a proportion of the triangle 0AB on Figure 24.3a. Musgrove

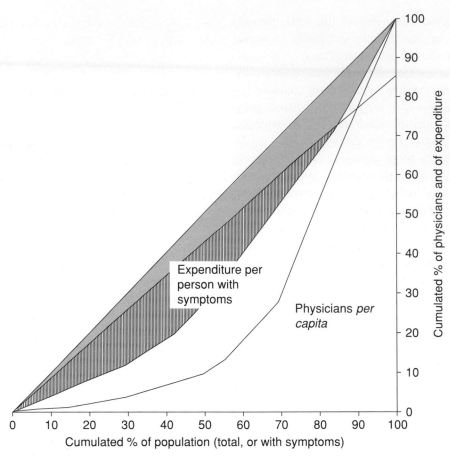

Figure 24.3b Health sector resource distribution in Peru, 1978
Source: Musgrove (1986).

(1986) has depicted the inequity of health sector resource distribution in Peru by adapting the technique (Figure 24.3b). The figure shows that inequities in the distribution of physicians *per capita* and in the distribution of expenditure per person with illness symptoms are marked. The Gini coefficient for the distribution of physicians is 0.51 – for income distribution this level would be interpreted as extremely inequitable (Todaro 1989). Musgrove's data are based on geographical inequity only – the data used are based on health regions rather than individuals. Further disaggregation by groups of individuals with

access to different sub-systems of the Peruvian health system could only increase the measure.

In the US the well-served group of the population constitute the majority and those without insurance cover will not be denied emergency and some other forms of care but can find themselves with no access to expensive treatment for chronic or incurable conditions. The poorest in the US are covered by social insurance. The uncovered group is made up of those whose health status excludes them from coverage, those who are irregularly employed or self-employed, or work for small employers who do not provide coverage or pay sufficiently to cover its cost, or those who exclude themselves as part of the adverse selection process (see Box 22.1). In poor countries without a social insurance sector, those whom the public sector does not reach at all are remote rural dwellers, often coincidental with the poorest population groups in the country. Their use of unregulated out-of-pocket reimbursed private providers is the option available to that proportion of the population who can raise the necessary money. Also effectively uncovered in many countries are population groups who use poor-quality and public providers that fail to provide appropriate care – because drugs are out of stock, staff absent or other necessary components of care are unavailable. Those with a little more money or geographical luck have access to moderately priced services in the NGO sector (reputedly but not always demonstrably better than in the public sector), and the formally employed may have access to employer-sponsored services where these have been organised. For a small urban elite, expensive private services can be purchased, or privileged access to public services may be obtained. For example, senior civil servants may use their authority to command a greater than equitable use of public services, or a private ward system may give higher public subsidy to those paying a higher fee, as has been documented in Indonesia (Gani 1996).

In the segmented Latin American parallel systems the main difference is the additional recourse to a social security sector of variable quality for the formally employed and the slightly more extensive private insurance system. Maceira (see Box 24.4) has charted the way that coverage patterns have typically developed over recent decades in Latin American countries. The analysis highlights the way that external economic shocks can dramatically change the extent and type of coverage of large population groups, and is relevant to any parallel health system.

24.5 The Interaction of the four Sub-systems: Efficiency

These patent inequities are also important inefficiencies – in themselves and in what they reflect. Allocative efficiency is achieved where the marginal value of expenditure is equated across the range of health interventions available. There are several reasons to suppose that this will be less the case in a parallel health system than in a universal one. Figure 24.4 shows how the three sub-sectors – public, social security and private – may increasingly diverge from a social welfare potential curve. According to this analysis, reallocating resources from the private sub-sector to the public one could increase the total social value generated through the health sector.

This analysis relates to allocative efficiency alone. Arguments that technical efficiency is likely to be greater in the private sector imply that the value of marginal activity in the three sub-sectors might be closer. The public sector may be trying to allocate resources to higher-priority activities but is so inefficient that the net value of its output per unit of resource is no higher than in the technically efficient but allocatively inefficient private sector. The shortage of evidence with respect to the hypothesis that the private sector exhibits higher levels of technical efficiency has been discussed in Chapter 22.

To the extent that the social insurance system and even the private system is subsidised with resources originating in general taxation (often in the form of tax breaks in the private sector), the inequities and inefficiencies are compounded. Trying to prevent the rich from spending their money inappropriately is likely

Box 24.4   *Movement between Sub-systems in Parallel Health Systems*

Maceira (reported in IADB 1996) describes movement in population coverage by different sub-sectors in response to external pressures. In the representations of the diagram, the population is ordered by income level along the horizontal axis, and its distribution is shown on the vertical axis. Sector 1 of the diagram shows the initial distribution of the population between the three sub-sectors, public, social security and private. Sector 2 shows the effect of crisis in the public system – quality and quantity of services offered there decline and a proportion of those initially covered by the public sector turn to the private sector. Sector 3 shows the effect of falling incomes in the social security sector, for example as a result of declining formal sector employment, or as a result of lower formal sector incomes. In the latter case the number affiliated to social security does not fall but the quality and quantity of services do and the effect is the same – people previously covered by social security services start to seek care in the public sector, placing more pressure there. Sector 4 shows the combination of the effects of the changes of the previous two stages – public sector services are even further stretched, more private sector services are sought by both ex-public service users and

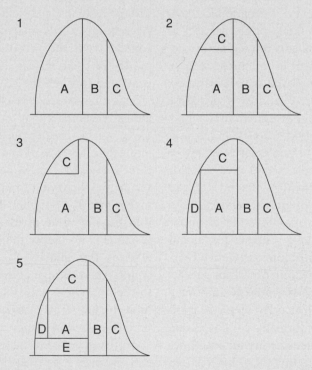

Figure B5   Movement between sub-systems in parallel health systems. Key: A: public health services, B: social security services, C: private health services, D: excluded population, E: non-governmental organisations
Source: adapted from Maceira, cited in IADB (1996).

Continued

ex-social security service users and a group unable to access private services – for example, because of inability to pay or lost access to social security services – become excluded from all services. In sector 5 the existence of large excluded groups and the stress on public services creates conditions for expansion of activities of non-governmental organisations.

The details of the analysis – for example, whether the 'initial' situation ever pertained, or the order of events – are less important than the message of this analysis, that the sub-systems making up a parallel health system are highly interdependent. Population groups move between sub-systems and pressures on one part of the system have knock-on effects on other sub-systems. Public sector adequacy has a major impact on the development of the private sector. While the richest members of society remain protected from this process, the poorest suffer the most extreme effects.

to be a futile pursuit and some people would consider it to be an inappropriate extension of the role of the state. The same argument does not apply to the spending of the tax dollar, shilling or peso. Spending these less rather than more efficiently and equitably is indefensible.

Inefficiency also arises from duplication between the various parallel sub-systems. On the financing side, there are several administration, information and collection systems. On the provision side, each system has to contain separate slack to deal with occasional

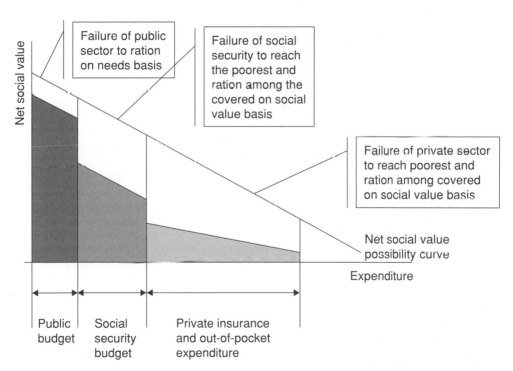

Figure 24.4 Achievement of social welfare potential in three sub-sectors of a segmented health system

demand surges. Each system has to start from zero in planning geographical access, resulting in phenomena like public, social security and private hospitals sitting side by side in a capital city while within the same country there may be no formal health services at all over a wide geographical area.

24.6 Conclusion

From a social welfare perspective the principal problem of parallel health systems is the loss of the solidarity provided in more universal systems. The lack of risk sharing, especially between social groups, reduces the availability of some of the most effective and needed services. Segmentation ensures the weighting of demands according to wealth by separating groups within which risks are pooled on the basis of economic power. The higher the proportion of the population using the out-of-pocket sub-sector, the more access to health resources depends on ability to pay. Within the sub-systems with insurance characteristics (in the broad sense: including public finance and provision), some market failures are avoided. For example, the provision of public goods at some level is enabled; patterns of supply are to some extent planned according to need (increasingly as the type of insurance is more public); 'catastrophic' costs are avoided at least by some groups. At the same time, rationing according to ability to pay is broadly maintained.

Choices about the degree of equity, solidarity and universality of health systems are fundamental political choices and reflect the culture and social values of societies. At stake is whether or not health services should properly be placed among the rewards for economic success, or whether they must be treated separately and distributed according to a commonly specified social welfare function. In the language of the political left, this involves the choice between treatment of health services and even health as a 'commodity' or as a 'right'.[1]

This choice is not ultimately a technical one. However, the extent to which different policies move health systems towards social or private demand-based values is, as we have seen, capable of technical assessment. The final chapter assesses the changes that have occurred in the reform of health sectors in the 1990s, in the context of this and other types of market failure.

Note

1. Up to this point, we have been assuming that what we have termed 'social values' are shared by policy makers globally. However, it is at this stage necessary to acknowledge that the implicit values of many systems and sub-systems contradict social values so greatly that we have to modify this assumption. Those divergences between private and social demand-based values classically included among 'market failures' are probably almost universally accepted as problems. In contrast, the relative weights which private demand-based values place on service delivered to the poor and the rich implicitly at least are accepted in systems which take very limited measures to redistribute them. Nevertheless, few governments explicitly acknowledge sympathy with the implications of those weights in the health sector.

Chapter 25

Trends in Health Sector Reform

....

25.1 Introduction

Chapter 20 suggested that highest expenditure and health sector inflation were associated with health systems that rely heavily on private finance and provision (e.g. the US and Switzerland). Those with social insurance generally have higher costs than mainly public health systems. We have been cautious in giving a clear answer as to the appropriate level of health expenditure, and therefore health expenditure growth. It is, however, clear that some countries have identified current levels as excessive and unsustainable, and health expenditure inflation has become a central target of a number of reform measures.

At the same time, where private forms of insurance dominate, there is increasing policy debate focused on increasing the 'social' component of insurance – exemplified by Switzerland's move from private to social insurance. This suggests pressures to achieve greater universality. These pressures can also be discerned in the 'parallel' health systems and take a number of forms, including demands to close gaps between standards of care in different sub-systems (and especially

to improve the quality of care in the public sub-system), and to capitalise on overlooked strengths of the private sector.

Chapters 20–1 suggested that public health service systems have been most criticised, in contrast, as 'under-funded' and as offering lower public satisfaction than their social insurance system counterparts. From a technical point of view it is difficult to establish either appropriate levels of expenditure or the extent to which public satisfaction is a reasonable measure of health system performance. Satisfaction measures may reflect aspects of health system output that are broader than those captured by crude and narrow measures of health status. These concerns may reflect the extent to which health systems meet private rather than social demand. Nevertheless, reform responses in public health service systems suggest that better public responsiveness is an accepted policy goal, while cost control has not been a central focus. Furthermore, maintenance of tax-based finance suggests there is no desire to withdraw from a universal approach.

This chapter reviews some of the measures countries are introducing into their health systems in order to meet complex objectives.

The ground is too wide to cover the full range of innovations in a single chapter, and many good surveys are already available. The focus in this chapter is on a few of the most commonly introduced measures, and the contribution of the areas of economic theory that have been introduced in the rest of this book to analysis of their implications and advisability.

25.2 Introducing User Charges in Tax-financed Systems

Many tax-financed systems have introduced user charges to increasing degrees over recent years. There are two broad justifications for this. One is the need to reduce moral hazard in contexts where prices are otherwise zero. The second is the wish to increase the funding level of the health system without resorting to higher levels of taxation, or reallocating resources from other types of public expenditure.

We have already encountered much of the analysis relevant to the moral hazard argument in the analysis of co-payment within an insurance system. It was concluded that co-payment rationed according to private demand, and could fully control moral hazard, as defined by reference to private demand-based values, only if co-payment levels were set at 100 per cent of the marginal cost of the services provided (see Chapter 22). The same applies to user charges. If they were to be set at 100 per cent of marginal cost, public subsidy would be restricted to covering the deficit where downward-sloping cost curves apply, which might be roughly equivalent to providing for fixed costs.

We have seen that public health service systems have superior rationing methods from a social demand perspective and it is therefore likely that the need to raise revenues dominates moral hazard arguments in most of the cases in which user charges have been introduced. There may, however, be some exceptions. Much of the support from UK family doctors for the proposed introduction of user charges for their services seems to arise from their perception of high levels of 'wasteful' use of their services.[1]

There is no costless source of revenue, and there is little difference to society in paying the same amount of resources directly to health providers or via the taxation system. Furthermore, a single administrative system for the raising of revenues for health services has potential efficiency advantages over a multiplicity of systems.

However, we have seen that particular constraints apply to tax-based funding. Democracies operate imperfectly in allocating the levels of funding that populations want to be spent on particular types of publicly funded services. It is also important to consider the macroeconomic effects of higher taxation. If higher tax leads to people choosing to work less or take fewer risks, the effect is to lower incomes, and thereby to lower tax revenue. The phenomenon of 'capital flight' by which businesses and people transfer their savings and transactions to other economies imposes macroeconomic cost on increasing tax rates. However, it is also possible that higher taxes will lower people's disposable income, and thereby encourage them to work harder. This is a classic economic question – there is an 'income effect', in which lower income leads to more work, and a 'substitution effect', where we would expect people to choose more leisure, since higher income tax effectively makes leisure relatively cheaper. Although much of the observed tax policies in the 1980s and 1990s suggests that governments believe higher taxes generate work disincentives, the

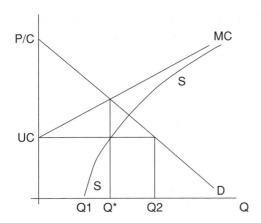

Figure 25.1 Potential role of user charges in a tax-constrained economy

empirical evidence is mixed, and many studies suggest that modest changes in tax have little effect on work effort and risk taking.

The implications of a user charge (which might also be considered a health service sales tax) are likely to be quite different from the implications of higher levels of general taxation. The greater willingness to pay for health services than for other components of public expenditure implies that user charges may be more acceptable to the majority of the population than general taxation increases. The fact that it is an individual's rather than general access to health services that is taxed changes the likely incentive effects on individuals' work effort and risk-taking choices, and therefore the supply-side macroeconomic implications.

Figure 25.1 explains the role user charges might play in enabling an improved total funding level of health services in a situation where public subsidy is constrained to below the optimal. Assuming (temporarily) that the demand curve measures social marginal value, Q* can be defined as in Chapters 21–3 as the optimal level of provision. However, the subsidy curve SS, which denotes possible

combinations of user charges and provision consistent with a given level of subsidy, shows that without user charges the maximum level of provision the public sector is capable of meeting is Q1. By introducing user charges, public expenditure can be increased along SS, so that at a user charge of UC the optimal total funding level can be achieved. This is consistent with a substantially subsidised price, depending on the level of the fixed public subsidy.

The important problem with this analysis, in common with the analysis of co-payments in Chapter 22, is that the demand curve cannot be assumed to represent marginal social value. Under the circumstances of Figure 25.1 demand will still have to be rationed using non-price methods, since demand at price UC is Q2. To this extent, those demands that are rendered effective will have to be sanctioned by a non-price rationing method. This may or may not effectively select only relatively high values of social demand. In either case, those needs which are not backed by ability to pay at least the subsidised price will be excluded irrespective of further rationing criteria.

As before, we would be likely to find that demands of high social value such as the demand for immunisation of the poorest lie in the 'rationed out' section of the private demand curve. In some settings it may also be possible to exempt from charges the utilisation of the poorest groups, but in the poorest countries this is extremely difficult to devise and implement. However, it is possible to levy user charges only on lower-priority health services and achieve effective cross-subsidy of higher-priority services. In principle both these measures could mitigate or remove the problems identified by this analysis. Consequently, much of the debate about user charges considers the extent to which these two measures are in place and succeed. In poor countries the highest-priority services are often excluded from charges but the extent to which other high social demands are rationed is contested. There is convincing evidence that the poor are most likely to reduce their utilisation and that at least some of the services excluded are those for which high costs of delayed treatment and communication apply (see Box 25.1). In richer countries, exemption policy is much more easily administered and the problems posed by charges are consequently much less severe. Nevertheless, there is evidence that many people are deterred from appropriate use of services as a result of charges (for example, Beck and Horne 1980).

25.3 Managed Competition, Regulated Competition and the Use of Public Sector Contracting

A plethora of definitions and terminology confront anyone interested in the phenomena of 'quasi-markets', 'internal markets', 'managed care', 'managed' and 'regulated competition' and other terms expressing options which mix public and market components within a regulated framework. Maynard and Bloor (1995) have defined 'regulated competition' as 'competition on the supply side only, with maintenance of a single source of public finance', while they define 'managed competition' as 'competition on both the supply and funding (demand) sides of the

---

International Case Study

Box 25.1   User Charges and Use of STD Services in Kenya

In Kenya, during 1989–90, user charges were first introduced and then withdrawn from public sector out-patient services. This provided a 'natural experiment' that was used by Moses *et al.* (1992) to study the impact of the charges. The authors collected data on the number, sex and diagnosis of users of a special treatment clinic for sexually transmitted diseases in Nairobi for twenty-three months before charges were introduced; the nine-month period in which they operated; and the fifteen months immediately after they were withdrawn. The table summarises the results of the study.

The data show significant reductions in utilisation associated with the introduction of charges, with an overall 60 per cent reduction in utilisation for men and 35 per cent for women. After the subsequent removal of charges, men's utilisation remained at the lower level, whereas women's increased. For gonorrhoea, women's utilisation increased significantly *during* the charge period.

The authors speculate that the reason for the observed increases is growing rates of infection resulting from falling rates of treatment. (The data show a steady rate of increase in utilisation for these two infections as the charge period progressed, which is consistent with this interpretation.)

Those users who were not diagnosed as suffering from a sexually transmitted disease reduced their utilisation most. However, the extent of the reduction in cases of diagnosed sexually transmitted diseases certainly implies that falling utilisation in response to user charges cannot be assumed to be restricted to 'trivial' cases.

Continued

Seasonally adjusted Mean (95% Confidence Interval) Monthly Patient Attendance at the Special Treatment Clinic before, during and after User Charges

Diagnosis	Period			Attendance in user charge period as % of attendance in pre-charge period	Attendance in post-charge period as % of attendance in pre-charge period
	Pre-charge	User charge	Post-charge		
Men					
Gonorrhoea	824 (711–955)	418 (438–503)	758 (647–888)	51 (44–58)[a]	92 (84–101)
Non-STD	848 (637–1129)	39 (20–76)	116 (78–173)	5 (2–9)[a]	14 (10–18)[a]
Chancroid	594 (511–690)	349 (290–419)	459 (389–541)	59 (51–68)[a]	77 (70–86)[a]
Syphilis	20 (14–29)	12 (7–18)	16 (11–24)	58 (43–78)[a]	82 (65–103)
Non-gonococcal urethris	572 (437–749)	374 (272–513)	521 (391–694)	65 (52–82)[a]	91 (77–107)
Total	2,890 (2,600–3,213)	1,164 (1,015–1,334)	1,838 (1,634–2,067)	40 (36–45)[a]	64 (59–68)[a]
Women					
Gonorrhoea	86 (41–121)	114 (79–164)	364 (264–501)	132 (102–171)[a]	422 (353–505)[a]
Non-STD	419 (283–619)	105 (62–179)	67 (40–114)	25 (17–38)[a]	16 (11–24)[a]
Chancroid	70 (44–110)	50 (30–84)	130 (82–205)	72 (51–102)[a]	186 (149–232)[a]
Syphilis	17 (10–27)	9 (5–16)	13 (7–21)	55 (38–81)[a]	76 (58–100)
Candidiasis	119 (72–199)	129 (73–227)	421 (258–687)	108 (73–161)	353 (217–450)[a]
Trichomoniasis	602 (478–759)	413 (317–539)	493 (385–631)	69 (57–82)[a]	82 (71–94)[a]
Total	1,278 (1,036–1,576)	830 (650–1,060)	1,560 (1,255–1,937)	65 (55–77)[a]	122 (109–137)[a]

Source: Moses *et al.* (1992).
Note:
[a] Significantly different (p = 0.05) from 100%.

market'. Both these types of competition may imply public sector contracting (although they may be entirely private sector based, as in the health maintenance organisation example of the US). These definitions are usefully broad and capable of encompassing important dimensions of reform in a wide range of countries. Box 25.2 compares the reform programmes of the UK, Colombia and Zambia and categorises them according to these definitions. However, it is important to understand the difference between contracting and competition. Public sector contracting need not imply competition on either side – governments or government agencies may choose to negotiate a contract with a single public or private provider. Contracting (at least implicit contracting – see Chapter 14) is necessary for competition, but can exist without it.

These types of arrangements offer the opportunity to combine public and private institutions in novel ways. It has been suggested in previous chapters that the strengths of private sector arrangements may lie in the 'high-powered incentives' more likely to be associated with profit-seeking organisations and competition (although there are dangers that these incentives may prove perverse in a health context). The strengths of public sector arrangements may lie in the ability to replace individual private demands as the basis for the allocation of resources with a 'social value'-based mechanism. The potential to combine private provision organisations with public purchasing (determining allocation of resources and limiting the operation of perverse incentives), or to approach this situation,[2] is the principal attraction of these types of arrangements.

Even without competition, many people believe that contracts in themselves are capable of exerting positive influence on a public

health system, organised in the manner described in Chapter 21. For example, the influential health economist Alain Enthoven (1985: 22) has argued:

> competitive tendering can be the entering wedge for a great deal of management improvement . . . It requires management to develop a precise work statement for each department, including quality standards. Avoidable costs in other departments must be estimated . . . Information and control systems must be established. Tendering requires a whole new style of management.

Contracting processes in the public sector may present opportunities to implement other innovations – such as changes to reimbursement systems – that are neither necessarily implied by contracts, nor impossible in a system without formal contracts.

Chapter 14 introduced Oliver Williamson's (1975, 1985) 'transaction costs' framework for the analysis of contracts. It was seen that some of the difficulties associated with contracts arise where there is asset specificity, bounded rationality and opportunistic behaviour. All these characteristics may be present in contracting within managed and regulated markets.

Asset specificity implies that it is difficult, if not impossible, for a competitive environment to thrive and therefore it is unlikely that the benefits of competition will apply. Suppose the council in a town with no hospital were planning to solicit bids from private companies for the provision of hospital services in the town. A number of companies might be interested, and the town council might select from a range of competitively priced and quality-specified contract proposals to purchase a flow of hospital services over a given time period (for example, five years). Because a hospital is a 'specific asset' in terms

International Case Study

Box 25.2 Managed Competition, Regulated Competition and Contracting in the UK, Colombia and Zambia

The UK

In the UK 'regulated competition' was introduced into an archetypal public integrated health sector model in 1991. The main rationales appear to have been the creation of competition between hospital-level providers and the development of a purchasing role that would be independent of concerns related to the management of provider institutions. It was expected that public purchasers would be able to identify the needs of the population and distribute resources accordingly (in contrast to a pure private market arrangement).

District Health Authority (DHA) purchasers who controlled the largest share of resources were unable to ignore the needs of their district hospitals, whose failure would pose a risk to populations whose interests they were charged with protecting. District purchasers therefore found themselves in a weak bargaining position, and hospitals were able to assume entitlement to a share of district budgets. Where a need for hospital closure was recognised, regulated competition has not been left to determine which hospital(s) should close. Rather, decisions were taken through the political process.

The 1997 changes in NHS structures (which fall short of 'reform' in that they do not fundamentally alter the contract-based model) seem to have recognised the purchasing role as that most in need of change, and have relocated the purchasing role to 'primary care groups' (PCGs), accountable to DHAs, in which general practitioners (GPs), community nurses and other interested parties participate.

At primary level the 1991 reforms offered GPs the opportunity to replace the DHA in purchasing certain hospital services for their patients. Those who did so became 'fund-holding GPs' (FHGPs). Unlike DHA purchasers, each individual GP *could* move contracts from one hospital to another without significantly affecting the hospital's viability. As a result, what competition emerged was competition for GP contracts. Allegations that patients funded by GP contracts received preferential treatment, including prioritisation on waiting lists, began to be heard. This form of GP-led purchasing has been abolished with the introduction of PCGs.

Sources: West (1997); Le Grand *et al.* (1998).

Colombia

In Colombia, until the reforms of 1996, a 'parallel' health system operated (see Chapter 20). The reforms seem to have had three overriding objectives – to increase the solidarity of the health system by merging public and social security sub-sectors; to introduce competition; and to introduce a contracting environment within a public health framework. In pursuit of the first objective, public health budgets have been redirected to subsidy of social insurance for those sections of the population who have been judged, according to a near-universal household survey, unable to pay. This constitutes the 'subsidised regimen' of the system. Competition is introduced on both provision and purchasing sides by the formation of 'health promotion enterprises' (EPSs) which offer packages of care for the insured (under both subsidised and

Continued

contributory regimens), by contracting with providers of all types. Colombia's example is therefore one of 'managed competition' according to our definitions. The EPSs are private enterprises that may be profit-seeking, or not-for-profit and sometimes community-based organisations. The latter have taken particular interest in competing for members of the sub-sidised regimen. This contract arrangement replaces integrated arrangements in both public and social security sectors.

A public health orientation for the system is sought through the extensive use of regulation that sets detailed rules for the operation of the system, through the leverage of substantial public funds flowing through the system and an 'equalisation mechanism' which serves to enforce solidarity despite the proliferation of EPSs. An important rule governing the operation of the market is the setting of a minimum package of care that all EPSs must offer. Rules also govern the levels of contribution in the contributory regimen and the levels of EPS reimburse-ment in both contributory and subsidised regimens and a mandatory cross-subsidy from the contributory to the subsidised regimen. Over time it is planned that the packages of care in subsidised and contributory regimens will become equal.

A number of problems have been encountered in implementation. For example, public hospitals have had to switch, with little opportunity for preparation, from an integrated to a contract mode of operation, and planned flows of finance around the system have not always been realised. These problems are at least partly due to an unrealistic reform timetable.

Source: Yepes and Sanchez (1998).

Zambia

In Zambia a purchasing agency, the Central Board of Health (CBoH), has been set up at central level, separate from the Ministry of Health but conceived of as the Ministry of Health's 'implementing agency'. The CBoH agrees contracts with district health boards (for primary- and district-hospital-level care) and hospital management boards (HMBs) for higher-level services. The CBoH also agrees contracts with NGO hospitals. This is an example of public sector contracting which does not imply regulated or managed competition, since no com-petition is implied on either side of the market.

A number of problems have arisen, some of which are due to the only partially legislated and ratified reform package, and others from what might be seen as an insufficient ambitious reform design. Most important, budgets are not directly related to the provision of services but still work on the basis of entitlement – a bed base formula in the case of hospitals and a capitation one in the case of districts. Difficulties in effectively monitoring activity levels are seen to preclude more sophisticated contract forms, but without these CBoH financing can be assumed to be independent of performance by districts and hospitals, and there is little leverage exercised by the contracts themselves. What leverage might be implied by the reporting requirements imposed by the contracts, which should demonstrate that services agreed have in fact been delivered, is undermined by the usual failure to pay the agreed budget in full. This arises from shortfalls in government revenue in comparison with require-ments. In the light of this, it is unsurprising that hospitals seem to pursue the implicit incent-ives to generate user charge revenue irrespective of the effects on the core patient business intended to be subsidised by the CBoH contract.

Source: Kamwanga *et al.* (1999).

of where it is located, the necessary buildings and installed equipment, each bid will have to include substantial costs for construction or conversion, and equipping the hospital. The competitive process can function. The public purchaser ensures that the flow of services is appropriate to the needs of the population, technically inefficient providers are unsuccessful in their bids because their price–quality specifications are uncompetitive, and prices close to marginal cost are achieved by the purchaser because those including too high a profit margin also make uncompetitive bids. One firm is chosen and builds its hospital in the town. At this point, what Williamson terms 'the fundamental transformation' occurs. The successful firm has become a monopoly. When the five years come to an end a new bidding process has only one possible winner. Only the successful bidder in the first round can offer prices that do not include the cost of building a new hospital. This bidder can substantially increase its prices above marginal cost without any risk that another firm can undercut. It can also insist on providing services that the public purchaser does not consider a priority.

All this occurs even without opportunistic behaviour in the sense of reneging on the first contract. However, if, in the first competition, bidding firms understood and predicted the 'fundamental transformation', they need not realistically estimate their price and quality specifications. The initial bidding could consist of a range of offers dependent on the firms' estimation of the gullibility of the town council purchasers. Once the hospital was built, the successful bidder could immediately increase prices, lower quality specifications, decide to invest in profitable (or interesting to physicians) but low-priority service provision and hold up the completion of the contract until the town council agreed to the revised terms.

Could the town council resort to law? To the extent that contracts were fully specified in detail, and contract performance was observable to the courts, possibly. Even under those circumstances, however, it might not be in the best interests of the town council to force the firm into bankruptcy and start all over again. Negotiating a revised contract might well make more sense – and if the hospital company had no alternative use for the hospital (could not, for example, turn it into a purely private hospital instead) the town council would have negotiating strength. More likely, however, 'bounded rationality' would ensure that no contract components could be fully specified in the contract, observed by all parties to the contract, and observed by the courts. Monitoring of quality especially is inevitably imperfect. The town council would be likely to enter into a series of negotiations with the company, amending prices, agreeing monitoring procedures, seeking out behaviour that the hospital aims to conceal and negotiating improvements in practice where problems are discovered.

This scenario makes the initial optimism in relation to the ability of managed and regulated markets to combine the best features of private and public systems look naive. All may not be quite so gloomy, and an astute town council starting out with a better understanding of the terrain might fare better. One of the major constraints on unqualified opportunism is the need for firms operating in this kind of environment to build a reputation for honest dealing. A more astute town council would look to the experience of counterparts in other towns with the bidding firms – good reputation would be a major asset to an initial bid. Knowing this, and assuming that the gains from a series of contracts performed honestly are greater than the gains from a single contract performed opportunistically, a firm will be constrained in its opportunism. However, given the unobservability, especially to outsiders, of the underlying causes of contract disputes, this mechanism will operate imperfectly. More important for the case under examination, reputation does not come into play where at the instigation of a managed or regulated market a single provider is already in place and a second provider is not a sensible option for the purchaser.

In these circumstances, the managed or regulated market might instead be set up as a market for hospital management rather than a market for hospital services. This removes several types of asset specificity and therefore the prospect of fundamental transformation. Although human asset specificity is still present in hospital management, its degree is probably less marked and it is likely to be possible to replace a grossly under-performing management team with a team capable of improved performance.

Nevertheless, problems of observability remain, suggesting the need for closer relations between the contracting parties than the classical 'arm's length' relationship. Both parties to the contract have a substantial stake in ensuring contract continuation. The degree of human asset specificity suggests both that management teams have a significant stake in their jobs and that purchasers have a significant stake in the existing team. Such human asset specificity is likely to take the form of detailed understanding of the specific management issues in a specific hospital, ranging from the personalities of key actors to knowledge of the priorities of the public purchaser – components of 'on-the-job' learning. Since a new team would have to start the learning process anew, the purchaser will expect lower levels of performance than the *potential* performance of the existing team, at least for some period. From the team's perspective,

such learning would at best have to start again in a new hospital and in a high-powered incentive environment might translate into lower levels of remuneration over an initial period in a new job. Adding reputation effects to the mix of considerations, such team members might have to consider retraining, or much more poorly reimbursed work in another field altogether.

The conditions are conducive to 'relational contracting' in which, understanding that their relationship is likely to be a long-term one, the parties to the contract try to work together to ensure that it remains a satisfactory one. Contacts between the two parties may be frequent, monitoring may be jointly undertaken and reviewed alongside other problem solving. Most importantly the relationship is characterised by trust. While this may solve some of the contracting problems, it also removes many of the classical features of contracting and resembles relations between levels of authority within a traditional public system such as that described in Chapter 21. The relation implies extremely muted levels of competition or threat of forced exit penalising poor performance. It is possible to operate incentive payment schemes – but may not be much easier than operating such schemes within the public sector.

It might be concluded that the underlying problems of ensuring appropriate, efficient and quality services in the health sector cannot be solved in any structure. No general organisational principles obviate the need for skilled managers of purchasing and provision in any structure. Certain organisational features may make the job easier or more difficult but these features are likely to vary between contexts. The task of reforming the health sector is also a complex and skilled one. It is not helped by generalised recipes for success but requires a sound grasp of the principles expounded in this text, and the ability to apply them to specific settings.

Notes

1. The argument has to be weighed carefully from a social demand perspective. General practitioners are likely to sanction uses of their services which they consider medically justified, whereas a social justification which is not necessarily of low priority – the benefits of discussing an irresolvable problem, or valued reassurance – may have motivated the patient in seeking care. Nevertheless, this does not imply that all demands placed on GPs must necessarily be high-priority either. There is no gatekeeping prior to the GP visit, and the important rationing mechanism at this level is time (distance and waiting). This was not judged particularly effective in Chapter 21 at rationing provision towards high social demands.

2. For example, by granting autonomy to provider organisations while maintaining public ownership (as in all three countries in Box 25.2).

References

....

Abbott, T. A. and Crew, M. A. (1995) 'Lessons from public utility regulation for the economic regulation of health care markets: an overview', in T. A. Abbott III (ed.) *Health Care Policy and Regulation*, Boston MA: Kluwer.

Alchian, A. A. and Demsetz, H. (1972) 'Production, information costs, and economic organization', *American Economic Review* 64(5): 777–95.

Aljunid, S. (1995) The role of private practitioners in a rural district of Malaysia and their interactions with public health services, Ph.D. thesis, University of London.

Allsop, J. and Mulcahy, L. (1996) *Regulating Medical Work: Formal and Informal Controls*, Buckingham: Open University Press.

Ashton, T. and Press, D. (1997) 'Market concentration in secondary health services', *Health Economics* 6: 43–56.

Barber, J. A. and Thompson, S. G. (1998) 'Analysis and interpretation of cost data in randomised controlled trials: review of published studies', *British Medical Journal* 317: 1195–200.

Bartlett, W. (1996) 'The regulation of general practice in the UK', *International Journal of Health Planning and Management* 11: 3–18.

Baumol, W. J. (1995) *Health Care as a Handicraft Industry*, London: Office of Health Economics.

Baumol, W. J., Panzar, J. C. and Willig, R. D. (1982) *Contestable Markets and the Theory of Industry Structure*, New York: Harcourt Brace.

Beck, R. G. and Horne, J. M. (1980) 'Utilization of publicly insured health services in Saskatchewan before, during and after co-payment', *Medical Care* 18(8): 787–806.

Becker, G. S. (1983) 'A theory of competition among pressure groups for political influence', *Quarterly Journal of Economics* 93: 371–400.

Bennett, S. (1991) *The Mystique of Markets: Public and Private Health Care in Developing Countries*, PHP Departmental Publication 4, London: London School of Hygiene and Tropical Medicine.

Bennett, S., Dakpallah, G., Garner, P., Gilson, L., Nittayaramphong, S., Zurita, B. and Zwi, A. (1994) 'Carrot and stick: state mechanisms to influence private provider behaviour', *Health Policy and Planning* 9(1): 1–13.

Bennett, S., McPake, B. and Mills, A. (1997) *Private Health Providers in Developing Countries: Serving the Public Interest?* London: Zed Press.

Berman, P., Nwuke, K., Hanson, K., Kariuki, M., Mbugua, K., Ngugi, J., Omurwa, T. and Ong'ayo, S. (1995a) *Kenya: Non-governmental Health Care Provision: Data for Decision Making Project*, Cambridge MA: Department of Population and International Health, Harvard School of Public Health.

Berman, P., Nwuke, K., Rannan-Ehya, R. and Mwanza, A. (1995b) *Zambia: Non-governmental Health Care Provision: Data for Decision Making Project*, Cambridge MA: Department of Population and International Health, Harvard School of Public Health.

Bhat, R. (1996) 'Regulating the private health care sector: the case of the Indian Consumer Protection Act', *Health Policy and Planning* 11(3): 265–79.

Birch, S. (1988) 'Item of service remuneration in general practice in the UK: what can we learn from dentists?' *Family Practice* 5(4): 265–70.

Blendon, R. J., Leitman, R., Morrison, I. and Donelan, K. (1990) 'Satisfaction with health systems in ten nations', *Health Affairs* (Millwood) 9(2): 185–92.

Blendon, R. J., Benson, J., Donelan, K., Leitman, R., Taylor, H., Koeck, C. and Gitterman, D. (1995) 'Who has the best health care system? A second look', *Health Affairs* (Millwood) 14(4): 220–30.

Bond, P. (1999) 'Globalization, pharmaceutical pricing, and South African health policy: managing confrontation with US firms and politicians', *International Journal of Health Services* 29(4): 765–92.

Bowden, A. (2001) 'Variation in health-related quality of life: a case study of an Akamba population', Ph.D. thesis, University of Manchester.

Bowling, A., Jacobson, B. and Southgate, L. (1993) 'Health service priorities: explorations in consultation of the public and health professionals on priority setting in an inner London health district', *Social Science and Medicine* 37(7): 851–7.

Bradach, J. L. and Eccles, R. G. (1989) 'Price, authority and trust: from ideal types to plural forms', *Annual Review of Sociology* 15: 97–118.

Brazier, J. E., Harper, R., Thomas, K., Jones, N. and Underwood, T. (1998) 'Deriving a preference-based single index measure from the SF-36', *Journal of Clinical Epidemiology* 51(11): 1115–29.

Briggs, A. H. and Gray, A. M. (2000) 'Handling uncertainty in economic evaluations of health care interventions', *British Medical Journal* 319. 635–8.

Broyles, R. W., Brandt, E. N., Jr and Biard-Holmes, D. (1998) 'Networks and the fiscal performance of rural hospitals in Oklahoma: are they associated?' *Journal of Rural Health* 14(4): 327–37.

Busse, R. (1999) 'Priority setting and rationing in German health care', *Health Policy* 50: 71–90.

Cairns, J. (1992) 'Discounting and health benefits: another perspective', *Health Economics* 1: 76–9.

Campbell, E. S. and Fournier, G. M. (1993) 'Certificate-of-need deregulation and indigent hospital care', *Health Politics, Policy and Law* 18(4): 905–25.

Carr-Hill, R. A. (1991) 'Allocating resources to health care: is the QALY a technical solution to a political problem?' *International Journal of Health Services* 21(3): 351–63.

Chambers, R. (1983) *Rural Development: Putting the Last First*, London: Longman.

Chollet, D. J. and Lewis, M. (1997) 'Private insurance: principles and practice', in *Innovations in Health Care Financing: Proceedings of a World Bank Conference*, 10–11 March, Washington DC: World Bank.

Chow, G. C. (1997) 'Challenges of China's economic system for economic theory', *American Economic Review* 87(2): 321.

Cleverly, W. O. (1992) 'Competitive strategy for successful hospital management', *Hospital and Health Services Administration* 37: 53–69.

Coase, R. H. (1937) 'The nature of the firm', *Economica* 4: 386–405.

Courty, P. and Marschke, G. (1997) 'Measuring government performance: lessons from a federal job-training program', *American Economic Review* 87(2): 383.

Cowling, K. and Cubbin, J. (1971) 'Price, quality and advertising competition: an econometric investigation of the UK car market', *Economica* 38: 378–94.

Creese, A. L. (1991) 'User charges for health care: a review of the recent experience', *Health Policy and Planning* 6(4): 309–19.

Creese, A. and Parker, D. (1994) *Cost Analysis in Primary Health Care: a Training Manual for Programme Managers*, Geneva: World Health Organisation.

Cronin, E., Normand, C., Henthorn, J. S., Hickman, M. and Davies, S. C. (1998) 'Costing model for neonatal screening and diagnosis of haemoglobinopathies', *Archives of Disease in Childhood*, Fetal and Neonatal edition, 79(3): F161–7.

Culyer, A. J. (1976) *Need and the National Health Service*, Oxford: Martin Robertson.

—— (1989) 'The normative economics of health care finance and provision', *Oxford Review of Economic Policy* 5: 34–58.

Culyer, A. J. and Cullis, J. G. (1975) 'Hospital waiting lists and the supply and demand of in-patient care', *Social and Economic Administration* 9: 13–25.

Custer, W. S., Moser, J. W., Musacchio, R. A. and Willke, R. J. (1990) 'The production of health care services and changing hospital reimbursement: the role of hospital–medical staff relationships', *Journal of Health Economics* 9(2): 167–92.

Demsetz, H. (1993) 'The theory of the firm revisited', in O. E. Williamson and S. G. Winter (eds) *The Nature of the Firm: Origins, Evolution and Development*, Oxford and New York: Oxford University Press.

Donaldson, C., Shackley, P., Abdalla, M. and Miedzybrodzka, Z. (1995) 'Willing to pay for antenatal carrier screening for cystic fibrosis', *Health Economics* 4: 439–52.

Dranove, D. (1988) 'Pricing by non-profit institutions: the case of hospital cost-shifting', *Journal of Health Economics* 7(1): 47–57.

Drummond, M. F., Stoddart, G. L. and Torrance, G. W. (1997) *Methods for the Economic Evaluation of Health Care Programmes*, Oxford: Oxford University Press.

Ellis, R. P. and McGuire, T. G. (1986) 'Provider behavior under prospective reimbursement: cost sharing and supply', *Journal of Health Economics* 5(2): 129–51.

Enthoven, A. (1985) *Reflections on the Management of the NHS*, London: Nuffield Provincial Hospitals Trust.

Feldstein, M. S. (1967) *Economic Analysis for Health Service Efficiency: Econometric Studies of the British National Health Service*, Contributions to Economic Analysis 51, Amsterdam: North Holland.

—— (1968) 'Applying economic concepts to hospital care', *Hospital Administration* 13: 68–9.

Folland, S., Goodman, A. C. and Stano, M. (1993) *The Economics of Health and Health Care*, Basingstoke: Macmillan.

—— (1997) *The Economics of Health and Health Care*, second edition, Englewood Cliffs NJ: Prentice-Hall.

Fox-Rushby, J., for the Kenqol Group (2000) 'Operationalising conceptions of "health" amongst the Wakamba and Maragoli of Kenya: the basis of the Kenqol instrument', *Quality of Life Research* 9(3): 316.

Franks, P. and Fiscella, K. (1998) 'Primary care physicians and specialists as personal physicians: health care expenditure and mortality experience', *Journal of Family Practice* 47(2): 103–4.

Friedman, M. (1953) 'The methodology of positive economics', in *Essays in Positive Economics*, Chicago: University of Chicago Press.

Gafni, A. and Birch, S. (1997) QALYs and HYEs: spotting the differences', *Journal of Health Economics* 16: 601–8.

Gani, A. (1996) 'Improving quality in public sector hospitals in Indonesia', *International Journal of Health Planning and Management* 11(3): 275–96.

Gertler, P., Locay, L. and Sanderson, W. (1987) 'Are user fees regressive? The welfare implications of health care financing proposals in Peru', *Journal of Econometrics* 36: 67–88.

Gold, M. R., Seigel, J. E., Russell, L. B. and Weinstein, M. C. (1996) *Cost-effectiveness in Health and Medicine*, New York: Oxford University Press.

Gray, A. M., Marshall, M., Lockwood, A. and Morris, J. (1997) 'Problems in conducting economic evaluations alongside clinical trials', *British Journal of Psychiatry* 170: 47–52.

Grindle, M. S. and Hilderbrand, M. E. (1995) 'Building sustainable capacity in the public sector: what can be done?' *Public Administration Development* 15(5): 441–63.

Grossman, M. (1972) *The Demand for Health: a Theoretical and Empirical Investigation*, Occasional Paper 119, New York: National Bureau of Economic Research.

Gudex, C., Williams, A., Jourdan, M., Mason, R., Maynard, J., O'Flynn, R. and Rendall, M. (1990) 'Prioritising waiting lists', *Health Trends* 22(3): 103–8.

Hackey, S. (1993a) 'Regulatory regimes and state cost containment programs: commentary', *Journal of Health Politics, Policy and Law* 18(2): 491–502.

Harris, J. (1977) 'The internal organization of hospitals: some economic implications', *Bell Journal of Economics and Management Science* 8: 467–82.

Hart, O. (1995) *Firms, Contracts and Financial Structure*, Oxford: Oxford University Press.

Heckman, J., Heinrich, C. and Smith, J. (1997) 'Assessing the performance of performance standards in public bureaucracies', *American Economic Review* 87(2): 389.

Hodgkin, D. and McGuire, T. G. (1994) 'Payment levels and hospital response to prospective payment', *Journal of Health Economics* 13(1): 1–29. (Review.)

Hodgson, G. (1988) *Economics and Institutions*, Cambridge: Polity Press.

Holmstrom, B. (1989) 'Agency costs and innovation', *Journal of Economic Behaviour and Organisation* 12(3): 305.

Holmstrom, B. and Milgrom, P. (1990) *Multi-task Principal–Agent Analysis: Incentive, Contracts, Asset Ownership and Job Design*, Working Paper 6, Stanford CA: Stanford Institute for Theoretical Economics.

Hongoro, C. (2001) 'Costs and quality of services in public hospitals in Zimbabwe: implications for hospital reform', Ph.D. thesis, University of London.

Hongoro, C. and Musonza, T. G. (1995) 'Analysis of the Referral System in Zimbabwe's Health Care System, Harare: Blair Research Institute'. (Unpublished.)

Hornbrook, M. C. and Goldfarb, M. G. (1983) 'A partial test of a hospital behavioral model', *Social Science and Medicine* 17(10): 667–80.

Huang, P. (1995) 'An overview of hospital accreditation in Taiwan, Republic of China', *International Journal of Health Planning and Management* 10(3): 183–92.

Hughes, D. (1993) 'General practitioners and the new contract: promoting better health through financial incentives', *Health Policy* 25: 39.

Hurley, J. (1998) 'Welfarism, extra-welfarism and evaluative economic analysis in the health sector', in M. L. Barer, T. E. Getzen and G. L. Stoddart (eds) *Health, Health Care and Health Economics: Perspectives on Distribution*, Chichester: Wiley.

IADB (1996) *Economic and Social Progress in Latin America, 1996. Report: Making Social Services Work*, Baltimore MD: Johns Hopkins University Press.

Iverson, T. (1993) 'A theory of hospital waiting lists', *Journal of Health Economics* 12: 55–71.

Joseph, H. (1975) 'On economic theories of hospital behaviour', *Journal of Economics and Business* 27: 69–74.

Kamke, K. (1998) 'The German health care system and health care reform', *Health Policy* 43(2): 171–94.

Kamwanga, J., Hanson, K., McPake, B. and Mungule, O. (1999) *Autonomous Hospitals in Zambia and the Equity Implications of the Market for Hospital Services*, Phase 1 report, *A description of the current state of hospital autonomy*

policy, London: London School of Hygiene and Tropical Medicine. (Unpublished.)

Keeler, E. B., Melnick, G. and Zwanziger, J. (1999) 'The changing effects of competition on non-profit and for-profit hospital pricing behavior', *Journal of Health Economics* 18: 69–86.

Knapp, M. (1984) *The Economics of Social Care*, Basingstoke: Macmillan.

Kreps, D. M. (1997) 'Intrinsic motivation and extrinsic incentives', *American Economic Review* 87(2): 359.

Kumaranayake, L. (1997) 'The role of regulation: influencing private sector activity within health sector reform', *Journal of International Development* 9(4): 641.

Kumaranayake, L., Lake, S., Mujinja, P., Hongoro, C. and Mpembeni, R. (2000) 'How do countries regulate the health sector? Evidence from Tanzania and Zimbabwe', *Health Policy and Planning* 15(4): 357–67.

Laffont, J-J. and Tirole, J. (1993) *A Theory of Incentives in Procurement and Regulation*, Cambridge MA: MIT Press.

Lancaster, K. J. (1966) 'A new approach to consumer theory', *Journal of Political Economy* 74: 159–74.

Lancry, P. J. and Sandier, S. (1999) 'Rationing health care in France', *Health Policy* 50: 23–38.

Langham, S., Soljak, M., Keogh, B., Gill, M., Thorogood, M. and Normand, C. (1997) 'The cardiac waiting game: are patients prioritised on the basis of clinical need?' *Health Services Management Research* 10(4): 216–24.

Lee, L. (1971) 'Conspicuous production theory of hospital behaviour', *Southern Economics Journal* 38: 48–58.

Leffler, K. B. (1978) 'Physician licensure: competition and monopoly in American medicine', *Journal of Law and Economics* 21(1): 165–8.

Le Grand, J., Mays, N. and Mulligan, J. (1998) *Learning from the NHS Internal Market: a Review of the Evidence*, London: King's Fund.

Leibenstein, H. (1966) 'Allocative efficiency versus X-efficiency', *American Economic Review* 56: 397–409.

Leonard, K. (2000) 'Incentives and rural health care delivery, Cameroon', in D. K. Leonard (ed.) *Africa's Changing Markets for Health and Veterinary Services: the New Institutional Issues*, London: Macmillan.

References

···

Lin, B. Y. and Wan, T. T. (1999) 'Analysis of integrated health care networks' performance: a contingency–strategic management perspective', *Journal of Medical Systems* 23(6): 467–85.

Lindbeck, A. (1997) 'Incentives and social norms in household behaviour', *American Economic Review* 87(2): 370.

Liss, G. (1995) 'Comment', in T. A. Abbott III (ed.) *Health Care Policy and Regulation*, Boston MA: Kluwer.

Lowy, A., Kohler, B. and Nicholl, J. (1994) 'Attendance at Accident and Emergency departments: unnecessary or inappropriate?' *Journal of Public Health Medicine* 16(2): 134–40.

Lynk, W. J. (1995) 'Nonprofit hospital mergers and the exercise of market power', *Journal of Law and Economics* 38: 437–61.

Mackintosh, M. (1997) 'Informal regulation: a conceptual framework and application to decentralised mixed finance in health care', Conference on Public Sector Management for the next Century, Manchester: Institute of Development Policy and Management, 29 June–2 July.

Macneil, I. R. (1978) 'Contracts: adjustments of long-term economic relations under classical, neoclassical and relational contract law', *Northwestern University Law Review* 72: 854–906.

Marmor, T. R. (1999) 'The rage for reform: sense and nonsense in health policy', in D. Daniel and T. Sullivan (eds) *Market Limits in Health Reform*, London: Routledge.

Marshall, A. (1920) *Principles of Economics*, eighth edition, London: Macmillan. Reprinted Palgrave, 1960.

Matthew, G. K. (1971) 'Measuring need and evaluating services', in G. McLachlan (ed.) *Portfolio for Health*, London: Oxford University Press.

Maynard, A. and Bloor, K. (1995) 'Health care reform: informing difficult choices', *International Journal of Health Planning and Management* 10: 247–64.

Mays, N. (1995) 'Geographical resource allocation in the English National Health Service, 1971–94: the tension between normative and empirical approaches', *International Journal of Epidemiology* 24(30), supplement 1: S96–102.

McGuire, A. (1985) 'The theory of the hospital: a review of the models', *Social Science and Medicine* 20(11): 1177–84.

McGuire, A., Henderson, J. and Mooney, G. (1988) *The Economics of Health Care: an Introductory Text*, London: Routledge.

McIntyre, D. E., Bourne, D. E., Klopper, J. M. L., Taylor, S. P. and Pick, W. M. (1991) 'A methodology for resource allocation in health care for South Africa', *South African Medical Journal* 80: 139–45.

McPake, B. (1993) 'User charges for health services in developing countries: a review of the economic literature', *Social Science and Medicine* 36(11): 1397–405.

Meiland, F. J., Danse, J. A., Hoos, A. M., Wendte, J. F. and Gunning-Schepers, L. J. (1996) 'The use of the waiting list in a fair selection of patients for nursing home care', *Health Policy* 38(1): 1–11.

Milgrom, P. and Roberts, J. (1992) *Economics, Organization and Management*, London: Prentice-Hall.

Ministry of Health, Peru (1997a) *Analisis de la demanda por servicios de salud*, Seminario 'Modernización del sistema de financiamiento de salud', Lima: Ministerio de Salud.

—— (1997b) *Analisis del financiamiento del sector salud*, Seminario 'Modernización del sistema de financiamiento de salud', Lima: Ministerio de Salud.

Mooney, G. H. (1983) 'Equity in health care: confronting the confusion', *Effective Health Care* 1(4): 179–85.

—— (1994) *Key Issues in Health Economics*, Hemel Hempstead: Harvester Wheatsheaf.

Moran, M. and Wood, B. (1993) *States, Regulation and the Medical Profession*, Buckingham: Open University Press.

Morrison, G. C. (1997) 'HYE and TTO: what is the difference?' *Journal of Health Economics* 16: 563–78.

Moses, S., Manji, F., Bradley, J. E., Nagelkerke, N. J. D., Malisa, M. A. and Plummer, F. A. (1992) 'Impact of user fees on attendance at a referral centre for sexually transmitted diseases in Kenya', *Lancet* 340: 463–6.

Mullen, P. M. (1985) 'Performance indicators: is anything new?' *Hospital and Health Service Review* 81(4): 165–7.

Murray, C. J. (1994) 'Quantifying the burden of disease: the technical basis for disability-adjusted life years', *Bulletin of the World Health Organization* 72(3): 429–45.

Murray, C. J. L. and Acharya, A. K. (1997) 'Understanding DALYs', *Journal of Health Economics* 16(6): 703–30.

Musgrove, P. (1986) 'Measurement of equity in health', *World Health Statistics Quarterly* 39: 325–35.

Muurinen, J. M. (1986) 'Modelling non-profit firms in medicine', in A. Culyer and B. Jonsson (eds) *Public and Private Health Services: Complementarities and Conflicts*, Oxford: Blackwell.

Nalbantian, H. R. and Schotter, A. (1997) 'Productivity under group incentives: an experimental study', *American Economic Review* 87(3): 314.

Naylor, C. D. (1988) 'Private medicine and the privatisation of health care in South Africa', *Social Science and Medicine* 27(11): 1153–70.

Neumann, J. von and Morgenstern, O. (1947) *The Theory of Games and Economic Behavior*, second edition, Princeton NJ: Princeton University Press.

Newhouse, J. (1970) 'Theory of non-profit institutions: an economic model of a hospital', *American Economic Review* 60: 64–74.

—— (1993) *Free for all? Lessons from the RAND Health Insurance Experiment*, Cambridge MA: Harvard University Press.

Ng, Y. K. (1983) *Welfare Economics: Introduction and Development of Basic Concepts*, Basingstoke: Macmillan.

Ngalande-Banda, E. and Walt, G. (1995) 'The private health sector in Malawi: opening Pandora's box?' *Journal of International Development* 7(3): 403–22.

Normand, C. and Busse, R. (2001) 'Social health insurance financing', in E. Mossialos, A. Dixon, J. Fugureras and J. Kutzin (eds) *Funding Health Care: Options for Europe*, Buckingham: Open University Press.

Norton, E. C. (1992) 'Incentive regulation of nursing homes', *Journal of Health Economics* 11: 105.

OECD (1992) *The Reform of Health Care: a Comparative Analysis of Seven OECD Countries*, Health Policy Studies 2, Paris: Organisation for Economic Co-operation and Development.

—— (1994) *The Reform of Health Systems: a Review of Seventeen OECD Countries*, Health Policy Studies 5, Paris: Organisation for Economic Co-operation and Development.

Ogus, A. (1994) *Regulation: Legal Form and Economic Theory*, Oxford: Clarendon Press.

O'Neill, C., Malek, M., Mugford, M., Normand, C., Tarnow-Mordi, W., Hey, E. and Halliday, H. (ECSURF Study Group) (2000) 'A cost analysis of neonatal care in the UK: results from a multi-centre study', *Journal of Public Health Medicine* 22(1): 108–15.

Pannarunothai, S. and Mills, A. (1997) 'Characteristics of public and private health-care providers in a Thai urban setting', in S. Bennett, B. McPake and A. Mills (eds) *Private Health Providers in Developing Countries: Serving the Public Interest?* London: Zed Press.

Parsonage, M. and Neuberger, H. (1992) 'Discounting and health benefits', *Health Economics* 1(1): 71–9.

Paul, C. (1984) 'Physician licensure and the quality of medical care', *Atlantic Economic Journal* 12: 18–30.

Pauly, M. and Redisch, M. (1973) 'The not-for-profit hospital as a physicians' cooperative', *American Economic Review* 63: 87–100.

Pauly, M. V. and Satterthwaite, M. A. (1981) 'The pricing of primary care physicians' services: a test of the role of consumer information', *Bell Journal of Economics and Management Science* 12(2): 488–506.

Peltzman, S. (1976) 'Toward a more general theory of regulation', *Journal of Law and Economics* 19: 211–40.

Posner, R. A. (1974) 'Theories of economic regulation', *Bell Journal of Economics and Management Science* 5(2): 335–58.

Propper, C. (1993) 'Quasi-markets, contracts, and quality in health and social care: the US experience', in J. Le Grand and W. Bartlett (eds) *Quasi-markets and Social Policy*, Basingstoke: Macmillan.

—— (1995) 'Agency and incentives in the NHS internal market', *Social Science and Medicine* 40(1): 1683–90.

Propper, C. and Bartlett, W. (1997) 'The impact of competition on the behaviour of NHS trusts', in R. Flynn and G. Williams (eds) *Contracting for Health: Quasi-markets and the National Health Service*, Oxford: Oxford University Press.

Quirk, J. and Saposnik, R. (1968) *Introduction to General Equilibrium Theory and Welfare Economics*, New York: McGraw-Hill.

Rawls, John (1971) *A Theory of Justice*, Cambridge MA: Belknap Press of Harvard University Press.

Reder, M. (1965) 'Some problems in the economics of hospitals', *American Economic Review* 55: 472–80.

Reich, M. R. (1995) 'The politics of health sector reform in developing countries: three cases of pharmaceutical policy', in P. Berman (ed.) *Health Sector Reform in Developing Countries*, Boston MA: Harvard School of Public Health.

Reinhardt, U. (1978) 'Comment on *Competition and Physicians* by F. A. Sloan and R. Feldman', in W. Greenberg (ed.) *Competition in the Health Care Sector: Proceedings of a Conference sponsored by the Bureau of Economics, Federal Trade Commission*, Germantown MD: Aspen Systems.

Rice, R. G. (1966) 'Analysis of the hospital as an economic organism', *The Modern Hospital* 106(4): 87–91.

Roberts, J. A. (1993) 'Managing markets', *Journal of Public Health Medicine* 14(4): 305–10.

Rodrigues, J. (1989) 'Hospital utilisation and reimbursement methods in Brazil', *International Journal of Health* 4(1): 3–15.

Roemer, M. I. (1961) 'Bed supply and hospital utilisation: a natural experiment', *Hospitals*, 1 November: 35–42.

—— (1993) *National Health Systems of the World* II, Oxford: Oxford University Press.

Rogowski, J. (1998) 'Cost-effectiveness of care for very low birth weight infants', *Pediatrics* 102(1): 35–43.

Rosenblatt, R. A., Hart, L. G., Baldwin, L. M., Chan, L. and Scheweiss, R. (1998) 'The generalist role of specialty physicians: is there a hidden system of primary care?' *Journal of the American Medical Association* 279(17): 1364–70.

Rowland, D., Lyons, B., Salganicoff, A. and Long, P. (1994) 'A profile of the uninsured in America', *Health Affairs* (Millwood) 13(2): 283–7.

Russell, S. (1996) 'Ability to pay for health care: concepts and evidence', *Health Policy and Planning* 11(3): 219–37.

Ryan, M. and Hughes, J. (1997) 'Using conjoint analysis to value surgical versus medical management of miscarriage', *Health Economics* 6: 261–73.

Samuelson, P. A. (1938) 'A note on the pure theory of consumers' behaviour', *Economics* 5: 61–71.

Samuelson, P. A. and Nordhaus, W. D. (2000) *Economics*, seventeenth edition, New York: McGraw-Hill.

Scitovsky, T. (1941) 'A note on welfare propositions in economics', *Review of Economic Studies* 9: 77–88.

Scrivens, E. F., Klein, R. and Steiner, A. (1995) 'Accreditation: what can we learn from the anglophone model?' *Health Policy* 34(3): 193–204.

Sen, A. (1979) 'Personal utilities and public judgements, or, What's wrong with welfare economics?' *Economic Journal* 89: 537–58.

—— (1981) *Poverty and Famines*, Oxford: Clarendon Press.

Sheldon, T., Davey-Smith, G. and Bevan, G. (1993) 'Weighting in the dark: resource allocation in the new NHS', *British Medical Journal* 306: 835–9.

Simborg, D. W. (1981) 'DRG creep: a new hospital-acquired disease', *New England Journal of Medicine* 304(26): 1602–4.

Simon, H. (1957) *Models of Man, Social and Rational: Mathematical Essays on Rational Human Behavior in a Social Setting*, London: Wiley.

Sloan, F. A. (1980) 'The internal organization of hospitals: a descriptive study', *Health Service Research* 15(3): 203–30.

Ssengooba, F., Atuyambe, L., Okuonzi, S. *et al.* (2000) *Prospects for Autonomy of Public Hospitals in Uganda: a Baseline Assessment*, Kampala: Institute of Public Health, Makerere University.

Stebbins, K. R. (1991) 'Tobacco, politics and economics: implications for global health', *Social Science and Medicine* 33(12): 1317–26.

Steinwald, A. B. and Dummit, L. A. (1989) 'Hospital case mix change: sicker patients or DRG creep?' *Health Affairs* 8(2): 35–47.

Stepan, A. and Sommersguter-Reichmann, M. (1999) 'Priority setting in Austria', *Health Policy* 50: 91–104.

Stewart, F. (1975) 'A note on social cost–benefit analysis and class conflict in LDCs', *World Development* 3(1): 31–45.

Stigler, G. J. (1971) 'The theory of economic regulation', *Bell Journal of Economics and Management Science* 2: 137–46.

Street, A. and Duckett, S. (1996) 'Are waiting lists inevitable?' *Health Policy* 36(1): 1–15.

Strong, N. and Waterson, M. (1987) 'Agents and information', in R. Clarke and T. McGuiness (ed.) *Economics of the Firm*, Oxford: Blackwell.

Strong, P. and Robinson, J. (1990) *The NHS: Under New Management*, London: Taylor & Francis.

Suárez, R., Henderson, P., Barillas, E. and Vieira, C. (1994) *Gasto nacional y financiamiento del sector de la salud en América Latina y el Caribe: desafíos para la década de los noventa*, Serie informes técnicos 30, Proyecto de Economía y Financiamiento de la Salud, Washington DC: Organización Panamericana de la Salud.

Todaro, M. P. (1989) *Economic Development in the Third World*, fourth edition, Harlow: Longman.

Townsend, J. (1987) 'Cigarette tax, economic welfare and social class patterns of smoking', *Applied Economics* 19: 355–65.

Trigg, A. B. and Bosanquet, N. (1992) 'Tax harmonisation and the reduction of European smoking rates', *Journal of Health Economics* 11: 329–46.

UN Development Programme (1999) *Human Development Report, 1999: Globalization with a Human Face*, New York: United Nations Development Programme.

Valdmanis, V. G. (1990) 'Ownership and technical efficiency of hospitals', *Medical Care* 28(6): 552–61.

Van den Heever, A. (1997) 'Regulating the funding of private health care: the South African experience', in S. Bennett, B. McPake and A. Mills (1997) *Private Health Providers in Developing Countries: Serving the Public Interest?* London: Zed Press.

Vitaliano, D. F. and Toren, M. (1994) 'Cost and efficiency in nursing homes: a stochastic frontier approach', *Journal of Health Economics* 13: 281–300.

Ware, J. E. and Sherbourne, C. D. (1992) 'The SF-36 short-form health status survey, I: Conceptual framework and item selection', *Medical Care* 30: 473–83.

Wennberg, J. E. and Gittelsohn, A. (1973) 'Small area variations in health care delivery: a population-based health information system can guide planning and regulatory decision making', *Science* 182: 1102–7.

—— (1982) 'Professional uncertainty and the problem of supplier-induced demand', *Social Science and Medicine* 16(7): 811–24.

West, P. A. (1997) *Understanding the NHS Reforms: the Creation of Incentives?* Buckingham: Open University Press.

Wilensky, G. R. and Rossiter, L. F. (1983) 'The relative importance of physician-induced demand in the demand for medical care', *Millbank Memorial Fund Quarterly* 61(2): 252–77.

Wilkin, D., Metcalfe, D. H. and Marinker, M. (1989) 'The meaning of information on GP referral rates to hospitals', *Community Medicine* 11(1): 65–70.

Williams, A. (1991) 'Allocating resources to health care: is the QALY a technical solution to a political problem? Of course not', *International Journal of Health Services* 21(3): 365–9.

Williamson, C. (1985) 'Consulting consumers: a managers' guide to consumers', *Health Services Journal* 105(5481): 28–9.

Williamson, O. E. (1975) *Markets and Hierarchies: Analysis and Antitrust Implications*, New York: Free Press.

—— (1985) *The Economic Institutions of Capitalism: Firms, Markets, Relational Contracting*, New York: Free Press.

World Bank (1993) *World Development Report 1993: Investing in Health*, New York: Oxford University Press.

WHO (2000) *The World Health Report 2000: Health Systems, Improving Performance*, Geneva: World Health Organisation.

Yang, B. (1991) 'Health insurance in Korea: opportunities and challenges', *Health Policy and Planning* 6(2): 119–29.

Yepes, F. J. and Sanchez, L. H. (1998) 'Reforming pluralist systems: the case of Colombia', in A. Mills (ed.) *Reforming Health Sectors*, London: Kegan Paul.

Yesudian, C. A. K. (1994) 'Behaviour of the private sector in the health market in Bombay', *Health Policy and Planning* 9(1): 72–81.

Zwanziger, J., Melnick, G. and Eyre, K. M. (1994) 'Hospitals and anti-trust: defining markets and setting standards', *Journal of Health Politics, Policy and Law* 19(2): 423–47.

Zwarenstein, M. F. and Price, M. R. (1990) 'The 1983 distribution of hospitals and hospital beds in RSA by area, race, ownership and type', *South African Medical Journal* 77: 448–52.

Index